Attachment, Trauma and Multip.

Valerie Sinason's *Treating Survivors of Satanist Abuse* addressed a subject that many professionals working in the field had been uncomfortable discussing. Her work in disability and abuse has consistently broken new ground in addressing subjects that many people have found initially hard to deal with. This new book covers the equally unexplored subject of Dissociative Identity Disorder (DID), and is the first major British book available for both clinicians and the intelligent lay public on this subject.

Attachment, Trauma and Multiplicity explains the phenomenon of DID, the conflicting models of the human mind that have been found to try to understand it, the political conflict over the subject, and, with the permission of patients, clinical accounts. Valerie Sinason, along with an impressive array of contributors, covers:

- The background history and a description of the condition
- Issues of diagnosis
- Treatment issues
- The stages of dissociation that lead to full-blown DID
- The legal and management problems

Attachment, Trauma and Multiplicity will be indispensable to professionals in the UK increasingly concerned about their lack of training in this subject and the fear it evokes in them and their teams.

Valerie Sinason is a psychoanalyst and Consultant Research Psychotherapist at the Psychiatry of Disability Department at St George's Hospital Medical School, London. She is Director of the Clinic for Dissociative Studies, Harley Street, London. She is the author of *Treating Survivors of Satanist Abuse*, Routledge, 1994.

Contributors: Arnon Bentovim; Nicholas Midgley; Felicity de Zulueta; Peter Fonagy; John Southgate; Howard Steele; Jean Goodwin; Sue Richardson; Peter Whewell; Phil Mollon; Joan Coleman; Patricia Pitchon; Claire Usiskin; R.D. Hinshelwood; Leslie Swartz; Brett Kahr and Survivor poets.

Attachment, Trauma and Multiplicity

Working with Dissociative Identity Disorder

Valerie Sinason

First published 2002 by Brunner-Routledge
27 Church Road, Hove, East Sussex BN3 2FA

Simultaneously published in the USA and Canada
by Taylor & Francis Inc
29 West 35th Street, New York, NY 10001

Reprinted 2002

Brunner-Routledge is an imprint of the Taylor & Francis Group

Typeset in Garamond by M Rules, London
Printed and bound in Great Britain by TJ International, Padstow,
Cornwall
Cover design by Louise Page

British Library Cataloguing in Publication Data
A catalogue record for this book is available
from the British Library

Library of Congress Cataloging-in-Publication Data
Attachment, trauma and multiplicity: working with dissociative
identity disorder / edited by Valerie Sinason.
       p. cm.
    Includes bibliographical references and index.
1. Multiple personality. 2. Multiple personality–Treatment.
I. Sinason, Valerie, 1946–

RC569.5.M8 A845 2002
616.85′236–dc21   2001037582

ISBN 0-415-19555-1 (hbk)
ISBN 0-415-19556-X (pbk)

To my Senior and Junior Guardian Angels,
Pearl King and Tina Carlile.

Contents

Notes on contributors

Arnon Bentovim MBBS, FRCPsych, FRCPCH, Associate Member of the Institute of Psychoanalysis and Member of the Institute of Family Therapy, is a consultant child and family psychiatrist, and has honorary appointments at Great Ormond Street Children's Hospital and the Tavistock Clinic, and is Director of the London Child & Family Consultation Service. He is Psychiatric Consultant to the Clinic for Dissociative Studies, and Consultant to SWAAY (Social Work for Abusing and Abused Youth). He and his colleagues founded the first comprehensive treatment service for sexually abused children and their families in 1980, and he continues to work with colleagues at the Institute of Child Health, University College, London, on work developing an understanding of processes which lead abused children and young people to develop offending patterns of behaviour.

Beverly, **Miki** and **Toisin** are brave women who have survived ritual abuse by means of DID. Beverly's Mum is Beverley's Mum.

Joan Coleman graduated MB, ChB in Edinburgh in 1956. She worked mainly in general practice, casualty and general medicine until 1969, when she started working in psychiatry. She qualified DPM in 1974, and MRCPsych in 1975. She worked in psychiatry and clinical medicine from 1969 to 1994. In 1989, with several others, she founded Ritual Abuse Information Network and Support (RAINS). She has been Membership Co-ordinator of RAINS since 1991 and has continued to work voluntarily for this organisation, dealing with all telephone calls and any enquiries from therapists, survivors, police, lawyers and journalists since retirement in November 1994. She contributed an article to *Child Abuse Review* entitled 'Presenting features in adult victims of satanist ritual abuse', and also a chapter in *Treating Survivors of Satanist Abuse*, Valerie Sinason (ed.), both in 1994.

Felicity de Zulueta BSc, MA (Cantab), MbChB, FRCPsych is a senior honorary consultant psychiatrist in psychotherapy in the Traumatic Stress Service in the Maudsley Hospital, London, and a clinical lecturer in traumatic studies at the Institute of Psychiatry. She is a trained individual psychoanalytic psychotherapist, a group analyst and a systemic family therapist. She also has a biology degree.

She has written a book entitled *From Pain to Violence, the Traumatic Roots of Destructiveness* (Whurr: London), and many chapters and articles on the subject of violence and Post-traumatic Stress Disorder. She is also a founder member of the International Attachment Network, a consultant to CAPP and trustee for WAVE (Worldwide Alternatives to Violence), and is a member of the European and International Societies for Traumatic Stress Studies and of the International Association for Forensic Psychotherapy.

Peter Fonagy PhD, FBA is Freud Memorial Professor of Psychoanalysis and Director of the sub-Department of Clinical Health Psychology at University College London. He is Director of the Clinical Outcomes Research and Effectiveness Centre and the Child and Family Centre, both at the Menninger Foundation, Kansas. He is a clinical psychologist and a training and supervising analyst in the British Psychoanalytical Society in child and adult analysis. His clinical interests centre around issues of borderline psychopathology, violence and early attachment relationships. He has published over 200 chapters and articles and has edited and authored several books. His most recent books include *What Works for Whom: A Critical Review of Psychotherapy Research* (with A. Roth, published 1996 by Guilford), *Psychoanalysis on the Move: The Work of Joseph Sandler* (co-edited with A. Cooper and R. Wallerstein, published 1999 by Routledge) and *What Works for Which Child* (with M. Target, D. Cottrell, J. Philips and Z. Kurtz – in press).

Jean M. Goodwin MD, MPH is in private practice in Galveston, Texas. She is Clinical Professor of Psychiatry at the University of Texas medical branch and is on the faculty of the Houston/Galveston Psychoanalytic Institute. She has authored five books; the most recent, *Splintered Reflections*, was written with R. Attias (Basic Books 1999).

R.D. Hinshelwood is a Member of the British Psychoanalytical Society, and currently Professor in the Centre for Psychoanalytic Studies, University of Essex. He was previously Director of the Cassel Hospital, Richmond, London. He is the author of *Dictionary of Kleinian Thought* (1989), and other books on Melanie Klein. He has written extensively on therapeutic communities and other social science applications of psychoanalysis (recently publishing with Wilhelm Skogstad *Observing Organisations*), on psychiatry and psychotherapy in the NHS, and on a psychoanalytic view of ethics, publishing *Therapy or Coercion: Does Psychoanalysis Differ from Brainwashing?* in 1997.

Brett Kahr is Senior Lecturer in Psychotherapy in the School of Psychotherapy and Counselling at Regent's College in London, and a

tutor in the Department of Primary Care and Population Sciences of the
Royal Free and University College Medical School of the University of
London, and a psychotherapist in private practice. His book on *D.W.
Winnicott: A Biographical Portrait* received the Gradiva Award for
Biography from the National Association for the Advancement of
Psychoanalysis. He is a patron of the Squiggle Foundation, and an adviser
to the Winnicott Clinic of Psychotherapy. His books include *Exhibitionism*
and *Forensic Psychotherapy and Psychopathology*. He is the Couple
Psychotherapist for the Clinic for Dissociative Studies and regularly con-
sults to TV and films. He has just been appointed as the Inaugura
Winnicott Senior Research Fellow.

Nicholas Midgley works at the Marlborough Family Service in North
London. He was previously a visiting lecturer in the Department of British
Studies at Tokyo University, Japan. While training as a child psychotherapist at the Anna Freud Centre, he is completing a doctorate on the
long-term follow-up of child psychoanalysis, at University College London.

Phil Mollon is a psychoanalyst (British Psychoanalytical Society), a psychotherapist (Tavistock Society) and also a clinical psychologist. He works in
a general NHS mental health setting, as well as in private practice. His
book on multiple personality, *Multiple Selves, Multiple Voices*, was published in
1996 (Wiley). He has also written widely on issues of narcissism, trauma and
memory, and served on the working party of the British Psychological Society
investigating the controversies regarding recovered memory. His most recent
book is *Releasing the Self. The Healing Legacy of Heinz Kohut* (Whurr).

Patricia Pitchon is working towards her MA in Integrative Psychotherapy
and has worked as clinic manager at the Clinic for Dissociative Studies. She
has also worked with war refugees. She has an abiding interest in the plight
of refugees and many Third World issues which stem from her South
American background. She has published articles covering these and other
topics and has translated several books in the fields of philosophy, anthropology and psychology, including *The Fundamentals of Psychoanalytic
Technique* by Horacio Etchegoyen, Karnac Books, London.

Sue Richardson is an attachment-based psychotherapist, trainer and consultant with almost 30 years experience in the helping professions. She has
integrated her extensive knowledge of child care and child protection into
her work with adults who have suffered childhood trauma. Sue is part of an
international network of professionals who have raised awareness of child
sexual abuse. She is co-editor and co-author of *Child Sexual Abuse: Whose
Problem?* (Venture Press, 1991) and a number of published papers. She is a
regular contributor to national and international conferences on child abuse
and related issues and a founder member of the UK Study Group of the
International Society for the Study of Dissociation.

Valerie Sinason is a child psychotherapist and an adult psychoanalyst registered with both the UKCP and BCP. She works especially in the field of learning disability and abuse. She was a consultant psychotherapist at the Tavistock Clinic, involved in the Learning Disability Workshop for almost twenty years and held part-time consultant psychotherapy posts at both the Anna Freud Centre and Portman Clinic. She currently works at St Georges Hospital Medical School in the Psychiatry of Disability Department and as founder and Director of the Clinic for Dissociative Studies. She has written 11 books and over 60 papers on abuse and disability.

Her books include *Treating Survivors of Satanist Abuse* (Routledge), *Memory in Dispute* (Karnac), *Mental Handicap and the Human Condition* (Free Association Books), *Understanding Your Handicapped Child* (Tavistock Clinic) and several books for learning disabled adults together with Professor Sheila Hollins in the *Language Beyond Words* books published by the Royal College of Psychiatry. She was a *Guardian* columnist for five years writing on family problems, and her articles and poems have been widely published.

She is Clinical Director of BATO, the British Anti-trafficking Organisation and President of the Institute of Psychotherapy and Disability.

She is an Honorary Consultant Psychotherapist at the University of Cape Town Child Guidance Clinic working on trauma and disability projects and was honoured with Life Membership of POMS, the Swedish organisation for psychodynamic psychologists working in the field of learning disability. She is a regular international keynote speaker in Australia, America, Sweden, Denmark, Finland, Belgium, Italy, Cyprus and South Africa.

John Southgate is the founder and Chair Emeritus of the Centre for Attachment-based Psychoanalytic Psychotherapy. He was supervised by John Bowlby until Bowlby's death in 1990. Formerly Head of Applied Behavioural Science at the University of North London, he is currently working on a synthesis based upon Lacan, Bowlby, Bion and Winnicott.

Howard Steele is Senior Lecturer in Psychology at University College London, where he is also Director of the Attachment Research Unit. He is the Founding Editor of *Attachment & Human Development*, a journal devoted to the presentation of clinical, research and theory-review papers on attachment issues. Together with his wife and colleague, Miriam Steele, he pursues longitudinal research on intergenerational attachment patterns and has written widely on the subject.

Leslie Swartz is Professor of Psychology at the University of Stellenbosch, South Africa. He has an interest in cultural issues in mental health, and in the provision of appropriate services in under-resourced societies. He is a major international lecturer on culture and mental health. Recent publications include *Culture and Mental Health: A Southern African View* (Oxford University Press 1998).

Claire Usiskin currently works for the Parents Information Service at the charity YoungMinds. She previously worked as a research assistant and administrator at the Clinic for Dissociative Studies. She has also worked at the Young Abusers Project (NSPCC), the Child Sexual Abuse National Research Project (NCH Action for Children and the Tavistock Clinic) and the Specialist Child Care Mediation Project (Tavistock Clinic, National Family Mediation, Brunel University and the Department of Health).

Peter Whewell is Consultant Psychotherapist at the Regional Department of Psychotherapy, Newcastle where he has developed and now co-leads a team specialising in the treatment of borderline personality disorder. He is founding course director of the North of England Association for Training in Psychoanalytic Psychotherapy, a four-year intensive course in psychoanalytic psychotherapy with membership of the British Confederation of Psychotherapists. He is a member of the Scottish Association of Psychoanalytical Psychotherapists and an Associate Member of the British Psychoanalytical Society.

Part I

Mapping the territory: childhood aetiology, dissociation, Post-traumatic Stress Disorder and Dissociative Identity Disorder

Peel away the layers
And find the real me
I've been hiding here for so long
It frightens me to see
Behind the mask is somebody
A vulnerable little child
Who desperately seeks a mother's love
To stop her from feeling so wild

Toisin

Introduction

Valerie Sinason

To begin at the end. The telephone rings at 10pm. A terrified child voice can be heard on the other end of the phone. There is a train noise in the background and the sound of people talking. 'Please, please stop her from going back. He's going to hurt us. He puts stingy stuff in me and I go all sore. Don't let her go back. I am frightened'.

The voice rises in terror until I remind her that she is not going to be taken back, that her abuser is dead, that she is safe. The voice softens and relaxes. The panic subsides. The 6-year-old voice on the telephone belongs to a professional woman of 40 with Dissociative Identity Disorder.

The woman could not avoid a train journey in order to attend a crucial meeting concerning her new work. At one point on the journey the train was going to stop at the town she had lived in as a child. Rationally she knew her abusers were long since dead. However, the severity of her early abuse had led to fragmentation. Merely stopping at that station was enough to bring back a state of panic.

Instantly, to aid the woman, out of cold storage came the brave 6-year-old friend. Frozen in a terrible state of now-ness that had not changed for over 30 years she emerged. The woman had only just come to therapy. Many of her inside people, alters, self-states, whatever language we wish to use, had autonomous existence. Created to protect her, they hid the discrepancy between the sadism of her attachment figures and her need for love. They came out when she could not manage, to hold the memories of trauma (both actual and corroborated as well as fantasy and flashback – see Jean Goodwin, Chapter 8) and help her survive. Some states were truly frozen – not just in time but in their emotional states, pointing to disorientated disorganised attachments (see Peter Fonagy, Chapter 4) and even earlier infantile trauma.

After two years of treatment they began to thaw, began to grow and discard their old strictures. Some of the frozen friends could then melt into their host bringing their strength, fragments of memory and courage back to the core personality.

HOW DOES IT BEGIN? 'STICKS AND STONES MAY BREAK MY BONES BUT NAMES WILL NEVER HURT ME'

What happens when a child has to breathe in mocking words each day? What happens when a parent, an attachment figure utters those words: someone the child needs in order to emotionally survive? Sometimes, that mocking voice gets taken inside and finds a home. It then stays hurting and corroding on the inside when the original source of that cruelty might long ago have disappeared or died.

'You stupid idiot, thick disgusting dunce!' Ella shouted when she accidentally spilled her tea on the floor. Ella was 60 and had a severe learning disability. Whenever she made any mistake she mocked herself with the words of her sadistic father even though he had died more than 20 years ago. By keeping his angry words she was keeping him alive and sparing herself from the helplessness of being a victim on the receiving end. By shouting at herself she was identifying with him, being him and therefore not having to remember being the frightened unwanted helpless little child. This is not schizophrenia or 'another person' inside. This is ordinary development made unpalatable by the toxic nature of what has had to be taken in.

DISSOCIATION AND FRAGMENTATION AS A CHILDHOOD DEFENCE

What happens when the toxic nature of what is poured into the undeveloped vulnerable brain of a small child is so poisonous that it is too much to manage? Little children, who have had poured into them all the human pain and hate adults could not manage, somehow grow up. There is a shadow side to this. Legions of warriors are lost to society through suicide, psychiatric hospitals, addiction and prison. What happens to them, especially when those who hurt them are attachment figures? (See chapters by Fonagy, de Zulueta, Richardson, Mollon, Whewell, Southgate and Steele.)

This book is about one way of surviving. It is about a brilliant piece of creative resilience which comes with a terrible price. It is a way of surviving so difficult to think about and speak about that, like the topic of learning disability, its name changes regularly. Dissociative Identity Disorder is the newest term. Where and in whom the disorder lies, however, is a crucial issue in its own right.

DISSOCIATIVE IDENTITY DISORDER

Dissociative Identity Disorder is the Mad Cow Disease of the mind. Despite the clear description of what constitutes DID in DSM-IV (see p. 10), this condition is still seen by some mental health professionals as a hysterical con-fabulation. It is 10–20 years too early for it to be picked up and dealt with well. What is it like to be suffering from something that is not yet recognised? And not only is the DID not recognised, but the nature of the sadistic abuse that has caused it in the majority of cases is even less recognised.

'I'm an attention seeker, don't you know?' said one patient bitterly. 'And I'm hysterical and full of delusions. Amazing isn't it. My abusers can rape and tor-ture me for years and they are wandering the streets perfectly happy and I am the one with a life sentence, the one who is scared to leave the house, the one who has to apologise for her illness.'

In the last decade I have assessed and treated children and adults, largely female, who have Dissociative Identity Disorder (DID). There is a very sig-nificant gender bias in this condition. Indeed, abused boys are far more likely to externalise their trauma although both sexes (see Bentovim, Chapter 1) use internalising and externalising responses. Cultural issues, as well as gender issues, need exploring (see Swartz, Chapter 15).

The majority of female children and adults I assessed had been diagnosed or misdiagnosed as schizophrenic, borderline, anti-social disorder or psychotic. Despite the fact that anti-psychotic drugs had little or no effect on them, that they experienced their voices as coming from inside and not outside (see Joan Coleman, Chapter 12), and they did not manifest thought disorder or distor-tions about time and place except when in a trance state, mental health professionals could not perceive flaws in diagnosis. Or rather, and more wor-ryingly, the diagnoses at times were correct but only applied to the 'state' that visited them. Hence one psychiatrist assessing 'Mary' correctly diagnosed psy-chosis, and another who assessed the patient a week later correctly disputed that diagnosis and declared 'Susan' had borderline personality disorder. Without a holistic approach professionals are attacking each other's contra-dictory diagnoses without realising the aptness of Walt Whitman's words – 'I am large. I contain multitudes'.

HIDING SELVES

In the face of professional confusion and societal denial some patients have man-aged to hide their multiplicity when told they were making it up. In answer to the key question concerning the small number of children who present in severe dissociative states (see chapters by Arnon Bentovim, Nicholas Midgley and Peter Fonagy) patients confirmed negative responses to their childhood dis-closures that led to hiding their symptoms (see Valerie Sinason, Chapter 7). Children were told they 'would grow out of it' or 'it was just like an imaginary friend'. Adults report similar past experiences and these are confirmed by my researching past medical files. The pain such misdiagnoses or denial of symptoms causes patients can be seen in the patients' poems (pp. 1, 69, 123, 195).

Unfortunately, when practitioners, shocked at the sight of dissociative identity disorder, misuse behavioural techniques without adequate specialist
training and give sanctions when 'alters' appear, the host personality learns to
hide them. This is often perceived as a treatment success. It is not understood
that for the patient, who is an expert in learning how to survive denial of DID
by clinicians, it is experienced as a psychically annihilating secondary trauma.

To survive, the host incorporates and imprisons within the different states.
'Don't you understand', says Ellen, 'it is unbearable having to keep everyone
imprisoned and not allowed out. But that is what I have to do to survive there.
To survive outside I have to let them out so they can get therapy and we can
link up. But if I was to show them inside I would just be seen as mad and
everything would be ruined. Even though they see that as winning their nasty
little behavioural game there is no alternative while my condition is not
understood.'

This book, bringing together experienced clinicians, aims to consider the
developmental, attachment and adaptive structure of DID as well as the controversy around its aetiology and manifestation.

WHAT IS DISSOCIATIVE IDENTITY DISORDER AND HOW DOES IT HAPPEN?

A loved child of 2 toddled around the kitchen. He put his hand up to almost
touch the gas heater. 'Hot!' he shouted. He shouted in the voice of his mother
who had been frightened for his safety when she had left the heater unguarded
the day before. He paused. 'Be careful sweetie', he added in the voice of his
older sister. Like young children all over the world he was taking in the language and intonation of his attachment figures. His family could amusedly
point to where his vocabulary, intonation and facial expressions came from.
However, just a short time later, in an ordinary developmental process, the
words and concepts and gestures and knowledge taken in from the outside
became truly his in an apparently seamless way.

When all goes well we take for granted the existence of the outside network
in each of us. Ironically, it is when things go wrong and become writ large that
we notice the amazing process of what we are linguistically made of.

'Stupid piece of shit. Edward! Stupid piece of shit. Get under.' This was the
verbal calling-card of a severely learning disabled man I worked with. He said
it over and over and because he was learning disabled it was called echollalia.
Once I met him and listened he was able to show me he was repeating the
cruel words said to him by a real external person. They hurt so much he could
not assimilate them except by becoming them and repeating them. I now see
them as a verbal flash-back. The childhood refrain 'sticks and stones may
break my bones but names will never hurt me' is not true. Names enter us like
weapons.

How do we account for these changed faces and voices? Again, if we go back to our 2-year-old loved boy we get some answers. When his mother shouts 'Hot!' in a frightened angry voice her face does not look the same as when she is beaming lovingly at him. Nor is her voice the same. A baby and a child get used to seeing their primary caretaker's face change dramatically into some-thing quite different, even though it does not have another name. However, Cross Mummy and Loving Mummy are very different people even though they are Mummy. Hence dissociative mothers with children (see Miki's description, p. 170) are able to consider their child's predicament.

Following sadistic abuse Jenny, aged 24 and with Down's syndrome, devel-oped different 'states' to help her survive. 'I cried in my bed last night. I cried because of those men who hurt me. When I cried and cried I felt hugged in my body. Maggie cuddled me because I was sad and she stroke my hair and help me put my head on pillow. When I wake up I am alright for my day centre.' 'How good that Maggie could help you and that you knew she was helping you', I replied. Jenny's face changed. It looked older but sweeter. Her voice changed too. 'Hello love', she said to me. 'I am glad you noticed I helped. Poor Jenny had a really hard time last night. A really hard time. I had to help her.' 'Thank you, Maggie', said Jenny, with facial expression and voice returning. Suddenly Jenny's face became hard and cruel and she smashed at her head with her right arm. 'Thank you Maggie! Thank you Maggie!' mimicked a mocking sadistic voice—Myra. 'Fucking idiots both of you. I will show you what hurts.'

Faced with memories of unbearable helplessness and shame (see Peter Whewell, Chapter 10) Myra represented the identification with the abuser as a defence against pain, leaving Maggie to represent the loving caretaking self and Jenny the vulnerable victim.

Such sights and sounds provide painful visual re-enactments of past trauma. 'Sibyl' and 'The Three Faces of Eve', however dated, remain the main public image (see Brett Kahr, Chapter 16) of dissociation. Somehow it has remained easier to consider the subject safely contained in a Hollywood film or a book rather than on the street and in the homes, schools, universities, workplaces and psychiatric hospitals of the country. DID (Dissociative Identity Disorder) people become successful professionals, writers, dancers, artists, scientists, shopworkers, singers (like Joan Baez) and parents. They also become prosti-tutes, drug addicts, criminals and pornstars. They also die. Sometimes they cover the range of possibilities within their one frame. Jane, for example, was a successful part-time university lecturer but dissociatively, as Enya, ran a sado-masochistic brothel, as Mel was involved in small-time theft, as Janet was a computer programmer and as Annette was a drug addict. Each had their own friendships, clothes and homes.

How do we make sense of the paradox of this mental position? At one level the idea that five different people could all have timeshares in one body seems absurd. And yet, it is both delusional and real and all at the same time. (See R.D. Hinshelwood, Chapter 14).

To understand this paradox takes us into a new way of conceptualising the human mind, the resilience of the human spirit and the profound need to find defences that can protect against unbearable events.

As an intellectual defence measure some professionals use diagnostic concepts to avoid considering traumatic aetiology. Border-line personality disorder, a description that applies to many such patients has an 81 per cent chance of major trauma (Herman 1992). Indeed, Professor Jean Goodwin (personal communication 2000) informs me that worn out American workers in some states are trying to treat symptoms and bypass aetiology to avoid controversy and political conflict. This is similar to the legal situation in the UK where evidence of ritual abuse can be removed in court cases because a jury is seen as more likely to take the evidence seriously if it is confined to the sexual aspects of abuse.

• Can we ever really manage to consider the meaning of trauma – something that breaks through our defences and cannot be properly processed? Think of the way someone breaks their leg and talks of 'the leg'. It is not 'my leg'. It is dissociated from as it has felt pain and caused pain. Think too of the encouragement offered by society to 'think about something else' – sometimes helpfully – to the hurt person. •

Now think of a child being bullied in a school playground. Everything goes into slow motion. The child feels it is not happening to them. That too is dissociation. Take it further. The child is an 8-year-old called Mary. She is being kicked and feels she is watching from a great height. It is not her. The person kicking her is an attachment figure, her father. She cannot see this properly because she needs the support of her father to survive. The only way she can manage this inescapable experience it is to dissociate further. She is 8 whereas that girl being kicked cannot be her because that girl is only 5. What's more, as the kicking goes on and turns into rape, her name is Mary and she has a father who loves her while that girl on the floor is only 5 and her name is Jane and she does not feel anything. Gradually the story becomes more fleshed out as the dissociation provides her with means of survival. If the abuse turns into torture it might be that even with 'Jane' Mary cannot psychically survive and a further 'state' is created. Jane, who appears when Mary cannot manage, then creates a big brother who is tall and strong and will protect her, called Peter.

This brilliant survival mechanism helped when facing the trauma of the abuse but it is maladaptive when the trauma is over. Mary aged 25 presents at her GP's surgery with terrible memory loss and signs of self-injury. Sometimes she does not know where she is when she wakes up. Jane and Peter are still appearing in Mary's life because no new way has been found for the system's survival. The multiplicity is hardwired, as brainscans are starting to show. To help Mary regain her spirit that is fragmented into her dissociative states means that she had to cognitively take on board her past. Without a safe environment and skilled staff how is it possible to re-experience the very trauma that led to fragmentation? And yet all over the UK these heroic and troubled survivors – mainly women – have to deal with a lack of specialist resources and disbelieving discrediting staff. It is hard to underestimate the impact on vulnerable people of facing the disbelief and even attack of professional staff when trying to have their problems heard.

JOHN BOWLBY AND DID

In 1988, in a clinical supervision, John Bowlby looked at drawings of little children being abused and pictorially delineating terrible stories. The artist was a middle-aged female patient who was being treated by John Southgate, the founder and former Chair of the Bowlby Centre for Attachment-based Psychoanalytic Psychotherapy. The patient had been feeling that her therapist did not understand the drawings. Dr Bowlby mused and finally said – 'I think this woman is a multiple personality.' Southgate commented, 'He said there was a lot of work in the US on Dissociation and proposed that I should talk to these children and listen to the story they were trying to tell me' (see Southgate 1996 and Chapter 5).

John Bowlby was the world-famous psychoanalyst who created attachment theory (see chapters by Felicity de Zulueta, Sue Richardson, Peter Fonagy, Howard Steele and John Southgate) and proved to the western world that separation of young children from their attachment figures was psychically damaging (whether in hospital or in evacuation) in proportion to the nature of their attachments, age and degree of separation.

Bowlby's work on separation and attachment did not find an immediate positive response. Indeed, upper class English Christian psychiatrists, doctors and psychoanalysts who had been sent away to boarding school found his ideas as disturbing as their Jewish counterparts who had lost their safe family links through the holocaust.

DID AS A PARADIGM SHIFT

As Bowlby himself tells us, we cannot see what we cannot bear to see. How then do we best educate each other and tolerate the conceptual and clinical gaps? Kuhn's work shows us how, when an older paradigm cannot account adequately for a subject, we find it problematic. Multiple Personality Disorder (MPD) or the newer term Dissociative Identity Disorder (DID) is such a subject.

The impact on professionals of extreme childhood trauma and multiplicity is far more severe than the impact of childhood separation was and so the response to this subject has been even less positive than to Bowlby's words of almost half a century ago. It remains disturbingly under-studied by all professions and both undiagnosed and misdiagnosed in this country (see Joan Coleman, Chapter 12) and a continued object of controversy in the USA.

DSM CRITERIA

The DSM-IV criteria specify that DID is

> The presence of two or more distinct identities or personality states (each with its own relatively enduring pattern of perceiving, relating to, and thinking about the environment and self).

> At least two of these identities or personality states recurrently take control of the person's behaviour.

> Inability to recall important personal information that is too extensive to be explained by ordinary forgetfulness and not due to the direct effects of a substance (e.g. blackouts or chaotic behaviour during alcohol intoxication) or a general medical condition (e.g. complex partial seizures).

Although the international psychiatric criteria in DSM-IV describe very clearly what constitutes this condition, British clinicians have on the whole ignored or condemned both the condition and the clinicians who recognise it and offer treatment. Indeed, the *British Journal of Psychiatry* has published only five papers on DID since 1989, all of which are unanimously critical. Psychiatric training (see Joan Coleman Chapter 12) offers little understanding both in the past and now (see Peter Whewell, Chapter 10; Phil Mollon, Chapter 11). This leaves British professionals uniquely vulnerable to emotional stress when encountering such patients.

A curious small ray of light appeared on the British television programme *Tomorrow's World* in 1999 when the Maudsley Psychiatrist Dr Raj Persaud declared that psychiatrists would now have to recognise DID because brainscan research at Harvard had proven its existence. Dr Persaud, who, like many of his psychiatric colleagues, did not consider DID could exist, changed his mind because of brain research results rather than the direct clinical experience of being with such patients. It could be that our recent social interest in brain research allows a face-saving way of changing our clinical paradigms. However, what is the emotional experience of children and adults living in a country at a time where the condition that is troubling them (and its traumatic aetiology) is linked to a paradigm shift rather than an area of clinical resourcefulness?

TRAUMATIC AETIOLOGY

North et al. (1983) found that this condition was not only linked to a high childhood sexual abuse rate but also to a 24–67 per cent occurrence rate of rape in adult life, and to a 60–81 per cent rate of suicide attempts. Thus it is clear that DID is part of a substantial grouping of trauma-based conditions. Putnam et al. (1986) in the USA, looking at 100 DID patients, found that 97 of the hundred had experienced major early trauma with almost half having witnessed the violent death of someone close to them. Compared with Freud's ability to recognise the traumatic aetiology of hysteria one hundred years ago (Freud 1896), contemporary clinicians have found it extremely hard to bear the horrors of patients' objective lives. Sometimes (Hale and Sinason 1994) psychotherapists' focus on the internal narrative is a defence against the historic external reality.

However, as de Zulueta (1993; see also Chapter 3) comments:

> A refusal on the part of psychiatrists and therapists to validate the horrors of their patients' tortured past implies a refusal to take seriously the unconscious psychological mechanisms that individuals need to use to protect themselves from the unspeakable. Such a denial is, however, no longer ethical, for it is this human capacity to dissociate that is part of the secret of both childhood abuse and the horrors of Nazi genocide, both forms of human violence, so often carried out by 'respectable' men and women.
>
> (p. 190)

PSYCHOANALYSIS AND THE BODY

In the adolescent and adult psychoanalytic field there is relatively little published work involving the physical body as opposed to the metaphoric or fantasy body. Exceptions include those who have to acknowledge the physical body through working on pregnancy and gender body issues, such as Raphael-Leff (1993), Perelberg, Pines (1982) and Susie Orbach; those working with violence and suicide, such as Eglé and Moses Laufer (1995); blindness and diabetes (Burlingham, Moran and Fonagy et al. from the Anna Freud Centre); as well as those who have worked with perversions and abuse, such as Glasser, Hale, Campbell, Welldon (at the Portman Clinic), Mario Marrone, Nicola Diamond, R.D. Hinshelwood, Roger Kennedy; plus colleagues Sheila Hollins, Brett Kahr, Nigel Beail, Pat Frankish, Sophie Thompson, Nicola Chad, Tamsin Cottis, Al Corbett and others working with disability.

Within the child field, in the last decade, by contrast, there has been a significant increase in writing about physical trauma. This is partly due to protective feelings for children who are not responsible for their external environment and partly as a result of health service statutory requirements since the existence of sexual abuse was accepted. Within the psychoanalytic community from the 1980s clinicians such as John Bowlby, Brendan MacCarthy, Judith Trowell, Juliet Hopkins, Arnon Bentovim (see Chapter 1), Eileen Vizard, Peter Fonagy (see Chapter 4) and Mary Target have been essential here in changing social views with their research as well as providing more focused case studies.

However, it is important to remember that only 15 years ago most major training schools did not accept the existence of child abuse and condemned what they saw as the unhealthy excitement that was considered to emanate from the earliest exponents. The language of their criticism is very similar (see R.D. Hinshelwood, Chapter 14) to what greets the clinician of today who speaks of DID. It has been a later knowledge that understands the way the shame and trauma of abuse become projected into the professional network leading to splitting and blame.

While professionals and patients can be blamed for 'believing' in an illness or having one, patients also report problems when they are believed. Some professionals, they commented, have worryingly simplistic ideas of 'integration'. Ignoring the separately named alters in effect offers a psychic death sentence rather than aiding integration. If anything it can create a compliant false-self 'main person' who answers to her name and keeps all other 'states' in silent terror internally. This iatrogenic damage is inevitable where professionals have a unitary model of the mind theories. Perhaps DID raises problematic philosophical and psychological concerns about the nature of the mind itself (see R.D. Hinshelwood, Chapter 14). Ideas of a unitary ego would incline professionals to see multiplicity as a behavioural disturbance. However, if the mind is seen as a seamless collaboration between multiple selves – a kind of trade union agreement for co-existence – it is less threatening to face this subject. This is an issue that continues to be debated internationally (see chapters by Southgate and Hinshelwood) and is crucial in considering many psychological problems.

The psychoanalyst Bion took great care to differentiate psychotic from non-psychotic personalities. New work on the changing roles between brain stem, left brain and right brain during infancy may soon clarify these issues without threatening established concepts of mind (Mary Sue Moore personal communication 2000).

Whatever the theory, it is important to note that clinicians such as Kluft draw attention to the clinical error of insisting that all alters talk as one or that only the alter with the legal name should be validated. 'Such stances are commonly associated with therapeutic failure.'

FRAGMENTATION IN THE TEAM

The primary split of DID creates a curious secondary splitting between staff. The psychiatrist who meets a frozen DID patient who shows only one state (as a result of correctly assessing their psychiatrist's inability to deal with the subject) and proclaims it is borderline personality disorder then attacks the other psychiatrist/social worker/psychologist/psychotherapist who points out the fragmentation into states. In having one professional pronounce that a condition does not exist versus another who does we are witnessing the trauma-organised systems (see Bentovim, Chapter 1) that systemically mirror the DID experience. The conflict between states is accurately and ironically mirrored in the conflicts between professionals. One state cannot believe that another exists, disputes its sense of reality and at times wishes to destroy it.

This polarisation extends to writing on the subject. Some clinicians show a remarkable ignorance of the current state of work in this country and the relative lack of interest by psychoanalytic practitioners. Aldridge-Morris (1989) sees those of us who are dealing with the reality of this condition as 'practitioners who generally favour hypnotherapeutic techniques, are psychoanalytic or neopsychoanalytic in orientation'. As Mollon (1996 and Chapter 11) points out: 'In fact most contemporary writers on the treatment of MPD favour techniques derived from cognitive-behavioural approaches. The concept of MPD is not part of the psychoanalytic tradition. Relatively few psychoanalysts make use of the concept of dissociation.' Yet at the same time others are arguing that psychoanalysts and therapists are projecting dissociation onto the patients. Merskey (1992), in a review of past cases of DID, states that: 'suggestion and prior preparation of the patients are at the root of this condition'.

With the advent of concern about the boundary between true memory and false extrapolations (which has been exploited by various false memory exponents) there has been more room for views like Merskey's that DID is an iatrogenic disease created and instantly implanted by naïve therapists who expect to see it (see Mollon, Chapter 11).

While rigorously trained professionals are well aware of the suggestibility of traumatised clients, especially those who have been hypnotised, it is worth noting that all the patients who came to the Clinic for Dissociative Studies had already got a long knowledge of their own dissociation. Similarly, those alleging ritual abuse as a trigger for fragmentation had never lost such memories and had expressed them to other professionals long before attending the clinic.

It is worth noting that, in this subject, becoming more experienced by seeing several people with the same condition is highlighted as a matter of concern rather than a useful building of knowledge. There is perhaps a wish to consider that the therapist is the toxic agent spreading this unbearable narrative. That would spare us all the pain of having to consider it might be true.

Whether fortunately or unfortunately, psychotherapists have negligible training in brainwashing, forcing of alien memories or distorted ideas. Military mind control experiments, brainwashing within religious cults and government programmes are not areas of mainstream professional training despite the profound influence such practices have on vulnerable minds. Thus psychotherapists do not have the competence to project states or traumatic narratives into their patients. Mental health professionals also do not have any basic grounding in this subject.

This book aims to redress that balance and to provide basic clinical and theoretical information for the mental health professional and the interested layman. It is of concern to all because while we consider that this brilliant but tragic adaptation to trauma is as rare as the torture it stands witness to, extreme states show us writ large the stresses and responses of ordinary life.

There are many fearful societal templates about this subject. But I would like to consider it through fairytale – 'The Shoemaker and the Elves'. The link (see Sinason, Chapter 7) came to me in the first meeting with a patient and helped to transform the session. As you may recall there was a poor shoemaker facing eviction and poverty and yet because he was hardworking he worked to the very end, leaving out the last two shapes of leather to make into shoes for the morning. In the morning, to his shock, there are two perfectly made pairs of shoes. They catch the eye of a rich customer and the money paid allows the shoemaker to buy leather for four pairs of shoes. These too appear perfectly made in the morning, are sold and bring in money for eight pairs of shoes. It carries on and on with the elves completing whatever the shoemaker leaves out for them.

He is shocked at first but then grateful and finally decides to stay up to meet his benefactors. When he spies the elves, who don't see him, he sees they are in rags and poorly fed. He and his wife then make lovely sets of clothes and shoes for them all and leave out food and, as they can see he is now rich and successful, the elves happily go away. He carries on making his excellent shoes.

The point of the story I want to illustrate is that the shoemaker did know how to make good shoes. His success was not fake. He was able to acknowledge the secret night-time help he got. When people with DID acknowledge their night-time help, they can then at some point be happy with the shared gifts they had and that helps them deal with the pain of their situation.

THE ORGANISATION OF THE BOOK

To understand the process and aetiology of DID Part I deals with origins in childhood and developmental issues. How does dissociation begin? Arnon Bentovim looks at the developmental precursors and gender issues followed by Nicholas Midgley of Great Ormond Street and the Anna Freud Clinic. Felicity de Zulueta of the Maudsley Hospital Traumatic Stress Service describes the continuum from dissociation to Post-traumatic Stress Disorder to full-blown Dissociative Identity Disorder.

Part II takes an attachment theory focus. Peter Fonagy provides a conceptual overview of the origins of dissociation. He sees the deactivation of attempts to understand the world as a defence from trauma. John Southgate offers an attachment-based model that combines his work with Bowlby and his interest in Bion. Leading University College London and Anna Freud Clinic researcher Howard Steele discusses the research potential of the Adult Attachment Interview in his work with patients from the Clinic for Dissociative Studies.

Part III looks at clinical practice. It includes leading psychoanalysts from the public sector Peter Whewell, Phil Mollon and Jean Goodwin. Peter Whewell describes both theoretically (especially using the work of Fairbairn) and clinically the work of the Newcastle NHS specialist team in dealing with clients. Phil Mollon provides a theoretical assessment of the nature of memory and assessment and the dangers of taking on this work. He provides many important cautions. Psychoanalytic therapist Sue Richardson provides an attachment theory method of working clinically. I provide a first meeting with a patient in which the story of the shoemaker and the elves provided a powerful therapeutic aid.

In Part IV we look at practical issues. Joan Coleman speaks of the lack of psychiatric training in this subject, Patricia Pitchon looks at how a telephone can offer help, and Claire Usiskin highlights administrative issues. Some legal pointers are also provided.

In Part V Bob Hinshelwood provides a thoughtfully sceptical look at the theoretical issues and social debate, Leslie Swartz offers an anthropological South African cultural experience, and Brett Kahr concludes with an interview with a pioneer on this subject – Flora Rheta Schreiber.

Poems by survivors also feature in the book, and at the end there is a brief information section.

THEORETICAL FORMULATIONS

Many of the authors provide particular reviews of literature that influence their understanding so I shall only provide a brief historical summary here.

There are many shades of dissociation that lead all the way to full-blown DID. It was Charcot, the great nineteenth-century neurologist who first brought the concept of hysteria and its symptoms of neurological damage and amnesia to public attention. While he demonstrated the psychological aetiology of hysteria as opposed to an organic aetiology, he was not particularly interested in the meaning, and it was Janet and Freud who became interested in taking the work further. By the mid-1880s (Herman 1992) both recognised that altered states came from trauma and that somatic symptoms represented disguised representations of events repressed from memory. Janet produced the term 'idée fixe' while Freud underpinned the concept of traumatic repetition as a way of working through. Breuer and Freud coined the term 'double-consciousness'. Breuer and Freud (1895) wrote that 'hysterics suffered from reminiscences' and Janet (1891) too described how one patient improved when, after removing the superficial layer of delusions, he realised the fixed ideas at the bottom of her mind.

However, it was Freud (1896) who in 'The aetiology of hysteria' firmly based the origins of hysteria in traumatic sexuality. He saw this as the key issue, the 'caput Nili'. Freud's shock at his own findings and his inability to conceive that abuse in his own social class was so widespread is not surprising. As I have written elsewhere (Sinason 1993), it is hard enough for professionals

100 years later than Freud to accept the extent of middle-class abuse. It is far easier to pick up the signs of abuse in working-class or 'underclass' children. In fact, Freud never gave up entirely on the significance of the abuse of early seduction.

However, Freud's modification and transforming of his clinical views came at a significant moment in European history. Charcot, before his death in 1893, was coming under attack concerning the scientific validity of his public demonstrations. There were rumours that the women were actresses pretending to go into trances; and Janet, who stayed faithful to the traumatic origins of hysteria, was not successful in having his ideas passed on. Breuer collaborated with Freud in publishing the case of 'Anna O' but did not like Freud's finding concerning early sexual trauma. After 'The aetiology of hysteria' was published, Freud wrote to Fliess: 'I am as isolated as you could wish me to be; the word has been given out to abandon me, and a void is forming around me' (4 May 1896).

The void that always forms around messengers with unwanted news was spreading and sadly returned the study of hysteria, hypnosis and altered states in Europe 'into the realms of the occult' (Herman 1992).

DID AND RITUAL ABUSE

In America the largest amount of DID is diagnosed in connection with allegations of ritual satanist abuse, hence the discrediting of or inability to perceive the possibility of the one existing automatically precludes rational thinking about the other. Hacking (1995) is concerned about this combination as well as the lack of external corroboration of ritual abuse. 'It would be a grave mistake for any therapist to believe memories of such events without conclusive independent corroboration' (p. 118). He adds, 'Ganaway thought that uncritical acceptance of memories of satanic abuse not only imperilled the credibility of multiple personality but put research on child abuse in general at risk'.

It is worth noting that both at the Portman Clinic and in the Clinic for Dissociative Studies we have not found evidence of fundamentalist religious beliefs, recovered memory or Munchhausen's Syndrome as issues in those alleging this kind of abuse. Indeed, the pilot study on patients alleging ritual abuse that Dr Rob Hale, Director of the Portman Clinic, and I submitted in July 2000 included the finding that the only two out of 51 subjects who had any link with evangelist religious groups did this after disclosing ritual satanist abuse because no one else would listen to them.

In our far more secular society with established churches in which leading members do not believe in a personal God, a personal Satan is incomprehensible. This leads the majority to conflate satanist abuse with Satan rather than with sadistic paedophilia carried out either by Satanists – people who do believe in Satan (Satanist paedophiles) – or those who draw on the frightening power of occult paraphernalia. To the child victim it is irrelevant which group carried out the abuse.

Van Benschoten (1990) comments that 'The issue of credibility is the first hurdle professionals and the public must confront when dealing with MPD patients' reports of satanic ritual abuse. Survivors' accounts reveal activities which are not only criminal but deliberately and brutally sadistic almost beyond belief.'

I have stated elsewhere (Sinason 1994) that the number of children and adults tortured in the name of mainstream religious and racial orthodoxy out-weighs any onslaught by satanist abusers. Wiccans, witches, warlocks, pagans and Satanists who are not abusive are increasingly concerned at the way crim-inal groups closely related to the drug and pornographic industries conflate their rituals.

In trying to deal with worrying patients who have to be treated regardless of the doubts around their disclosures, mental health professionals often have to face these contentious issues. This makes it much harder for a proper considered response because professionals, like everyone else, are affected by the consensus. In my past work at the Portman Clinic and in my clinic I have noted the sec-ondary traumatisation of professionals caused both by the impact of the patients' narrative and then by the disbelieving stance of colleagues. Indeed, both pro-fessionals and, more importantly, patients, suffer from societal discrediting processes (including the media) in addition to their primary trauma. This applies to lawyers and police officers as well as mental health professionals.

On the influential *Today* programme on 9 February 2000 I spoke of a clinic database of 76 children and adults who alleged to have witnessed appalling crimes within the context of ritual abuse. The programme correctly com-mented that I would separately be sending a pilot study report co-written with Dr Robert Hale to the Department of Health. I mentioned that some patients coming to the Clinic for Dissociative Studies brought proof that they had not been registered as children. This is a shocking fact and not surprisingly caused shock. Also included in the programme was a woman survivor with whom I have no connection who described seeing children kept in a cage. The *Daily Mail* provided a banner headline conflating these two episodes. 'Do Satanists really keep babies in cages in modern Britain – or has this woman [me] duped the BBC's most prestigious news programmes?'

In a curious process of Chinese whispers they then quoted Professor Sydney Brandon as saying that I had spoken of 12-year-old girls being kept in a cage, 'the proof being droppings under the cage. Words fail me. The terrible thing is that therapists influence people's lives and they can do harm as well as good.'

The media response to this topic with concerning distortions even, appar-ently, from mental health professionals, inhibits some colleagues from taking on this work. This also impacts on the police.

The public often fail to understand the difference between clinical concerns of what is heard in a session and the amount of proof necessary to prove beyond reasonable doubt in a criminal court. Only 2 per cent of rape cases even get to court. The *Today* programme interviewer was shocked to hear that photographic evidence of sites with mutilated animals, injuries that could not be self-inflicted, and remains of ceremonies do not lead to successful prosecutions.

However, the increase in referrals from worried clinicians and families all over the UK is moving towards the critical mass that is required to implement proper provision and treatment strategy.

In 1999 the Institute for Psychotherapy and Disability was launched at St George's Hospital Medical School under the mission statement 'Treating with Respect'. Professors Bicknell and Hollins, Dr Pat Frankish, Dr Nigel Beail, Brett Kahr and myself all declared that one essential pre-requisite for a specialist learning disability therapist was treating the client with respect. We found ourselves shocked by the lack of respect accorded to many adults in the mental health services and the dynamic of 'blaming the patient for their illness'. Sadly it has to be mentioned that learning-disabled patients with dissociative identity disorder have also been significantly represented. This concerns organisations such as RESPOND and VOICE.

Secondary traumatisation is a real danger in facing this work. I have found it essential to have weekly supervision from a senior training analyst as well as a long personal psychoanalysis. Additionally, I have benefited from the Psychoanalytic Study Group on Ritual Abuse and Dissociation and the support of clinic staff and consultants.

The clinical needs of this patient group are very different and it requires careful thought when considering where the frame needs altering to provide the adequate conditions of safety (see chapters by Mollon and Whewell). Sessions that last double time (100 minutes) with face-to-face patients who are too terrified to lie down on a couch are a very different experience for the average psychodynamic practitioner. Considering the clinical and technical issues of using emails and telephone calls to provide extra support at different times also takes a great deal of thinking. Many psychodynamic practitioners find they are using cognitive elements too.

If a lucky enough professional needs a multiplicity of supports to manage this subject we need to think very hard about the level of trauma the actual patient feels. Whatever we feel is only a shadow of that. If we cannot manage to bear the pain of these individuals what does that say about the level of pain that was forced into them at an early age?

One courageous ritual abuse survivor, on being told by the team psychiatrist that her behaviour and disclosures were upsetting the nurses commented: 'What do you expect me to say? I am the patient. That is why I am here in this case conference. I am sorry the nurses are upset. But I tell you. I would rather be the nurses who are upset than be me and have to deal with in my head what I have gone through.'

To conclude with the words of Toisin, a survivor:

> Please don't turn your head and walk away
> Have you the strength inside to stay
> I know it's hard to face the fact
> That human beings can do such violent acts.

The views expressed by any of the contributors, including myself as editor and chapter-writer, are individual opinions. Inclusion in this collection does not imply theoretical or clinical agreement.

With thanks to the following for crucial support in this work: to Pearl King for weekly supervision, clinical and ethical guidance and unwavering support, to the memory of Mervin Glasser, my psychoanalyst, who died in November 2000 for making the unbearable manageable, to the memory of my father Professor S.S. Segal whose steadfast pioneering led to the inclusion of disabled children within the education system and whose motto in standing up for stigmatised individuals was 'and shall not pass them by nor throw them crumbs', to David Leevers for personal, editorial and conceptual support, Tina Carlile, Joan Coleman, Carole Mallard, Peter Fonagy, Richard and Xenia Bowlby, Howard and Miriam Steele, Marcus and Jennifer Johns, Moira Walker, D.I. Clive Driscoll, D.C.I. Chris Healy, D.C.I. John Welch, D.C.I. Kate Halpin, Sarah Gordon, Rob Hale, Ainsley Gray, Jeremy Glyde, Harry Grant, Michael Curtis, Nancy Dunlop, Anthony Lee, Lee Moore and ACAL, Jeni Couzyn, Lynda Rycraft, Eddy and Heather Rowarth, John and Hazel Silverstone, Tamar and Alan Segal, Marek and Marsha, Patricia and Eduardo Pitchon, Susie Orbach and Joe Schwarz, LASA, Llin Golding MP, Lord Alton, Sheila Hollins, Arnon Bentovim and Marianne Tranter, Estela Welldon, Liz Lloyd, Shahnawz Haque and Respond, Lloyd de Mause, the Psychoanalytic Study Group on Ritual Abuse and Dissociation including Phil Mollon, Mario Marrone, Nicola Diamond, Elizabeth Campbell, Peter Whelan, John Southgate, Kate White, Liz London. Particular thanks for editorial assistance work from Claire Usiskin and Jill Duncan, the former and current Clinic Administrators. Thanks to all the contributors for both their written chapters and their many other emotional contributions, to Joanne Forshaw at Routledge for her patience and care and to Kristin Susser for production.

Thanks to all those with DID who have dared to face yet another professional with their gifts, their hurt and their courage.

REFERENCES

Aldridge-Morris, R. (1989) *Multiple Personality, An Exercise in Deception*. Hove: Erlbaum.

Breuer, J. and Freud, S. (1893–5) 'Studies on hysteria', in *The Standard Edition of the Complete Psychological Works of Sigmund Freud*, vol. 2. London: Hogarth Press.

de Zulueta, F. (1993) *From Pain to Violence: The Traumatic Roots of Destructiveness*. London: Whurr Publishers.

Freud, S. (1896) 'The aetiology of hysteria', in *The Standard Edition of the Complete Psychological Works of Sigmund Freud*, vol. 3, p. 203. London: Hogarth Press.

Hacking, I. (1995) *Rewriting the Soul: Multiple Personality and the Sciences of Memory*. London: Princeton University Press.

Hale, R. and Sinason, V. (1994) In Valerie Sinason (ed.) *Treating Survivors of Satanist Abuse*. London: Routledge.

Herman, J.L. (1992) *Trauma and Recovery*. New York: Basic Books.

Janet, P. (1891) *Néuroses et idées fixes*. Paris: J. Rueff.

Laufer, M. (ed.) (1995) *The Suicidal Adolescent*, for Brent Adolescent Centre, Centre for Research into Adolescent Breakdown. London: Karnac Books.

Merskey, H. (1992) 'The manufacture of personalities. The production of multiple personality disorder', *British Journal of Psychiatry* 160: 327–40.

Mollon, P. (1996) *Multiple Selves, Multiple Voices*. Chichester: John Wiley & Sons.

North, C.S., Ryall, J.-Em., Ricci, D.A. and Wetzel, R.D. (1983) *Multiple Personalities, Multiple Disorders, Psychiatric Classification and Media Influence*. New York: Oxford University Press.

Pines, D. (1982) 'The relevance of early psychic development to pregnancy and abortion', *International Journal of Psychoanalysis* 63: 311–320.

Putnam, F.W., Guroff, J.J., Silberman, E.K. et al. (1986) 'The clinical phenomenology of multiple personality disorder: Review of 100 recent cases', *J. of Clinical Psychiatry* 47: 285–93.

Raphael-Leff, J. (1993) *Pregnancy: The Inside Story*. London: Sheldon Press.

Sinason, M. (1993) 'Who is the mad voice inside?', *Psychoanalytic Psychotherapy* 7: 207–21.

Sinason, V. (ed.) (1994) *Treating Survivors of Satanist Abuse*. London: Routledge.

Southgate, J. (1996) 'An attachment approach to dissociation and multiplicity', paper presented at the Third John Bowlby Memorial Lecture, Centre for Attachment-based Psychoanalytic Psychotherapy, London.

Van Benschoten, S. (1990) 'Multiple personality disorder and satanic ritual abuse: the issue of credibility', *Dissociation* 3(1) March.

Chapter 1

Dissociative Identity Disorder
A developmental perspective

Arnon Bentovim

Richard Kluft, in his foreword to the text *The Dissociative Child: Diagnosis, Treatment and Management* edited by Joanna Silberg (1996), describes his struggle to understand the early origins of adults who are diagnosed as suffering from Dissociative Identity/Multiple Personality Disorder. He asked where this condition comes from. Clinical manifestations appear to have virtually erupted in many cases. He could not understand where these phenomena had been sequestered before the switch, which completely caught him by surprise. He wondered whether childhood forms of the disorder existed, did the developmental process gradually take shape, did they emerge fully developed, like Athena from the brow of Zeus?

He felt that his efforts to track the natural history of Dissociative Identity Disorder were successful, but his attempts to find childhood cases were an 'unmitigated fiasco'. He was able to describe an 8-year-old child who did appear to manifest 'a series of developed personality states', having witnessed a near drowning, and also suffered physical abuse. However, he realised with other colleagues that his scope was too narrow. He noted that Fagan and McMahon (1984) described a notion of incipient multi-personality disorder in children; they raised the possibility of a wider spectrum of dissociative phenomenology that children may manifest.

Perhaps it is appropriate that the text edited by Joanna Silberg is described as the 'Dissociative Child', rather than 'Dissociative Disorder of Childhood', and indeed Peterson, in the same collection of papers (Peterson 1996), described the struggles to persuade the DSM-IV task forces to include the notion of a Dissociative Disorder of Childhood. Finally, references to dissociative processes in childhood were included as part of the exclusion criteria for the diagnosis of Attention Deficit/Hyperactivity Disorder in Childhood.

When I consider my own experience as a child and adolescent psychiatrist who has been working in the field of child abuse and trauma since the end of the 1960s, having seen many hundred sexually abused children and adolescents since we became aware of sexual abuse at the end of the 1970s and 1980s, I realise that I have seen very few children and young people who I would unequivocally categorise as showing a classical Dissociative Identity Disorder.

I have seen a small number of children who would fulfil the criteria of demonstrating 'two or more distinct identities or personality states with such identities recurrently taking control of the person's behaviour, with the forgetfulness associated', as described in the DSM-IV criteria for Dissociative Identity Disorder/Multiple Personality Disorder. These are a rarity in my practice, but many of the features that perhaps develop into such separate identities are seen in children who have been extensively traumatised.

The study on boys who have been sexually abused, which I and colleagues at the Institute of Child Health/Great Ormond Street Hospital carried out, demonstrates the presence of dissociative phenomena in this particular group (Midgley 1997). It is also striking in that study that dissociative responses were seen not only in children experiencing sexual abuse, but also in children subject to physical or emotional abuse within the family context. In other words, dissociative responses occur in the context of children who are subject to and live in a climate of violence and abuse.

To look more systematically at the way personality develops in traumatised children and how this can contribute to what may be the fully formed Dissociative Identity Disorders of adulthood, it is helpful to examine the response of children and young people to abuse in a systematic way.

TRAUMA ORGANISED SYSTEMS

I have argued that the best model to understand the effects of abuse, whether physical or sexual, is to consider them as forms of what I described as 'Trauma Organised Systems' (Bentovim 1995). By this I meant that abusive events are traumatic in effect, and through a process of repeated cumulative actions, cause increasingly severe effects on the emotional lives of those children involved. I argued too that the perpetrator who traumatises the child is also caught up in a system that allows the maintenance of abusive action in secrecy. Those adults in the children's context who should be protective are caught up in the process as well, and are involved in a system of secrecy, denial and blame which, in turn, maintains abusive action.

I argued as follows:

1 Trauma organised systems are essentially action systems. The key actors are the victimiser and traumatiser and the victim who is traumatised.
2 There is an absence of a protector, or potential protectors are neutralised.
3 The victimiser is overwhelmed by impulses to actions of a physically, sexually or emotionally abusive nature that emerge from his or her own experiences. They are felt to be overwhelming and beyond control.
4 The cause is often attributed to the victim who, in line with individual family and cultural expectations, is construed as responsible for the victimiser's feelings and intentions.

5 Any action on the victim's part as a result of abuse or to avoid abuse, is interpreted by the abuser as a further cause for disinhibition of violent action, or justification for further abuse.

6 Thus there is a sense of entrapment for the victim and the victimiser, who feel there is no escape from the pattern of action which feels imposed from outside, an impulse which takes them over, or is pre-destined and from which they cannot escape.

7 Any potential protective figure is organised or neutralised by the process of secrecy, minimisation of victimising actions, blaming the victim. The process of silence, of dissociation, spreads to the victim, the victimiser and those who could potentially protect.

8 Thinking processes of both the victim and the victimiser alike are characterised by deletion of thought, minimisation of the experience, dismissal of the event, or blame of self or other. This process of dissociation and separation from the experience and the actions is a characteristic coping style which enables individuals to continue in what appears like a day-to-day existence.

9 The repeated nature of violent actions', traumatic stress effects comes to organise the reality and the perceptions of those participating, including potential protectors, professionals who become involved in the family situation.

10 The pressure not to see, not to hear, not to speak, means that there is no processing of experiences, and a range of coping strategies emerge which may well include a variety of identifications of a confusing nature.

It is interesting to note that Goodwin (1996) describes a series of male young people who themselves had been seriously abused, and whose abusive behaviour appeared to be associated with switching into a different personality style of an abusive nature; this is a process of identification with the aggressor. Clinical experience indicates that young people who are at the early stages of abusive behaviour, before a full perversion has developed, may well describe very similar phenomena.

Case examples

A young person of 15 who was admitted to the unit for young sex offenders for which I am a consultant (SWAAY) described his very considerable anxiety at starting in a college which was situated next to a school for young children. He described his intense sense of anxiety and fear that his abusive behaviour, 'the abuser within', as it were, would suddenly emerge and drive him to abuse against these children. The context reminded him of the setting where he had abused other children extensively. At the same time being within college also reminded him of his sense of vulnerability. The man who abused him targeted him, came into school, secreted him away and abused him on a number of occasions. For him the experience of being put in touch with his victim self, and also his abusive identification, was evoked by the particular context. This young person was describing the feeling of being overwhelmed by flashbacks of abusive experiences and impulses to abuse, characteristic of the psychological realities of trauma organised systems.

Another of the boys in the unit had been extensively, sadistically abused, and involved in ritual activities. He alternated between states of absolute terror when he was convinced that his father who was in prison would appear in the unit, reinforced by flashbacks and visualisations of his experiences. These victimisation states could switch suddenly into explosive violent attacks. Fire extinguishers would be thrown through windows, mirrors and crockery would be smashed, other young people and staff attacked. Psychotherapeutic work indicated that this boy became preoccupied with a desire to impose the terror to which he had been subjected on to those around him. His apparently impulsive actions were in fact planned, and carefully worked out to create the most shocking and terrifying action which he could himself perpetrate. He had previously abused other children in the setting where he had been placed.

THE MULTI-LAYERED EFFECTS OF TRAUMATIC ACTION

It is generally accepted that to understand the impact of traumatic events requires an understanding of the direct effect of abusive action, the development of a post-traumatic state, and an understanding of the associated long-term effects on personality. Finkelhor (1987) described these as 'Traumagenic Dynamic Responses'.

I have conceptualised traumatic responses as a systemic interconnected process with the three now well-known effects, 're-enactment', 'avoidance' and 'arousal' at the points of a triangle (see Figure 1.1).

I noted that each response leads to the other, re-enactment to avoidance, to hyperarousal, and around the cycle. Re-enactment is the intrusion of unwanted, painful and distressing memories of events into the thoughts of a child, reflected in drawing, conversation and play. They represent the events which cannot be coped with because they are outside the experience of the child, and the process of re-enactment is in part a biological response of fear, to sensitise the individual to similar dangers.

Given that abusive experiences and their responses occur over a significant length of time, they may become inextricably linked with traumagenic dynamic responses. These are usually described as 'powerlessness' (see Figure 1.2), associated with invasion and physical discomfort; 'betrayal', through the manipulation of trust, violation of care and lack of protection; 'stigmatisation', linked to the context of blame and denigration; and 'sexualisation', the premature and distressing arousal of sexual responses through inappropriate

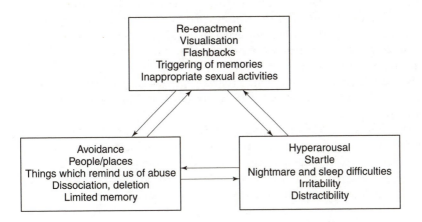

Figure 1.1 Trauma organised systems: traumatic response to sexual abuse

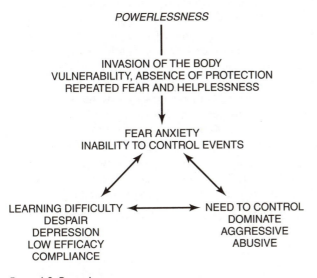

Figure 1.2 Powerlessness

responses being rewarded by means of induction into a sexual partner role. Inevitably there has to be a search for meaning in the face of such stressful and uncontrollable events. The child attributes what is happening to himself, the actions are his fault. Stable attributional sets emerge, and impact both on biological and psychological aspects of development.

I have noted, for instance, that boys who have been subject to extensive sexual abuse describe flashbacks of their abusive experience triggered during a phase of normal adolescent sexual arousal. The most difficult question for such boys is 'do you ever feel the abuser's hand on your penis at times when you are sexually aroused, when you have an erection?' This may be admitted with intense shame, and it becomes clear that the arousal associated with abuse becomes incorporated into the basic sexuality, the 'central masturbatory fantasy' of the young person. This may be experienced as an alien shameful desire to re-enact abusive actions with others which at the same time has to be repudiated.

One begins to see the development of different selves, the struggle to see such impulses and feelings as 'not oneself', the product of an alien other within, the concrete presence of the abuser. This is the pathway to the sort of experience triggered by the young person described earlier when faced with a context which reminded him of his previous abuse and abusive activities.

THE PROCESS OF DISSOCIATION AND AVOIDANCE

An important element of the primary response to abuse is avoidance, and the attempt to prevent thinking about the abusive experience, reinforced by an abuser who demands secrecy, or by the disbelief of members of the child's family to whom they may have tried to speak. The dynamics of powerlessness, stigmatisation, betrayal, sexualisation, may in turn also reinforce the struggle to 'avoid' thinking, feeling or action, which can take the form of dissociation. This is seen in extreme forms in 'Childhood Pervasive Refusal Syndrome' where the child inhibits speech, movement, refuses to eat, control urination or defecation, and shows an extreme passivity. In more minor forms the process of dissociation – temporary switching off, blanking out at times of stress – may be triggered by a spontaneous flashback or visualisation or when attempts are made to work therapeutically, by reminding children of abusive contexts. The development of an 'alternative self' as a way of coping may well be an under-standable response to reinforce the process of avoidance of thinking – the self without memory.

Case examples

The process of 'childhood pervasive refusal' was seen in extreme forms in the younger three siblings of a sibship of seven, aged 3, 4 and 6 years. The possibility of sexual abuse had been raised through the extreme sexualised behaviour of the eldest daughter. The older brother and second eldest sister began to describe being videoed, and abusive action perpetrated against them by both parents while they were in foster care.

But the three youngest children, a boy and two girls, were silent, monosyl-labic, passive in school and at home with carers and family members. They were silent, frozen and unable to communicate in interviews. Although severe neglect was a factor, in addition there was extensive silencing and the response of extreme dissociation in the face of the extensive climate of violence and abuse they grew up in.

The third major response of arousal, fearfulness and tension associated with poor sleep may also be triggered as part of the fight or flight response to abuse. Explosive action may be reinforced to counter a sense of powerlessness. One young person who threw fire extinguishers did so particularly towards night-time, the time of darkness when the sense of reality is disturbed by the nightmares within.

THE IMPACT OF ABUSE, OF LIVING IN A CLIMATE OF VIOLENCE, AND OF EXTENSIVE ABUSIVE EXPERIENCES ON DEVELOPMENTAL PROCESSES

It is necessary to develop an understanding of trauma organised systems and the intertwined, enmeshed relationship of the victimiser and victim, both in the external world and in the internal world of the child. In this way it becomes possible to conceptualise multiple personality development, and the way for different selves/alters seen in Dissociative Identity Disorder to emerge. I have found it helpful to conceptualise responses as internalising or external- ising following widely used models. Figure 1.3 demonstrates the process. To understand the complexity of response, it is helpful to consider the three major areas of personality function of children and young people:

1   The regulation of emotion
2   The development of attachments
3   The development of an adequate sense of self.

Although these three areas are considered separately, they in fact reinforce each other and are intertwined and come to underpin the relationship models of the individual child and young person both within his family and within the social context. Increasingly there is an awareness of the biological underpin- ning to these areas. The description of the 'conditioned fear response' to overwhelming stress leads to an interrelated biological and psychological response. Thus the child or young person living in a world invaded by fear and anxiety has ways of relating that are coloured and directed by such experiences. It is not surprising that different selves develop as a way of coping with the overwhelming processes which remain locked in the psychic structure of the seriously traumatised child.

The effect of being extensively abused is that the abuser literally inserts themselves into the self of the victim; they are omnipresent in the form of flash- backs, visualisations, reminders. The relationship between the perpetrator and victim is constantly interplayed, and may be one of the factors accounting for

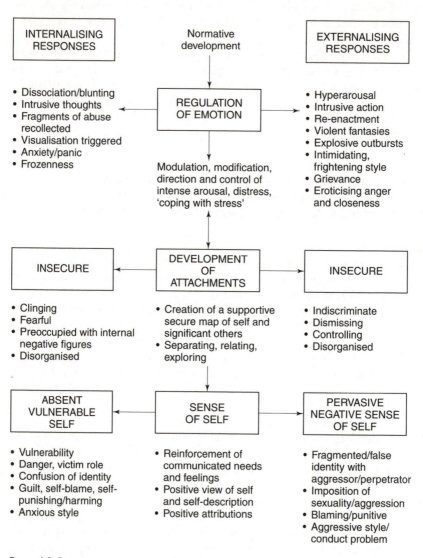

Figure 1.3 Responses to traumagenic contexts

an internalising process whereby the abuser is felt literally as an internal figure occupying the total space of the personality, or in externalising processes when there is an identification with that abusive figure turning outwards to project the victim self on to another. In those individuals who are prone to develop a Dissociative Identity Disorder, a number of selves develop, representing both the abusive figures and the victim, exploding into consciousness through the processes to be described. It is likely that factors of severity and extensiveness of abuse play a part in determining which young person will demonstrate such responses, taking each aspect of development in turn (see Midgley, Chapter 2).

Regulation of emotions

Regulation of emotions during development is to do with the modulation, modification, direction and control of intense arousal, distress, i.e. developing modes of coping with stress. 'Good enough care' and containing is required to facilitate this process. Adequate care-giving and the parental capacity to empathise with the infant's overwhelming distress, fussing, crying, enables the growing infant and young child to internalise a supportive parental figure and to take control of overwhelming distress for themselves. By definition, abusive care fails to deal adequately with distress, and replaces containing calmness and coping with frustration, anger, rage, withdrawal, ignoring, disruption, physical shaking, hitting, pinching, burning. The parent whose resources are limited through failures of their own care-giving can only feel crying and fussing to be aversive, punitive responses that they themselves were subject to and so retaliation is justified.

At later stages of development, specific abusive experiences, sexual abuse, physical abuse, the induction of illness states, result in overwhelming arousal – emotional responses, e.g. sexuality and anger, that the infant has no capacity to contain or deal with. The child's responses are unmodulated and uncontained, and inevitably trigger and justify the parents repeating abusive action – the core of a trauma organised response.

It is helpful to group such responses into externalising and internalising responses. Internalising responses describe the sense of being overwhelmed and intruded upon. Blanking out, deleting, dissociating, blunting is the response. However there are intrusive thoughts, fragments of abuse are recollected, flashbacks of intense overwhelming experiences occur. Anxiety, panic, states of frozenness result. Avoidance of people, places and things which remind is the predominant mode of relating or clinging to perceived 'safe' figures, including the abuser!

Externalising responses represent the opposite to this. Instead of blunting there is hyperarousal; instead of recollections or fragments of abuse which feel thrust into mind, the impulse is towards intrusive action, re-enactment towards others to contain overwhelming emotions. Violent fantasies, explosive outbursts are seen, and an intimidating, frightening style of relating results. The emotional states which predominate are those to do with grievance. Anger may be eroticised in an intertwining of sexuality and anger. Closeness evokes overwhelming desires to intrude, attack, sexualise.

Although internalising and externalising responses are described as if they were alternative emotional states, both are seen in individuals who have been subject to extensive abusive experiences. Overwhelming distress and a sense of being intruded upon, switches to hyperarousal, grievance, and violent outbursts against the other and the self. Such alternating emotional states form the bedrock of the personality states later seen in Dissociative Identity Disorder. Dissociation blunting of affect and feelings is a characteristic coping mechanism of children subject to severe pervasive abusive experiences. This response forms a buffer between states, and between different personality characteristics and selves. Such emotional states become personified through other processes including the development of attachment and self-development.

Development of attachments

Closely associated with the regulation of emotion and the development of emotional responses is the development of attachments. Attachments develop both as a means of creating proximity, and evoking care-giving. Attachment style arises out of coping with the particular emotional state of the care-giver and results in the characteristic attachment patterns. The interactive context during the first year of life and subsequent development results in the infant creating a map of themselves and significant others. In a secure relationship this results in satisfactory separation and individuation, the bedrock to relating to and exploring the world around.

Aversive parenting evokes insecure patterns of the self and others. If relationships are sufficiently disrupted attachments will be indiscriminate, seeking anyone to attach to. Response to a context of fear, anxiety and unpredictability, can lead to a clinging insecure attachment – fearful, maintaining closeness and intensity as a mode of coping, leading to a preoccupation with internal negative experiences and figures. These responses are reinforced by the internalising responses, augmented by intrusive fragments of recollected abuse, visualisations, flashbacks triggered. A process of disorganisation takes over, switching from state to state results from the process of being overwhelmed with uncontrollable emotional experiences as a consequence of living in a context of pervasive abuse.

Alternatively, coping may be dismissive, aversive in character, avoiding contact, or alternately attempting to take control. Again this mode of relating, if linked with the externalising emotional responses of hyperarousal, intrusive action, explosive outbursts, comes to characterise the style of relating. Such patterns can become highly disorganised, with switching from a clinging state of being preoccupied with internal figures, to a state of controlling, dismissive, or indiscriminate ways of relating; again forming a bedrock for the switching of states which becomes crystallised into the identities seen in adult lives.

Sense of self

The sense of self arises through the reinforcement by parents providing good enough care, and responding to communicated needs and feelings. Out of this a positive view of self develops a description of self as worthy of care and love, with associated positive attributions.

Children growing up in a climate of violence develop a profound absence of self. In the internalising mode, the image and presence of the abusive parents occupy all the psychological space. There is a sense of vulnerability, danger, identification with a victim role, intense confusion of identity and responsibility. The feeling that if the child is subject to anger, to rage, to punishment, then he or she must be an appropriate subject for such treatment, results in guilt, self-blame, and a self-punitive harming style. Self-harm becomes a distraction, a way of distracting from emotional pain, and becomes a way of taking control; to cause pain oneself gives an illusory sense of control over the environment rather than feeling like the passive vessel evoking anger in an inconsistent unpredictable way.

The sense of vulnerability, victim self or absence of self is associated with blunted, dissociated affect, and a preoccupation characteristic of internalising modes of coping with emotions and attachments. Switching may be seen between the absent vulnerable sense of self to a state of invulnerability, from powerlessness to omnipotence. The pervasive negative sense of self can predispose to an identity with the aggressor, or the perpetrator. Sexuality and aggression may be imposed on others, a blaming, punitive, aggressive style may develop with fragmentation of self, the development of false selves, and a variety of different identifications. The basic model of coping with a context of pervasive violence results in switching between a state of vulnerability and powerlessness and a powerful, oppressive role which identifies with the aggressor.

Such polar shifts form the basis for personality style. Moving through the developmental phases of childhood and adolescence results in the crystallisation of one or more of these identities, internalising roles which identify with the victim that the child or young person is or has been, to the externalising roles identifying with the perpetrator/abuser role.

Case example

To illustrate the process of identity development in childhood a case example will be given. The father of the family abused his stepdaughter sexually over a number of years. When she reached 16 years of age he ran away with her, they married and subsequently had seven children. The family were well known to social services over the years because of the very poor standard of care given to the children; they went to school poorly clothed with inappropriate shoes, clothing suitable for summer in the winter months. There were growth problems, the children were often dirty, unkempt, late for school, or absent without reason. There were extensive investigations when concerns were raised, but no action was taken.

The father's response to authorities was angry, rejecting, uncooperative, bullying to social workers and professionals and clearly in control of the family.

His wife said nothing, no adequate explanation was ever given for the state of the children. There were brief interventions, periods when the children seemed to be better cared for, then lapses. The oldest daughter who was aged 18 at the time of referral managed to 'escape' from the family and insisted on being fostered by an ex-neighbour. Despite attempts by the parents to get her to return she refused and was protected by the social services department.

She eventually began to speak about what was happening in the family, and revealed that there was extensive sexual abuse going on. Children were made to be sexual with each other, and were abused regularly by both parents, they were videoed and abused by a ring of over 30 adults, she alleged. There followed an extensive investigation, the children were removed into care, and the parents prosecuted. The children confirmed the story that their older sister had given. They also reported that there was rigid control of sleeping times, what they ate, when they were allowed to get up, when they were allowed to come out of their rooms. They revealed a family atmosphere of extensive oppression, multiple sadistic and sexual abuse in an atmosphere of threat and violence. Their mother found herself caught between wanting to agree with the children's statements and to see her husband as the abusive figure in her own life. But she was also pulled towards a strong alliance with him against authority, to deny what was being alleged, blaming the oldest daughter for behaving vindictively, wanting to prove their innocence and blaming the professionals for feeding stories to the children.

It is interesting to review briefly the behavioural patterns, attachments, emotional life and sense of self that each of these children revealed. They illustrate the considerable range of patterns which are seen in children who have grown up in a context of secrecy, pervasive violence, threat and extensive abusive sexual activities both with each other and with each of the parents in a sadistic and intensive fashion.

Cathy, the youngest of the children, was aged 7 years and the youngest girl. Her attachment pattern and relationships were described as follows. She was perceived as her father's favourite. This falsely positive relationship was reflected by her identifying with his bullying style. She bullied her 13-year-old sister who was living in the same home as she was, appearing to adopt her father's style. At the same time in foster care she made calculated sexualised advances to men and women. She rubbed against people, and whenever she saw her siblings she made sexualised contact with them. The term 'traumatic attachment' has been used to describe a mode which adopts and adapts as to the abuser role.

In her emotional life, although she could be outgoing and friendly, she could also behave in a strikingly regressed fashion. She became preoccupied with urination and defecation. She would soil and wet, her sleep became restless and poor, as well as demonstrating a bullying style with her sister. When challenged she would crumple, go to pieces. Yet at other times she could behave explosively and angrily.

Her sense of self was again revealed through opposites, she could be attractive, friendly, bubbly, and appeared to demonstrate a real sense of herself. Then she could behave defiantly or withdraw. She saw herself as a sexual object, desirable, a favourite and if rejected would become distressed.

Thus it can be seen that this 7-year-old was already showing a pattern of responses which switched from one state to another, from brightness, bubbly attractiveness to withdrawal, from crumpling in the face of challenge to angry hitting out. She could take on her father's role, bullying her older sisters, identifying with the sexualised patterns of behaviour which are the expected norm for which she had been groomed and inducted into. It is hoped that therapeutic work will help this child become more integrated, and find a true self-image from these fractured modes of being.

Her 13-year-old sister Barbara's attachments were also intensely sexualised. As a young adolescent, she was preoccupied with 'love' relationships with her peers at school. She rapidly sexualised such relationships to a degree which was uncomfortable and embarrassing for boys at a similar stage of development who did not have the maturity and understanding to respond to the sexualised behaviour. She began to blossom in foster care, and began to get in touch with a real self, but she stated that she felt she did not exist, she had no importance, she should be treated as nothing.

It was hard to be in contact with her emotional life. She was secretive, she exploded, had tantrums in a wild way. When attempts were made to discuss her abuse, she glazed over and appeared dissociated.

Her sense of self was characterised by a pervasive negative sense. She had poor self-confidence, she had poor self-esteem, she cared for herself poorly. She allowed herself to be scapegoated and beaten by her younger sister and became confused about the reasons they were in foster care, not with their own family. She felt guilty that her father was in prison, felt that they should all be returned, that what happened was their fault, the father was not to blame, nor her mother. As another child I saw said, 'they could not have realised what they were doing was wrong otherwise they would have stopped'.

Barbara has already begun to develop a personality style and identity in adolescence with poor self-esteem and self-confidence. She comes to life in intense love relationships with peers. At the same time she feels as though she is nothing, should be treated like a thing. The danger of this role can be seen through the risk of her being targeted, used and abused by adults. The fact that she blossomed in foster care gives some sense of hope that she could find a real self, begin to integrate the various sides of herself, and find re-parenting from her foster carers with whom she is beginning to develop a trusting relationship.

Of the boys, Stanley, aged 11, demonstrated an almost immediate, compliant adaptive mode of attachment to his foster family. He behaved as if the past did not exist, his old family did not exist. He was like a compliant, trained child, who immediately saw himself as part of his new family. He behaved in school as if he had relationships, friendships. He appeared to be talking to people in the playground, but he was alone, there was no one there, he was living a totally false self-existence.

Emotionally he found it extremely difficult to talk about feelings, it was as if they did not exist. Gradually it was noticed that he became increasingly aroused, sexual in his ways and modes of relating, touching, secretive in his responses. At times he was overwhelmed with panic; it seemed as though he was expecting the sort of treatment that he received in his own family.

His sense of self reveals an emptiness, he did not exist, he had no past, no family, he trusted no one and was constantly on the watch. In a pre-adolescent phase Stanley has negated his past experiences, they did not exist, only his present family and relationships exist. Where there is absence he creates a false presence. At times it is as if he is in the grip of his old family, and he behaves as if he expected the punitive, highly sexualised form of relating into which he was inducted. He began to show elements of sexualisation in his relating.

Kenneth was 13 at the time he was taken into care. His attachments during this middle adolescent phase revealed that he took on the role of his father in an active fashion. He rejected and was enraged with the social workers' attempts to take him and his siblings into care when his parents were imprisoned. Before his mother was imprisoned he tried to protect her; he attempted to control the children, showing the same mode and style as his father did. He wanted to keep the family together, and got into intense power battles with foster parents when he was placed.

His emotional life was explosive, objects were smashed, there were moments when he seemed chaotic, bizarre, responsible for everything that had gone wrong. Slowly he began to demonstrate a more appropriate angry response towards his parents, as he began to perceive they may have used and abused him rather than providing adequate care. One sees here the stark total introjective identification with a dominating, controlling parental style: a young person identifying in word and deed with the role model provided and shaping a sense of self which recreated his father's role.

Derek, the 15-year-old, shows quite a different pattern. In his attachments, he too like his younger brother showed the compliant, adaptive role in the foster family. He warmed to his foster parents and they to him. He was a blue-eyed boy who seemed perfectly to adapt to the foster carer's family life. Slowly he revealed a desire to take control.

His emotional life was full of grievance, of anger, despite his apparent surface compliance. He was desperate for possessions, for material goods to give him some sort of sense of himself. Like his siblings he felt empty, did not exist, his life felt ruined, he felt only a shell remained. Again a real sense of self was emerging from this ruined landscape of self and other.

Thus these children – all of whom have grown up in a context of pervasive abuse, violence, sexual abuse, being sold for sex with other adults, videoed, humiliated – show both differences and common themes. There may be differences in relationship to gender; males and females may respond differently. However, the themes of compliant adaptation, various modes of sexualisation of relationships, explosiveness and anger directed to self or other, intense preoccupations with body states, focus on defecation and urination, or on sexual arousal, are common features. These features become gathered into alternating states of being – the foci for personality styles which can become the core of different states of self.

Hopefully therapeutic work and good care can interrupt the processes of taking on abuser and victim role, and a variety of false selves (alters), as a way of coping with what cannot be safely contained. Preventative work in childhood may ensure that the switching from state to state does not result in switching from one self to another. Dissociation is a common defensive mode in children subject to pervasive violence, and is also seen in these children and young people.

Prospective research on factors which increase the risk of young males who have been sexually abused becoming abusers (Skuse et al. 1999), has confirmed the role of pervasive family violence, disruptions of care, and rejection in orienting a young person to take an abusive role. However, parallel research on protective factors has indicated that such risk can be lessened by the provision of adequate alternate care, of supportive attachment figures and of adequate therapeutic care.

ADULT CASE OF DISSOCIATE IDENTITY DISORDER

It is interesting to look at a recently assessed adult patient in her fifties who was referred to the Clinic for Dissociative Studies. Her most recent concern was having found herself soaked on a beach with no memory or awareness of how she had reached there. She gave a history of self-harm, internal voices urging towards destruction. She described a childhood which was very similar to the children already described. She described polyincestuous abuse, and associated ritual abuse.

She remains in a partly dissociated state as far as childhood is concerned and remains unable to recall many periods of her early life. She has few memories of the conception of her first child. She described the development of both serious anorectic and self-harming behaviour, and intense sexualisation during adolescence. It seemed she remained unaware of her abusive background until she had her own children.

Her self-harming behaviour then increased to such an extent that she sought help through her children. She would appear in hospital with burns, cuts, and realised in therapeutic work that she was using an alter which she named to express feelings and experiences she was unable to convey or recall in her ordinary waking state. She realised that this must have been the explanation when she found herself in dangerous situations. She became aware that such actions could result in death. She had worked with a number of therapists who had either sexualised the relationship, or had gone too fast, and overwhelmed her capacity to contain and deal with overwhelming abusive and traumatic memories. Her dissociative identities were modes of survival, of dealing with emotional states which could not be dealt with, finding a way of living with powerful and dangerous identifications. They maintain the reality of abusive experience through flashbacks, re-enactments and overwhelming flooding of memories, alternating with states of identification. Alters have to contain overwhelming psychic realities to help the individual survive.

The struggle to integration in adult life is a far longer and more arduous task. In childhood and adolescence it is difficult enough before firm identities have been formed. It is essential that we recognise these processes early in children who have been subject to pervasive abuse so that they can be helped to integrate at an early stage; to process and to expose experiences in a context of care. Their true selves, which are often hidden and protected, can then emerge and a different lifescript written of survival and growth.

It is important to find ways to create a healing narrative from destructive forces unleashed by the effects of pervasive violence on children and young people's development. Seeing the development of different personality states as modes of coping with the uncopable can begin the development of such a healing narrative.

REFERENCES

Bentovim, A. (1995) *Trauma Organised Systems*. London: Karnac.

Fagan, J. and McMahon, P. (1984) 'Incipient Multiple Personality in Children: Four Cases'. *Journal of Nervous and Mental Diseases*, 172: 26–36.

Finkelhor, D. (1987) 'The Trauma of Child Sexual Abuse: Two Models'. *Journal of Interpersonal Violence*, 2: 348–366.

Goodwin, J. (1996) 'Childhood Dissociative Identity Disorder: The Male Population'. In *The Dissociative Child*, ed. J. Silberg. Lutherville, Maryland: The Sidran Press.

Midgley, N. (1997) 'Dissociation and Abuse: A Study of Dissociation Among Sexually and Physically Abused Adolescent Boys'. Unpublished MSc thesis at University College, London.

Peterson, G. (1996) 'Diagnostic Taxonomy: Past to Future'. In *The Dissociative Child*, ed. J. Silberg. Lutherville, Maryland: The Sidran Press.

Silberg, J.L. (1996) *The Dissociative Child*. Lutherville, Maryland: The Sidran Press.

Skuse, D., Stephenson, J., Hodges, J., Bentovim, A., Richards, A., McMillan, D., Salter, D. and Moore, T. (1999) 'Risk Factors for the Developmental of Sexually Abusive Behaviour in Sexually Victimised Males'. Institute of Child Health, London. Submitted to the Department of Health.

Chapter 2

Child dissociation and its 'roots' in adulthood[1]

Nicholas Midgley

THE CONCEPT OF DISSOCIATION

According to the *Oxford English Dictionary*, the term 'dissociation' dates back to 1611, in the sense of cutting off from association or society, the action of severing or disuniting. As a psychological concept, however, the term was not taken up until the eighteenth century, when the British empiricists argued that 'ideas (i.e. mental states) have associative links to one another, and that when these links are broken (e.g. in amnesia), certain ideas may be said to be split off or dissociated from the rest' (Braude 1991: 93). Influenced by these 'associationist' theories, especially the work of Hobbes and Hartley, the American, Benjamin Rush, was probably the first to use 'dissociation' as a medical term, in his psychiatric text of 1812 (Carlson 1986), but it was only at the end of the nineteenth century, amidst the exciting new discoveries of Charcot and Freud, that the term became widespread, thanks largely to the work of one man, Pierre Janet (Ellenberger 1970; Ross 1989; Decker 1986; Haule 1986).

Janet's ideas about dissociation derived from his work with a series of remarkable patients during the period 1882–88, and were published in his doctoral dissertation on *Psychological automatism* in 1889. Janet argued that subconscious fixed ideas, often caused by traumatic or frightening events early in life, could be split off from consciousness and become 'psychological automatisms', which interfere and sometimes even take control of the person. They might infiltrate personal consciousness in the shape of dreams or traumatic flashbacks, or in more extreme cases take over entirely in the shape of a second personality ('double consciousness' or, as it later became known, 'multiple personality').

The work of Pierre Janet is important because it gave the first trauma-based model of dissociation, similar in many ways to the work of Freud and Breuer in *Studies on Hysteria* published a few years later (Breuer and Freud 1895; Ross 1989; Mollon 1996).[2] After a brief period of popularity, however, Janet's work, along with the anglicised versions of dissociation championed by William James and Morton Prince, was largely forgotten. 'Freudian theory has flooded the field like a full rising tide', wrote Morton Prince, 'and the rest of us were left submerged like clams buried in the sands at low water' (quoted by Nemiah 1989: 1527). When Henri Ellenberger, in his monumental work on *The Discovery of the Unconscious* (1970), compared Janet's work to 'a vast city buried beneath ashes, like Pompeii', he wondered whether its fate was to 'remain buried forever', or to be 'unearthed some day and brought back to life' (p. 409).

Less than twenty years later, on the 100th anniversary of the publication of his original thesis, the *American Journal of Psychiatry* answered that question by devoting an entire issue to Janet's work, entitled 'Janet Redivivus'. In its editorial, Nemiah describes Janet as 'one of the most seminal psychiatric clinicians and thinkers of the last two centuries', arguing that the anniversary of his book's publication was 'perhaps of equal magnitude' to that other anniversary – the French Revolution (Nemiah 1989). If this seems hyperbolic, Nemiah is not alone. Both Ross (1989, 1996, 1997) and Gelinas (1995) evoke Thomas Kuhn's concept of a 'paradigm shift' in thinking from the Freudian model of 'intrapsychic conflict' to the 'trauma paradigm' as a major event in twentieth-century psychiatry (and one, we might note, that parallels certain strands within psychoanalysis itself, including the work of Ferenczi, Fairbairn and American self psychology).

The two events which most authors agree did most to re-awaken interest in Janet's dissociation theory and the 'trauma paradigm' were the Vietnam war (which created a new interest in the psychological effects of extreme trauma) and the rise of the Women's Movement (which helped to bring child abuse, and especially incest, into the open). The work of Ellenberger himself (1970) and Hilgard (1977) brought dissociation as a topic into the realm of academic research, and by the 1980s there was official recognition by the psychiatric community (the DSM-III diagnosis of 'dissociative disorder' was introduced in 1980), the creation of an International Society for the Study of Multiple Personality and Dissociation (ISSMP&D) with an annual conference since 1984, and the establishment of a theoretical and research journal, *Dissociation*, in 1988 (Ross 1989).[3] By the 1990s the topic had entered popular culture, with films such as Richard Gere's *Primal Fear*, the story of a murderer who fakes multiple personality to escape conviction (playing on a common anxiety about multiple personality, like hysteria 100 years earlier, being a kind of play-acting), or David Lynch's film, *Lost Highway*, described by the *Village Voice* as the 'only film to put the viewer inside the experience of disassociation [sic]' (Taubin 1997).[4]

Contemporary definitions of dissociation, however, following the general shift in mainstream psychiatry towards the description of symptoms rather than the explanation of underlying processes, do not follow Janet in his thoughts about 'fixed ideas', 'psychological automatism' or the subconscious. The *Diagnostic and Statistical Manual of Mental Disorders* (DSM-IV, American Psychiatric Association 1993) speaks of 'a disruption in the usually integrated functions of consciousness, memory, identity, or perception of the environment', and classifies the field of dissociation into the following disorders: dissociative amnesia; dissociative fugue; depersonalisation disorder, dissociative identity disorder (as 'multiple personality disorder' [MPD] is now officially known, although both terms are still widely used); and dissociative disorder not otherwise specified (p. 477).

Although diagnostically distinct, it is generally accepted that there is considerable overlap between dissociation and post-traumatic stress, and some authors choose to see multiple personality as 'a chronic post traumatic stress disorder' (Classen et al. 1993), in which dissociation is seen as a defence 'often mobilized against the pain and helplessness engendered by traumatic experiences such as rape, incest and combat' (Spiegel 1986: 123). Frank Putnam enumerates the protective functions of dissociation as '(a) automatization of certain behaviors; (b) resolution of irreconcilable conflicts; (c) escape from the constraints of reality; (d) isolation of catastrophic experiences; (e) cathartic discharge of certain feelings; (f) analgesia; and (g) alteration of sense of self, so that a traumatic event is experienced as if "it is not really happening to me"' (Putnam 1993: 40). As a defence, dissociation is seen to have a double edge: it provides protection from immediate experiences, but results in long-term fragmentation of the self. Vincent and Pickering (1988) offer the following example of a woman describing her experience at the age of 3 or 4 years old, repeatedly molested by her foster father:

> It became her habit to stand still and wait for the switch in her mind to transport her from a gray agony to a former calm or even happy state. She did this without knowing that she was saving her life each time, at the cost of nourishing two selves within her, each unknown to the other . . . to love what is killing you is impossible. She cannot do it. An infernal Mitsein is spawned in the child's soul. She keeps herself free to love, and lets 'the other' hate.
>
> (Vincent and Pickering 1988: 525)

CHILD ABUSE AND DISSOCIATION

In reviewing the literature on the long-term effects of child sexual abuse and on dissociation we come across a paradox: almost all articles on dissociation speak of childhood abuse, both physical and sexual, as a prime causal factor, and yet the converse does not hold: the majority of articles on child abuse barely even mention dissociation – a situation that has only begun to change in the last few years.[5] Just how widespread is dissociation as a mechanism for coping with experiences of childhood abuse, and in particular sexual abuse, or is it even correct to focus on abuse as the aetiological basis of dissociation?

Although Pierre Janet may have developed a trauma model of dissociative disorders, the kind of trauma he refers to is very different to those described in the modern literature: in one case, two men hidden behind a curtain who jump out and frighten a 7-year-old girl; in another, a cold bath that stopped a 13-year-old girl's menstruation (Ellenberger 1970). Janet was quite clear (indeed this was one of his disagreements with Freud) that sexuality was not central to the dissociative process. Nor was Janet the only author to hold this view. In a review article on dissociation by Taylor and Martin written in 1944, the possible causes of MPD are given as 'head injury, marked intoxication, extreme fatigue, lowered general energy, unbalanced urges, severe conflicts, and excessive learnings and forgettings' (quoted by Ross 1989: 41).

It was not until the 1970s, with the new concepts of 'child abuse' and 'sexual abuse', that cases of multiple personality and dissociation began to be linked with childhood sexual trauma (Hacking 1995), yet very soon the link was seen as inevitable. 'Never in the history of psychiatry', declared Richard Loewenstein, then president of the International Society for the Study of Multiple Personality and Dissociation (ISSMP&D), in 1989, 'have we ever come to know so well the specific etiology of a major illness' (quoted by Hacking 1995: 81). As Goodwin and Sachs put it, in their valuable essay on 'Child Abuse in the Etiology of Dissociative Disorders':

> Since the early 1980s, the hypothesis that this high frequency of prior abuse is somehow intrinsically related to the development of dissociative symptoms has become central to theory and research in the field.
>
> (Goodwin and Sachs 1996: 91)

Certainly the research figures seem to bear this hypothesis out. Several studies of MPD patients, psychiatric inpatients and non-clinical populations have found high levels of sexual and physical abuse, neglect and traumatic childhoods among those with dissociative symptoms (Goodwin and Sachs 1996; Putnam et al. 1986; Chu and Dill 1990; DiTomasso and Routh 1993). Fonagy and Target (1995), in a survey of the literature, report that 90 per cent of patients meeting DSM-IV criteria for Dissociative Identity Disorder report histories of physical and sexual abuse, and note that in one such study 17 of the 20 patients had their reports independently corroborated. Likewise, Colin Ross, in a 1997 lecture in London, offered statistics from five major studies suggesting that between 68 per cent and 92 per cent of MPD patients had reported sexual abuse histories, while between 60 per cent and 82 per cent reported histories of physical abuse (Ross 1997).

More specifically, dissociation may be related to certain aspects of abuse, such as the severity, duration or identity of the perpetrator (Chu and Dill 1990; Irwin 1996, 1999; Friedrich et al. 1997). At this point, however, the research is inconclusive, with several studies questioning the relation between dissociation and specific aspects of abuse, or even whether a history of sexual abuse should be considered the 'specific etiology' of dissociative disorders (Nash et al. 1993; Maynes and Feinauer 1994; Mulder et al. 1998). Tillman et al., in their provocative essay, 'Does trauma cause dissociative pathology?' (1994), note 'the fervor with which some dissociation theorists and lay press adhere to the trauma–dissociation link' despite the 'equivocal research basis for this view' (Tillman et al. 1994: 409). They make several points, including the following: that there has been too great an emphasis on external events as efficient causation, without considering the patient's internal construction of the event; that high scores on the Dissociative Experiences Scale (the most widely used and respected self-report checklist) may be attributable to gross psychopathology rather than specifically to dissociative pathology; that research designs are often poor, especially in respect of weak control groups; that the wider pathogenic factors in a child's environment are often ignored, though these might be of great significance to dissociative behaviour; and that some self-reports of abuse as a child may be of questionable validity. In conclusion, they argue that there 'does appear to be some kind of a relationship between childhood trauma and later dissociative disorders, but many studies have failed to control for other contributing pathogenic factors that could explain this association' (ibid.: 407).

Despite these qualifications, it does seem possible to offer some provisional model of the aetiology of dissociative disorders, and in particular Multiple Personality Disorder/Dissociative Identity Disorder. Braun and Sachs (1985) offer a 'Three-P theory' of MPD, in which the stress is laid on Predisposing, Precipitating, and Perpetuating factors. This model largely overlaps with the more widely-used 'Four factor theory' proposed by Kluft, which covers: (1) the capacity to dissociate; (2) overwhelming life experiences during childhood that cannot be dealt with by other defences; (3) the idea that the dissociative defence is shaped toward personality formation by being linked with other intrapsychic structures; and (4) a lack of nurturing and healing support before the process becomes relatively fixed (Kluft 1984).

The first of these factors, the predisposition or capacity to dissociate, has been the cause of much controversy, ever since the debate between Janet and Freud/Breuer over the relative importance of 'mental degeneracy' and 'hypnoid states'. Several contemporary authors have attempted to see this predisposition as equivalent to a person's susceptibility to hypnosis, with research suggesting an overlap between hypnotic and dissociative ability (Breuer and Freud 1895; Hilgard 1977; Spiegel 1988; Ross 1989; and for the counter-argument, Putnam 1996); others have argued for the significance of genetic inheritance, passed on within certain families to a greater degree than in others (Ludwig 1983), though preliminary results from a twin study suggest that family inheritance is more likely to be environmental than genetic (Putnam 1996).

A more promising line of thought, one which has emerged in the last few years, is that certain types of attachment pattern in early childhood, especially the more recently recognised 'disorganised/disoriented' attachment pattern (Main and Solomon 1986), may predispose a child to dissociative defences when faced with abusive or traumatic experiences later in life (Barach 1991;

Liotti 1992, 1995; Main and Morgan 1996; Putnam 1996; Ogawa et al. 1997). Alexander (1992) makes the important observation that, while child sexual abuse is associated with severe long-term sequelae, there is no evidence of a specific constellation of symptoms unique to sexual abuse victims. She suggests that family variables such as levels of family support and cohesion may be more predictive of long-term effects of abuse than abuse-specific variables such as the severity or duration of the abuse itself. More specifically, she argues that particular attachment patterns antecedent to the abuse itself may predict how a child responds to an abusive or traumatic experience, and that a disorganised/disoriented attachment ('D' type), in which the attachment figure is often both the source of and solution to the child's anxiety, a frightened and/or frightening figure, is especially likely to produce the defence of dissociation, or what Bowlby himself called 'defensive exclusion'. Liotti (1995) points out that the behaviour of such 'D' type infants – contradictory intentions, lack of orientation and moments of immobility or dazed expressions – are somewhat analogous to dissociative symptoms, and that these children do often have histories of severe neglect and/or physical and sexual abuse. He postulates that a child's experience of such a parent may lead to 'multiple internal working models of attachment', and that this could be a 'factor of vulnerability to dissociation' in the developmental process. Fonagy (1997a, b) has taken this argument one stage further, arguing that the dissociative defence may be seen as a 'failure of mentalisation' commonly found among disorganised/disoriented infants, for whom conceiving of the parent's mind is simply too terrifying, creating a defensive disruption of their capacity to depict thoughts and feelings in themselves and others.

The attachment model offers the possibility of a developmental approach to understanding dissociation, an approach that Frank Putnam, in a series of papers and books, has also been developing over the last decade (Putnam 1989a, 1991, 1993, 1994, 1996, 1997). Basing his argument on Wolff's study of infants' discrete behavioural states, Putnam argues that we are 'all born with the potential for multiple personalities and over the course of normal development we more or less succeed in consolidating an integrated sense of self' (1989a: 51). Trauma, however, creates a disruption of the developmental tasks of consolidation of self across behavioural states, not so much a developmental arrest as, in Judith Armstrong's phrase, 'a developmentally complex difference . . . a case of growing up strangely' (Armstrong 1994).

The models provided by Kluft and Putnam take for granted that dissociative disorders have their onset in childhood, as developmental, trauma-based disorders, but until very recently almost all of the literature on dissociation was based on retrospective studies of adult cases.[6] As Ian Hacking notes, in his excellent book, *Rewriting the Soul* (1995), working with children became, by the end of the 1980s, both a theoretical necessity – in order to confirm the hypotheses developed in work with adults – and also a therapeutic imperative, for the developmental model assumes that early intervention could have a higher chance of influencing patterns of defence that by adulthood are often deeply entrenched. 'The hunt was on for child multiples' (Hacking 1995: 90).

CHILDHOOD AND ADOLESCENT DISSOCIATION

In an editorial to a special issue of the journal, *Dissociation,* published in 1992 and dealing specifically with research on dissociative disorders in children and adolescents, Richard Kluft wrote:

> Although there are many important and compelling concerns in the dissociative disorders field, the recognition and treatment of youngsters with dissociative disorders deserves to be among its highest priorities.
>
> (Kluft 1992: 2)

But what reasons could there have been for the inability to recognise (and treat) children and adolescents with dissociative disorders? Various hypotheses have been proposed. One likely cause is professional attitudes. As Lynda Shirar points out, children adaptive enough to develop a dissociative identity disorder are rarely obvious about it, and professionals 'may not be as likely to systematically evaluate for childhood trauma and dissociative disorders as for other problems' (1996: 23). Often such children's symptoms will be given some other diagnosis, such as attention deficit hyperactivity disorder, conduct disorder, oppositional defiant disorder or schizophrenia (Putnam 1993), depression or post-traumatic stress disorder (Hornstein and Putnam 1992), or borderline personality (Dell and Eisenhower 1990; Atlas and Wolfson 1996). It has been estimated that on average a child with a dissociative identity disorder has received between 2.7 and 3.6 previous diagnoses (McElroy 1992). We might wonder what it is that makes dissociative disorders in children so easy to miss? Peterson suggests that some clinicians 'just do not ask the questions which will lead to the diagnosis – questions regarding missing blocks of time or other phenomena of dissociation, appearing to be in a trance, events which are not being discussed for fear of not being believed or for fear of punishment' (1990: 4). Without some 'index of suspicion', clinicians and researchers may simply fail to recognise the signs of dissociative disorder (Armstrong and Loewenstein 1990).

But there are other reasons for the lack of dissociative diagnoses among children. Some authors have argued that there are atypical presentations in child and adolescent cases, or that personalities are not well enough developed to be classified as MPD, or even that there is relatively little difference between young alters and age-appropriate behaviours of children, such as playing with imaginary friends (Tyson 1992). Frank Putnam has made an impassioned argument that 'DSM operated under the misguided principle that whenever possible, adult criteria should be applied to children and adolescents', but in the case of children's dissociative disorders, such 'adult diagnostic criteria are grossly inappropriate and misleading' (1994: 178). Clinicians tend to report more ambiguous dissociative symptoms among children, which involve less fully developed MPD, and are inappropriate for the label 'dissociative disorders not otherwise specified' (DDNOS).

To counter these problems, various checklists of childhood dissociation have been proposed, including Kluft's 16-point checklist of symptoms (1984), Putnam's 1981 checklist and Fagan and McMahon's 20-point checklist of teacher and parent observation (1984). More recently, attempts have been made to develop a dissociation sub-scale in the widely-used Child Behaviour Checklist (Malinosky-Rummell and Hoier 1991; Midgley 1997), and a whole range of scales have been developed, both self-report and parent-report, to specifically measure levels of dissociation in children, the most popular being the Child Dissociation Checklist (CDC) (Putnam et al. 1993), which has been widely used and validated in the last few years (Putnam and Peterson 1994). The CDC measures behaviour in the following domains: (1) dissociative amnesias; (2) rapid shifts in demeanour, knowledge, abilities or behaviour; (3) spontaneous trance states; (4) hallucinations; (5) identity alterations; and (6) aggressive and sexual behaviour.[7]

In the published case histories of children with dissociative disorders, some attempt has been made at a more appropriate description of the dissociative symptoms. Fagan and McMahon (1984) use the term 'incipient multiple personality', indicating that childhood behaviours that might be interpreted as normal, such as being in a daze, depressed, having an abundance of physical complaints or imaginary playmates, might be a sign of potential multiplicity. Others have used such terms as 'MPD in evolution' or 'precursors to multiple personality' (Peterson 1990).

The most thorough attempt to provide a diagnostic tool appropriate for children is that of Gary Peterson, who worked (unsuccessfully) on the DSM-IV Task Force Dissociative Disorders Work Group for a 'Dissociative Disorder of Childhood' diagnostic criterion to be included in the DSM-IV categories (Peterson and Putnam 1994). His work is important partly because he introduces a *developmental* perspective which is often missing when adult criteria are applied to children (as in the case of DSM-IV). By making an analysis of all previous checklists, Peterson proposes three areas of dissociative experience relevant to children and adolescents: amnestic experiences, fluctuations in behaviour, and developmental issues (Peterson 1990).

Research is also underway to explore the hypothesis that adolescence is a crucial period for the consolidation of dissociative disorders. Several authors have made important theoretical contributions to the understanding of adolescence and dissociative experiences (Hornstein 1996; Putnam 1994; Armstrong et al. 1997), while others have published valuable empirical and case studies of adolescents with dissociative disorders (Allers et al. 1997; Coons 1996;

Bowman et al. 1985; Sanders and Giolas 1991; Ross et al. 1989; Dell and Eisenhower 1990; Hornstein and Putnam 1992).

In the last few years, Armstrong, Putnam and Carlson have been working on an Adolescent Dissociative Experiences Scale (A-DES), a 30 question self-report form for use with adolescents between the ages of 12 and 18, and covering experiences in the following domains: dissociative amnesia; absorption and imaginative involvement; passive influence; and depersonalisation and derealisation (Armstrong et al. 1997; Smith and Carlson 1997). In a report on the checklist the authors point out that adolescence 'may well be a transition point for dissociation', the period at which 'normal' dissociative tendencies, such as identity confusion and imaginative involvement, begin to diminish as adolescents move towards adulthood, while pathological dissociation may well interfere with the construction of a cohesive sense of self and solidify into the more fixed patterns of adult dissociative disorders. Dissociative adolescents often present with depression, suicidality, self-mutilation, learning difficulties, auditory hallucinations and aggression and sexual promiscuity, and may have been previously diagnosed as having a conduct disorder, borderline personality, attention deficit hyperactivity disorder or post-traumatic stress disorder. Yet the authors freely admit that 'the nature and frequency of dissociation in adolescence has yet to be mapped' (Armstrong et al. 1997).

CONCLUSION

In 1984 Richard Kluft, a leading worker in the field, wrote of childhood dissociation and the essential paradox it presents: although adult dissociative disorders are generally felt to have their roots in childhood, there is a paucity of literature on childhood dissociation itself. Fifteen years after Kluft first drew attention to the paucity of literature on child and adolescent dissociation the situation has been transformed, with the creation of research tools, the publication of numerous articles and several books specifically on this topic, and the growth of clinical and theoretical understanding of the problems young people face.

Why has it taken so long for this understanding to emerge? Is it a question of cultural preconceptions, professional attitudes or the personal resistance to recognising such states in children? Ironically, it was only with the growing understanding and investigation of adults with dissociative disorders that the need to explore childhood dissociation became imperative. The hypothesis that adult dissociation had its roots in childhood obliged professionals to turn their attention to children themselves, in order to confirm or disprove this hypothesis. The whole field of child and adolescent dissociation, we could say, had its 'roots' in adulthood, and it is only now that the field is being understood in its own right. But it is not just understanding that is necessary: the recognition of the particular dilemmas faced by children and adolescents with dissociative

disorders is paving the way for more appropriate treatments, and more importantly early preventative interventions.[8] Childhood experience is no longer
simply seen as the aetiological root of adult dissociative disorders; it has come to
be recognised as a period in which dissociative defences and symptoms first
develop, and a crucial period for effective clinical and social policy interventions.

NOTES

1 The research for this chapter was undertaken while working with Dr Jill Hodges
   at the Institute of Child Health, Great Ormond Street Hospital, London, as part
   of a larger study into the influence of early experience of sexual abuse on the formation of sexual preferences during adolescence. I am grateful for her generous
   support and advice.
2 Breuer and Freud, in the 'preliminary communication' to the *Studies on Hysteria*,
   write that *'the splitting of consciousness which is so striking in the well-known classical
   cases under the form of* "double conscience" *is present to a rudimentary degree in every hysteria, and that a tendency to such a dissociation, and with it the emergence of abnormal states
   of consciousness (which we shall bring together under the term "hypnoid"), is the basic phenomenon of this neurosis.* In these views we concur with Binet and the two Janets'
   (1895: 63, italics in original). In later chapters, both Freud and Breuer criticise
   Janet for his idea of 'psychical inefficiency' or 'mental weakness', arguing that the
   patients appear weak-minded because their mental activity is divided, not the
   other way around (pp. 166, 311). Various authors, however, suggest that Freud and
   Breuer misrepresented Janet's position (Ellenberger 1970; van der Hart and Horst
   1989; Mollon 1996).
3 The society was recently renamed the International Society for the Study of
   Dissociation (ISSD), following the decision by the *Diagnostic and Statistical Manual
   of Mental Disorders* (DSM-IV) to re-classify 'multiple personality disorder' as 'dissociative identity disorder' in 1993.
4 For accounts of dissociation and multiple personality from the perspective of
   social history, see Ian Hacking's fascinating book, *Rewriting the Soul* (1995) and
   Elaine Showalter's much-publicised *Hystories: Hysterical Epidemics and Modern
   Culture* (1997).
5 Finkelhor's widely-used 'traumagenic dynamic model' of the long-term effects of
   child sexual abuse finds almost no place for dissociative symptomatology, except
   as a branch of post-traumatic stress (Finkelhor 1988), and dissociation is not mentioned in Finkelhor and Browne's extensive literature review of post-abuse
   symptomatology (1985), is given only one (bracketed) reference in Watkins and
   Bentovim's comprehensive review of sexual abuse of male children (1992), and is
   not cited in Friedrich et al.'s review of behaviour problems in sexually abused boys
   (Friedrich et al. 1988). Friedrich's more recent book on *Psychotherapy with Sexually
   Abused Boys* (1995), however, does include a section on dissociation. John Briere is
   a rare example of a researcher into the general effects of child sexual abuse who has
   always included dissociation as a significant issue (e.g. Briere and Runtz 1988),
   and his research suggests that dissociation and somatisation are the two forms of
   symptomatology most predictive of an abuse history (see also Maynes and Feinauer
   1994).
6 In his review of the period up until 1979, Kluft was only able to find one case of
   childhood multiple personality – that of an 11-year-old girl called Estelle
   described by Despine Pere in 1840 (Kluft 1984). In 1992, Gary Tyson found only

eleven articles and two book chapters on the subject written after 1979, covering a total of 21 cases of childhood MPD or other dissociative disorders, and just six cases of adolescent MPD (Tyson 1992). There is no doubt, however, that the numbers have increased exponentially since 1992, and there are now several reviews of childhood dissociation available (e.g. Hornstein 1996; Putnam 1997; Wallach and Dollinger 1999). Nevertheless, the discrepancy between the reports by adult dissociative patients of the childhood onset of their dissociative symptoms, and the actual number of childhood dissociative disorders actually diagnosed, still remains (Vincent and Pickering 1988; Peterson 1990; Dell and Eisenhower 1990).

7 Although the CDC is the most widely used tool, other dissociation checklists for children include the Children's Perceptual Alteration Scale (Evers-Szostak and Sanders 1992) and the Child/Adolescent Dissociation Checklist (Reagor et al. 1992). At this time there are no validated structured interviews for DSM-IV diagnoses of dissociative disorders in children, though Putnam refers to several in the course of development, including a possible module for inclusion in the Diagnostic Interview Schedule for Children (DISC) (Putnam 1994).

8 There is not space in this chapter to cover the therapeutic possibilities of work with children with dissociative disorders, but both Putnam (1997) and Shirar (1996) give excellent introductions to the type of clinical work possible. See also Richardson (1998) and Allers et al. (1997) for examples of particular therapeutic approaches to children and adolescents with dissociative disorders.

BIBLIOGRAPHY

Alexander, P. (1992) 'Application of Attachment Theory to the Study of Sexual Abuse', *J. of Consult. and Clin. Psych.* 60/2.

Allers, C., White, J. and Mullis, F. (1997) 'The Treatment of Dissociation in an HIV-infected, Sexually Abused Adolescent Male', *Psychotherapy* 34/2.

American Psychiatric Association (1993) *Diagnostic and Statistical Manual of Mental Disorders* (4th edition). Washington, DC: Am. Psychiatric Assoc.

Armstrong, J. (1994) 'Reflections on Multiple Personality Disorder as a Developmentally Complex Adaptation', *Psa. Study of Child* 49.

—— and Loewenstein, R. (1990) 'Characteristics of Patients with Multiple Personality and Dissociative Disorders on Psychological Testing', *J. of Nerv. and Ment. Dis.* 178/7.

——, Putnam, F. and Carlson, E. (1997) 'Adolescent Dissociative Experiences Scale' (unpublished).

——, Putnam, F., Carlson, E., Libero, D. and Smith, S. (1997) 'Development and Validation of a Measure of Adolescent Dissociation: The Adolescent Dissociative Experiences Scale', *J. of Nerv. and Ment. Dis.* 185/8.

Atlas, J. and Wolfson, M. (1996) 'Depression and Dissociation as features of Borderline Personality Disorder in Hospitalized Adolescents', *Psych. Reports* 78/2.

Barach, P. (1991) 'Multiple Personality as an Attachment Disorder', *Dissociation* 4/3.

Bernstein, E. and Putnam, F. (1986) 'Development, Reliability and Validity of a Dissociation Scale', *J. Nerv. Mental Dis.* 174/12.

Bowman, E., Blix, S. and Coons, P. (1985) 'Multiple Personality in Adolescence: Relationship to Incestual Experiences', *J. Am. Acad. Child Psychiatry* 24/1.

Braude, S. (1991) *First Person Plural: Multiple Personality and the Philosophy of Mind.* London: Routledge.

Braun, B. and Sachs, R. (1985) 'The Development of Multiple Personality Disorder: Predisposing, Precipitating and Perpetuating Factors', in Kluft, R. (ed.) *Childhood Antecedents of Multiple Personality.* Washington: Am. Psychiatric Press.

Briere, J. and Runtz, M. (1988) 'Post Sexual Abuse Trauma', in Wyatt, G. and Powell, G. (eds) *Lasting Effects of Child Sexual Abuse.* London: Sage Publications.

Breuer, J. and Freud, S. (1895) *Studies on Hysteria* (Vol. 3 of the Penguin Freud Library).

Carlson, E. (1986) 'The History of Dissociation Until 1880', in Quen, J. (ed.) *Split Minds/Split Brains.* New York: New York University Press.

Chu, J. and Dill, D. (1990) 'Dissociative Symptoms in Relation to Childhood Physical and Sexual Abuse', *Am. J. Psychiatry* 147/7.

Classen, C., Koopman, C. and Spiegel, D. (1993) 'Trauma and Dissociation', *Bull. of Menn. Clin.* 57/2.

Coons, P. (1996) 'Clinical Phenomenology of 25 Children and Adolescents with Dissociative Disorders', *Child & Adolesc. Psych. Clin. of N. Am.* 5.

Decker, H. (1986) 'The Lure of Nonmaterialism in Materialist Europe: Investigations of Dissociative Phenomena, 1880–1915', in Quen, J. (ed.) *Split Minds/Split Brains.* New York: New York University Press.

Dell, P. and Eisenhower, J. (1990) 'Adolescent Multiple Personality Disorder: A Preliminary Study of Eleven Cases', *J. Am. Acad. Child & Adolesc. Psychiatry* 29/3.

DiTomasso, M. and Routh, D. (1993) 'Recall of Abuse in Childhood and Three Measures of Dissociation', *Child Ab. & Neglect* 17/4.

Ellenberger, H. (1970) *The Discovery of the Unconscious.* London: Fontana Press.

Evers-Szostak, M. and Sanders, S. (1992) 'The Children's Perceptual Alteration Scale (CPAS): A Measure of Children's Perception', *Dissociation* 5/2.

Fagan, J. and McMahon, P. (1984) 'Incipient Multiple Personality in Children', *J. of Nerv. and Mental Dis.* 172/1.

Finkelhor, D. (1988) 'The Trauma of Child Sexual Abuse: Two Models', in Wyatt, G. and Powell, G. (eds) *Lasting Effects of Child Sexual Abuse.* London: Sage Publications.
—— and Browne, A. (1985) 'The Traumatic Impact of Child Sexual Abuse: A Conceptualization', *Amer. J. Orthopsychiat.* 55/4.

Fonagy, P. (1997a) 'Attachment, the Development of the Self, and its Pathology in Dissociative Disorders', paper presented at the 'Trauma and Dissociation' Conference, Chester, England.
—— (1997b) 'Multiple Voices vs. Meta-cognition: An Attachment Theory Perspective', *J. of Psychotherapy Integration* 7/3.
—— and Target, M. (1995) 'Dissociation and Trauma', *Current Opinion in Psychiatry* 8.

Friedrich, W. (1995) *Psychotherapy with Sexually Abused Boys.* London: Sage Publications.
——, Beilke, R. and Urquiza, A. (1988) 'Behavior Problems in Young Sexually Abused Boys. A Comparison Study', *J. Interpers. Violence* 3/1.
——, Jaworski, T., Huxsahl, J. and Bengtson, B. (1997) 'Dissociative and Sexual Behaviours in Children and Adolescents with Sexual Abuse and Psychiatric Histories', *J. of Interpersonal Violence* 12/2.

Gelinas, D. (1995) 'Dissociative Identity Disorder and the Trauma Paradigm', in Cohen, L., Berzoff, J. and Elin, M. (eds) *Dissociative Identity Disorders.* New Jersey: Jason Aronson.

Goodwin, J. and Sachs, R. (1996) 'Child Abuse in the Etiology of Dissociative Disorders', in Michelson, L. and Ray, W. (eds) *Handbook of Dissociation: Theoretical, Empirical, and Clinical Perspectives*. New York: Plenum Press.

Hacking, I. (1995) *Rewriting the Soul. Multiple Personality and the Sciences of Memory*. New Jersey: Princeton University Press.

Haule, J. (1986) 'Pierre Janet and Dissociation: The First Transference Theory and Its Origin in Hypnosis', *Am. J. Clin. Hypn.* 29/2.

Hilgard, E. (1977) *Divided Consciousness: Multiple Controls in Human Thought and Action*. New York: John Wiley & Sons.

Hornstein, N. (1996) 'Dissociative Disorders in Children and Adolescents', in Michelson, L. and Ray, W. (eds) *Handbook of Dissociation: Theoretical, Empirical, and Clinical Perspectives*. New York: Plenum Press.

—— and Putnam, F. (1992) 'Clinical Phenomenology of Child and Adolescent Dissociative Disorders', *J. Am. Acad. Child & Adolesc. Psychiatry* 31/6.

Irwin, H. (1996) 'Traumatic Childhood Events, Perceived Availability of Emotional Support, and the Development of Dissociative Tendencies', *Child Ab. & Neglect* 20/8.

—— (1999) 'Pathological and Nonpathological Dissociation: The Relevance of Childhood Trauma', *J. of Nerv. and Mental Disease* 187/3.

Kluft, R. (1984) 'Multiple Personality in Childhood', *Psych. Clin. of N. Am.* 7/1.

—— (1992) 'Editorial: Dissociative Disorders in Childhood and Adolescence: New Frontiers', *Dissociation* 5/1.

Liotti, G. (1992) 'Disorganized/Disorientated Attachment in the Etiology of Dissociative Disorders', *Dissociation* 5.

—— (1995) 'Disorganized/Disoriented Attachment in the Psychotherapy of the Dissociative Disorders', in Goldberg, S., Muir, R. and Kerr, J. (eds) *Attachment Theory: Social, Developmental and Clinical Perspectives*. New York: Analytic Press.

Ludwig, A. (1983) 'The Psychobiological Functions of Dissociation', *Am. J. of Clin. Hypnosis* 26/2.

McElroy, L. (1992) 'Early Indicators of Pathological Dissociation in Sexually Abused Children', *Child Ab. & Neglect* 16/6.

—— and Morgan, H. (1996) 'Disorganization and Disorientation in Infant Strange Situation Behavior', in Michelson, L. and Ray, W. (eds) *Handbook of Dissociation: Theoretical, Empirical, and Clinical Perspectives*. New York: Plenum Press.

Main, M. and Solomon, J. (1986) 'Discovery of a New, Insecure-Disorganized/Disorientated Attachment Pattern', in Brazelton, T and Yogman, M. (eds) *Affective Development in Infancy*. Norwood: Ablex.

Malinosky-Rummell, R. and Hoier, T. (1991) 'Validating Measures of Dissociation in Sexually Abused and Nonabused Children', *Behavioural Assessment* 13/4.

Maynes, L. and Feinauer, L. (1994) 'Acute and Chronic Dissociation and Somatized Anxiety as Related to Childhood Sexual Abuse', *Am. J. of Family Therapy* 22/2.

Midgley, N. (1997) 'Dissociation and Abuse: A Study of Dissociation Among Sexually and Physically Abused Adolescent Boys', unpublished MSc thesis at University College London.

Mollon, P. (1996) *Multiple Selves, Multiple Voices. Working with Trauma, Violation and Dissociation*. Chichester: John Wiley & Sons.

Mulder, R., Beautrais, A., Joyce, P. and Fergusson, D. (1998) 'Relationship between Dissociation, Childhood Sexual Abuse, Childhood Physical Abuse, and Mental Illness in a General Population Sample', *Am. J. of Psychiatry* 155/6.

Nash, M., Hulsey, T., Sexton, M., Harralson, T. and Lambert, W. (1993) 'Long-Term Sequelae of Childhood Sexual Abuse: Perceived Family Environment, Psychopathology, and Dissociation', *J. Cons. and Clin. Psychology* 61/2.

Nemiah, J. (1989) 'Janet Redivivus: The Centenary of *L'automatisme psychologique*', *Am. J. Psych.* 146/12.

Ogawa, J., Sroufe, A., Weinfield, N., Carlson, E. and Egeland, B. (1997) 'Development and the Fragmented Self: Longitudinal Study of Dissociative Symptomatology in a Nonclinical Sample', *Dev. and Psychopathology* 9/4.

Peterson, G. (1990) 'Diagnosis of Childhood Multiple Personality Disorder', *Dissociation* 3/1.

—— and Putnam, F. (1994) 'Preliminary Results of the Field Trial of Proposed Criteria for Dissociative Disorder of Childhood', *Dissociation* 7/4.

Putnam, F. (1989a) *Diagnosis and Treatment of Multiple Personality Disorder*. New York: Guilford Press.

—— (1989b) 'Pierre Janet and Modern Views of Dissociation', *J. of Traumatic Stress* 2/4.

—— (1991) 'Dissociative Disorders in Children and Adolescents', *Psych. Clin. N. Am.* 14/3.

—— (1993) 'Dissociative Disorders in Children: Behavioral Profiles and Problems', *Child Ab. & Neglect* 17/1.

—— (1994) 'Dissociative Disorders in Children and Adolescents', in Lynn, S. and Rhue, J. (eds) *Dissociation: Clinical and Theoretical Perspectives*. New York: Guilford Press.

—— (1996) 'Child Development and Dissociation', *Child & Adolesc. Psych. Clin of N. Am.* 5/2.

—— (1997) *Dissociation in Children and Adolescents: A Developmental Perspective*. New York: Guilford Press.

——, Guroff, J., Silberman, E., Barban, L. and Post, R. (1986) 'The Clinical Phenomenology of Multiple Personality Disorder: Review of 100 Recent Cases', *J. of Clinical Psychiatry* 47.

——, Helmers, K. and Trickett, P. (1993) 'Development, Reliability and Validity of a Child Dissociation Scale', *Child Ab. & Neglect* 17/6.

—— and Peterson, G. (1994) 'Further Validation of the Child Dissociative Checklist', *Dissociation* 7/4.

Reagor, P., Kasten, J. and Morelli, N. (1992) 'A Checklist for Screening Dissociative Disorders in Children and Adolescents', *Dissociation* 5/1.

Richardson, L. (1998) 'Psychogenic Dissociation in Childhood: The Role of the Counseling Psychologist', *Counseling Psychologist* 26/1.

Ross, C. (1989) *Multiple Personality Disorder*. New York: John Wiley & Sons.

—— (1996) 'History, Phenomenology and Epidemiology of Dissociation', in Michelson, L. and Ray, W. (eds) *Handbook of Dissociation: Theoretical, Empirical, and Clinical Perspectives*. New York: Plenum Press.

—— (1997) 'Understanding Trauma and Dissociation, Iatrogenesis of MPD and Memory', lecture in London, 10 February.

——, Ryan, L., Anderson, G., Ross, D. and Hardy, L. (1989) 'Dissociative Experiences in Adolescents and College Students', *Dissociation* 2/4.

Sanders, B. and Giolas, M. (1991) 'Dissociation and Childhood Trauma in Psychologically Disturbed Adolescents', *Am. J. Psychiatry* 148/1.

Shirar, L. (1996) *Dissociative Children*. New York: W.W. Norton & Co.

Showalter, E. (1997) *Hystories. Hysterical Epidemics and Modern Culture*. London: Picador.

Smith, S. and Carlson, E. (1997) 'Reliability and Validity of the Adolescent Dissociative Experiences Scale', *Dissociation* 9/2.

Spiegel, D. (1986) 'Dissociating Damage', *Am. J. Clin. Hypn.* 29/2.

—— (1988) 'Dissociation and Hypnosis in Post-traumatic Stress Disorders', *J. of Traumatic Stress* 1/1.

Taubin, A. (1997) 'Hanging in Park City', *Village Voice* 11 February.

Tillman, J., Nash, M. and Lerner, P. (1994) 'Does Trauma Cause Dissociative Pathology?', in Lynn, S. and Rhue, J. (eds) *Dissociation: Clinical and Theoretical Perspectives*. New York: Guilford Press.

Tyson, G. (1992) 'Childhood MPD/Dissociation Identity Disorder: Applying and Extending Current Diagnostic Checklists', *Dissociation* 5/1.

van der Hart, O. and Horst, R. (1989) 'The Dissociation Theory of Pierre Janet', *J. of Traumatic Stress* 2/4.

Vincent, M. and Pickering, M. (1988) 'Multiple Personality Disorder in Children' *Can. J. Psychiatry* 33/6.

Wallach, H. and Dollinger, S. (1999) 'Dissociative Disorders in Childhood and Adolescence', in Netherton, S. and Holmes, D. (eds) *Child and Adolescent Psychological Disorders: A Comprehensive Textbook*. New York: Oxford University Press.

Watkins, B. and Bentovim, A. (1992) 'The Sexual Abuse of Male Children and Adolescents: A Review of Current Research', *J. of Child Psychology and Psychiatry* 33/1.

Chapter 3

Post-traumatic Stress Disorder and dissociation

The Traumatic Stress Service in the Maudsley Hospital

Felicity de Zulueta

The Traumatic Stress Service at the Maudsley Hospital is one of the few NHS outpatient services in this country specialising in the treatment of people who suffer from Post-traumatic Stress Disorder (PTSD), a condition which is still poorly recognised in this country.

The core principle underlying our work is the view that PTSD is essentially an attachment disorder with all that this implies in terms of cognitive distortions, emotions and physical or somatic symptoms (Zulueta 1993, 1999). A brief review of the literature relating to both these fields of research highlights their common aspects and the underlying premises of our treatment programmes.

INTRODUCTION TO PTSD AND ITS UNDERLYING NEUROPSYCHOLOGY

Accounts of overwhelming stress on the body and mind of victims go back to the ancient Greeks and, over the years, PTSD has had many names – hysteria, shell shock, battle fatigue, battered wife syndrome, battered child syndrome, rape trauma syndrome – to name but a few. However, it was not until 1980 that the diagnosis of 'post-traumatic stress disorder' or PTSD entered the formal psychiatric lexicon of the *Diagnostic and Statistical Manual of Mental Disorders* developed by the American Psychiatric Association and it has now been brought up to date (1994).

PTSD involves the reliving of terrifying experiences with accompanying 'freeze–fight or flight' responses and parallel avoidance behaviour, numbing and dissociation. The 'freeze–fight or flight' response is a rapid autonomic response which we share with other animals when we are in danger. In order to prepare for immediate survival, the body releases numerous neurotransmitters such as adrenaline, and increased steroids as well as endogenous opiates which are pain relievers. People who have PTSD continue to respond in the same way, as if still in danger when in fact they are not.

Example 1 A group of eight Vietnam veterans suffering from PTSD were exposed to a 15-minute clip of a Vietnam war film: seven of the men showed a 30% reduction in their perception of pain and were found to have released the equivalent of 8 mg of morphine.

(Pitman et al. 1990: 542)

PTSD does also appear to alter brain function. Van der Kolk and his team have shown how – when exposed to the taped account of their traumatogenic experience – the brains of right-handed individuals suffering from PTSD displayed remarkable changes under positron emission tomography (Rauch et al. 1996). They noted a marked decrease in blood flow in Broca's area – the speech area in the dominant left hemisphere – and increased blood flow in the right limbic and paralimbic system as well as in the visual cortex. The latter may be associated with the visual component of PTSD such as the flashbacks. This also ties in with our clinical experience: traumatised patients often report an inability to speak when they relive traumatic experiences and many 'see things' relating to these experiences.

Case An Asian woman who had been through appalling experiences in her home country – witnessing the murder of most of her family and later the drowning of her friends and their children – was later attacked in her home and almost beaten to death. Following this last traumatic experience she developed PTSD and she complains that, when she is frightened, she becomes paralysed and unable to walk or talk for several hours.

PTSD also appears to result from the failure to integrate trauma into the declarative memory system. As a result, trauma can become organised at a sensory and somatic level and the traumatic response can be unconsciously triggered off and physically re-experienced without the conscious memories to accompany it. This represents a somatic form of dissociation. As a result, the traumatised individual is likely to be repeatedly exposed to states of high arousal which cannot be handled because of an associated inability to modulate such experiences, both biologically and psychologically. This leads to attempts to self-medicate the pain and dysphoria by resorting to drugs or alcohol.

(van der Kolk 1996)

These behaviours are particularly evident in victims of chronic adult or childhood trauma or 'complex PTSD'. Judith Herman defined the victims of this chronic form of PTSD as those who had survived

a history of subjection to totalitarian control over a prolonged period (months to years). Examples include hostages, prisoners of war, concentration camp survivors and survivors of some religious cults. Examples also include those subjected to totalitarian systems in sexual and domestic life, including survivors of domestic battering, childhood physical or sexual abuse, and organised sexual exploitation.

(Herman 1992: 121)

Herman goes on to outline the changes observed in people suffering from complex PTSD. Their symptoms involve changes in affect regulation including persistent dysphoria, chronic suicidal preoccupation, self-injury, explosive or extremely inhibited anger, compulsive or extremely inhibited sexuality.

Other symptoms involve changes in consciousness such as amnesia for traumatic events, transient dissociative episodes, experiences of depersonalisation or derealisation, reliving the experiences either through flashbacks and intrusive thought or through ruminative preoccupations.

Accompanying these symptoms are changes in self-perception such as a sense of helplessness, feelings of shame and guilt, a sense of having been defiled or stigmatised and of being completely different from others.

These cognitive changes are usually accompanied by perceptual changes relating to the perpetrator including an intense preoccupation with the relationship to the perpetrator who may be idealised, at least at times, and whose beliefs may be identified with. All these changes resulting from severe and chronic traumatisation are usually accompanied by a loss of faith and trust in others and a sense of hopelessness and despair.

In victims of childhood trauma, the repeated experience of terror in relation to their caregivers has many long-term and more specific effects. Van der Kolk points out that, when subject to deprivation, infants appear to develop fewer opioid receptors and therefore need higher levels of endogenous opiate secretion to feel soothed (Panksepp et al. 1985). They may attempt to self-medicate even more markedly than victims of simple trauma by artificially producing a release of endogenous opiates through re-traumatisation. This leads to the phenomenon of 'repetition-compulsion'. They will also achieve the same effect by cutting themselves and/or bingeing. Dissociative experiences are intrinsic to the experience of PTSD.

Example 2 One night in 1968, a Vietnam veteran lit a cigarette that led to the killing of his buddy by the Vietcong. Back in the USA, on the anniversary of his friend's death, this man carried out 18 yearly 'armed robberies' by putting his finger in his pocket and carrying out a hold-up which elicited police gunfire. This unconscious re-enactment only came to an end when he was treated with psychotherapy and remembered what had happened to him and his friend.

(van der Kolk 1996: 391)

This simple illustration highlights how individuals can cut themselves off from memories and feelings that are too painful to acknowledge. But, while they cannot recall these awful events, they are still present somewhere in their mind and can be brought back into action by external or internal triggers – such as an anniversary – often to recreate the very pain to which the victim was exposed, either to himself or to the other person involved.

This dissociation is particularly prevalent in individuals with a history of childhood abuse for reasons that will become clearer when we look at their attachment history.

Another phenomenon that also characterises sufferers of PTSD is the feeling of guilt they experience in relation to their traumatic experience. Even victims of natural disasters will feel responsible for what happened to them. This sense of guilt is of major importance in the treatment of these patients who may not only feel this way because they have survived when others have not, but also because by feeling they are to blame they are at least feeling more in control of what has happened to them. It's a normal response in the face of the terrible sense of helplessness they experienced at the time of the traumatic experience. This 'moral defence', as Fairbairn called it (1952: 65–67), is particularly prevalent in victims of childhood abuse and can best be understood by referring to research in the field of attachment.

While it is 'politically correct' to view PTSD as a disorder that can happen to any one of us, we know that certain people are more vulnerable than others. Those who have a history of mental illness or childhood trauma are more likely to develop PTSD. Recent research carried out by Yehuda and her team shows how the survivors of a road traffic accident who later developed PTSD had an immediate lower cortisol response than those who did not go on to develop post-traumatic stress disorder (Yehuda 1997). This result could be linked to earlier changes in the cortisol response of these individuals, a change that could be related to earlier damage to the attachment system. Abnormal responses to stressful experiences such as separation from mother have been observed in avoidant infants who showed low cortisol secretion in comparison with their secure counterparts who showed a high cortisol secretion (Tennes 1982)

Patients suffering from chronic PTSD have been observed to have a smaller hippocampus than normal (Bremner et al. 1995). This phenomenon has been linked to excessive cortisol secretion following long-standing PTSD.

PTSD AS AN ATTACHMENT DISORDER

The importance of the attachment system and its accompanying behavioural patterns cannot be underestimated in the study and treatment of post-traumatic stress disorder. In the severe cases of complex PTSD, recent research shows strong links between early attachment patterns and later psychopathology. Sroufe and his team have carried out a 19-year long prospective study showing how infants assessed as having disorganised attachment patterns, using the strange situation, develop dissociative disorders, such as borderline personality disorders or dissociative identity disorders as adults (Ogawa et al. 1997). The 1-year-old infant's disorganised behaviour is that of a child suffering from PTSD. Such a child has parents who are very frightening, either because they are abusive to their children or because they themselves suffer from frightening flashbacks and/or dissociative states (Main and Hesse 1990). The disorganised infant's unpredictable behaviour results from the fact that he or she has been threatened by his or her caregiver, the very same person who is supposed to provide the infant with a secure base. In a desperate need to preserve their life-giving attachment, these children will 'cut-off' or dissociate themselves from memories and experiences which could threaten this attachment bond. The terror and helplessness such children will experience when faced with a violent attacking or rejecting parent cannot be underestimated: they face death and/or loss of the vital parental figure on whom they totally depend for survival. When Lindemann defined psychological trauma in 1944 as the 'sudden uncontrollable disruption of our affiliative bonds', he was highlighting the marked changes that take place in most victims of trauma. Their capacity to relate to others – particularly in intimate relationships – is markedly affected, leading to a breakdown in their intimate relationships and disruption of their families' lives. Their distrust and sense of isolation can contribute to failure at work, loss of employment and loss of self-esteem.

In those who have suffered earlier abuse in childhood, the sense of guilt is compounded with earlier identifications with an abusing parent. To believe oneself to be bad gives the child a sense of power and control, which is desperately needed, but such an identification also implies that the child sees himself as 'wicked' and needs to be punished. As Fairbairn pointed out, the abused child will cling to this belief in his own badness because by becoming 'bad', such a child also makes the objects of his attachment 'good'. In this way, he has a part to play in his downfall and but also a sense that he can make things better in the future, hence the term 'moral defence' (Fairbairn 1952: 65–67). For the developing child, the developmental failure resulting from deprivation and abuse leads to internal 'splitting' of the parent into a 'good' idealised and desperately needed attachment figure and a 'bad' rejecting and traumatising figure. This split identification is clearly seen in people suffering from a borderline personality disorder or complex PTSD (Ryle 1997). The resultant inability to integrate these split models of attachment make people with this disorder unable to grieve and to mourn. In psychoanalytic language, they cannot move from the paranoid-schizoid position to the depressive position (Segal 1975: 73). They hang on to their bad internalised object-relations in order to retain the possibility of one day being good enough to be loved and cared for. In terms of attachment behaviour and PTSD, they hang onto their parental relationship because however insecure or abusive it is, it is their only hope: the dissociated traumatised child needs to cling onto this idealised caregiver in order to survive.

Only the prospect of alternative secure enough attachments can enable such an individual to abandon his lifelong parental attachments with all the suffering that this implies. It means realising that there never was and never will be a good enough parent and that some of the wounds of the past will probably always be there, albeit in an attenuated and more tolerable form.

TREATMENT APPROACH

The Traumatic Stress Service aims at providing all patients with a secure base. Following the approach taken by Sandi Bloom, treatment takes place in a series of stages, the first and perhaps most important being that of ensuring safety, followed by affect modulation, grief and evolution (1997).

Our permanent team comprises a full-time consultant psychiatrist and psychotherapist, a senior registrar in forensic psychiatry, a nurse therapist and a clinical psychologist as well as two half-time clinical psychologists – all trained in the treatment of post-traumatic stress disorder and associated disorders such as depression or anxiety.

ASSESSMENT

The assessment process is carried out with the following principles in mind.

Ensuring safety

The essential core of our therapeutic approach is to ensure that the patient is given a sense of control and responsibility throughout the treatment programme. This is crucial to counteract the sense of helplessness induced by traumatic experience. This means that the patient and therapist are to become engaged in a 'journey of exploration' in which the therapist informs and guides the client. He or she neither takes over the treatment nor invites regression by adopting the conventional psychoanalytic stance of remaining silent – at least not in the early phase of treatment. First and foremost, the victim of trauma wants to know that the therapist is affected and does care about what happened to him or her. This does not mean becoming emotional but simply and gently conveying compassion, respect and understanding of the victim's plight. The traumatic story is thereby validated.

The cognitive blueprint

Many of our patients have avoided talking about their symptoms to medical staff because they fear they are going mad. This fear is particularly marked in some people for whom the experience of flashbacks is tantamount to having hallucinations. For this reason, one of our first tasks is to explain to patients and their relatives or partners what are the symptoms of PTSD and why they occur.

Empowerment

To counteract the overwhelming sense of helplessness experienced by sufferers of PTSD, they are given simple advice as to what they can do to feel more in control. They are taught relaxation techniques using tapes or other methods and, in the case of simple PTSD, they are encouraged to let the memories of the traumatic event come to mind and observe them. If patients are able to do this many show an immediate positive response to this early intervention (Ehlers and Clark, 2000). Patients with complex PTSD often resort to self-destructive or destructive patterns of behaviour in order to cope with their symptoms. They may cut themselves, abuse drugs or alcohol or cling to destructive relationships. A thorough assessment needs to be done in relation to their capacity for self-harm or the dangers that they might bring upon themselves by engaging in treatment. When this isn't carried out, it can have tragic consequences.

> *Case* A young black woman called Susan was referred to our service with a history of having been sexually abused as a child. She had reported her father's abuse to the police in her teens but, when her family found out, they made her life such hell, she withdrew her statement and the abuse continued. She ended up having psychiatric care and, with support, was able to leave home and start working. When she came to the TSS she wanted to join a group with others who had been through similar experiences. For some reason, her mother was living with her again and, although this was raised as a cause for concern, no work was carried out to help Susan regain her earlier independence before beginning her treatment. A few weeks later, she became very disturbed and threatened to kill herself: she had to be sectioned under the Mental Health Act and admitted to her local psychiatric hospital. She complained that her mother had been constantly criticising her for attending the group and threatening her if she brought up the history of her abuse. What finally made Susan feel suicidal was finding out that her mother had been reading her diary. She became once again the helpless teenager whose mother was preventing her from getting the help she needed to escape her abusive relationships. The re-enactment of her past trauma was very clear and Susan could see it herself once she left hospital. Mother moved out of the home and treatment could be resumed. With more careful preparation, this destructive episode could have been avoided.

Battered women face similar dangers if they embark on treatment without prior preparation. Support and advice will be given to them so that they can establish a safety network beforehand. This may involve leaving the family home and seeking refuge as well as seeking legal advice. It must be borne in mind that it is at the time when a woman seeks to leave an abusive relationship where domestic violence is taking place, that she is in greatest danger of being attacked or killed by her partner.

In the case of substance abuse, patients will be advised to give up using alcohol or drugs and to seek specialised help if needed. In this case, they will not be taken into treatment until they have been treated for their addiction to alcohol or drugs.

Assessment of dissociative disorders

Dissociation refers to a wide variety of behaviours that represent lapses in the psychological and cognitive processing. Three main types of dissociative behaviour have been recognised: amnesia, absorption and depersonalisation. Dissociative amnesia involves suddenly finding oneself in situations or faced with evidence that you have performed actions for which you have no memory. Absorption implies becoming so involved in what you are doing that you are unaware of what is going on around you. Depersonalisation refers to experiencing events as if you are an observer, disconnected from your body or feelings. These various forms of dissociation are prevalent in patients who suffer from complex PTSD and can be assessed by giving them the Dissociative Experience Scale (DES). If they show high scores (of 30 and above), we need to take measures to deal with this phenomenon in our treatment plan.

> *Case* A young Asian woman presented to me for an assessment for psychotherapy. She appeared motivated for treatment. During our meeting, she began to talk about her experience of sexual abuse and then lost her voice. Realising that she could no longer speak and that her face became contorted with pain, I continued talking to her, telling her what I was seeing and experiencing. She regained her voice at the end of our meeting and returned for a second appointment when she told me that, although she could not speak, she found it helpful to listen to me. It enabled her to remain connected to me in the present.

For many of our patients, recognising that they do suffer from a Dissociative Identity Disorder comes as a shock and we get very few individuals who present to us with a constellation of previously identified self states with named personalities. In some cases, an awareness that therapy will involve exploring aspects of themselves they would rather not know about, makes them choose to refuse therapy or to postpone it until such time as they can find no other solution to their problems. Sroufe points out how the strength of the early self is negatively related to later dissociation, thereby underscoring his view that dissociation is a self-related process (Ogawa et al. 1997: 877). The vulnerable self will tend to adopt dissociation as a defensive process because it does not have the belief in its worthiness gained from a loving responsive early relationship. While the process of dissociation begins as a protective mechanism for the integrity of the self in the face of catastrophic trauma, it can develop into a direct threat to the optimal functioning of the self if it becomes a routine response to stress.

Our approach in the TSS is to acknowledge that a patient with a tendency to dissociate into different self states needs to be made aware of when this is happening, particularly if it is putting them at risk of being harmed or of harming others. In order to do this we gradually establish a procedure whereby it is recognised that these patients will take responsibility for themselves and the management of their dissociated self-states. This can mean involving friends, family or other carers in being available after therapeutic sessions and writing a diary to establish what are the triggers to these dissociative experiences. As many of these patients 'forget' what happens in their therapeutic sessions, they are also offered the possibility of taking home tape-recordings of their sessions. Most of our patients have found this extremely helpful while acknowledging that it means that they have to work harder at integrating the past with the present.

MODULATION OF AFFECT AND GRIEF WORK: THE CONSTRUCTION OF A NARRATIVE

Affect modulation is inherent to the treatment process. It requires a patient to confront their traumatic experience as well as the feelings and cognitive distortions that accompany it. The Traumatic Stress Service attempts to offer a treatment programme suited to each patient's needs. The underlying principle is to help our patients construct or re-construct the narrative of their shattered selves. They do so by confronting the past in the here and now of an attachment relationship with their therapist(s).

Patients who suffer from PTSD resulting from one or more traumatic experiences are offered a choice of cognitive-behavioural therapy or Eye Movement Desensitisation and Reprocessing (EMDR) over 12 to 24 sessions (Shapiro 1995). In this new approach, the patients are invited to imagine a safe place to which they can return if needed. After having been questioned about their emotional, cognitive and physical responses to their traumatic event, they are also asked to state how they would like to feel about themselves in relation to the traumatic event. The patients are then encouraged to follow the regular movements of the therapist's finger while focusing on the event itself. This technique need not use eye movement but can be modified by using alternate hand tapping or sounds if the patient prefers. In many cases this approach produces rapid results. It is particularly useful for patients who tend to experience a lot of physical symptoms or to intellectualise, and also in cases where patients find it hard to talk about their traumatic experience because it is too humiliating, such as in victims of rape or torture.

We also use EMDR when patients involved in other therapies appear to be stuck or as an adjunct to the treatment of patients with complex PTSD. In these cases, the patient's therapist may accompany the patient during this stage of treatment or be informed as to what took place so that the information that is brought up in the EMDR session can be integrated into the ongoing therapy.

One foot in the past and one foot in the present

If integration is essential to the treatment of PTSD, it is even more so in the treatment of patients suffering from complex PTSD. Such patients require a longer period of treatment and a carefully thought out programme involving a psychoanalytic approach with considerable cognitive input. The slow and painful construction of the patient's narrative requires the patient to focus on the past while recognising the presence of the therapist in the here and now of the present. Many patients suffering from complex PTSD will tend to dissociate and get lost in the horrors of their past – thereby recreating their past trauma within the therapeutic setting. In order to prevent this, the therapist may keep in verbal contact with the patient by commenting on what he or she sees or hears and reminding the patient that the event was in the past. Patients can be helped to stay in the room through various grounding techniques such as keeping eye contact, holding on to something, or pushing their feet into the floor.

Knowing how important it is for these individuals to feel that they are not over-dependent nor abused or helpless, we need constantly to watch for therapeutic situations that may precipitate destructive behaviour and, at the same time, help with the reintegration of earlier self–other experiences. According to Sroufe,

> when an experience is acknowledged and accepted, integration inevitably follows because the self cannot help seeking meaning and coherence from experience. When experience is dissociated, however, integration is not possible, and to the extent that dissociation prevails, there is fragmentation of the self. A coherent well-organised self depends on integration.
>
> (Ogawa et al. 1997: 857)

In order to prevent dependency in relation to one therapist and to attend to their difficulties in relating to others, patients with a tendency to dissociate are offered conjoint individual and group therapy. This form of 'contained splitting' allows patients to explore issues of intimacy and difficult experiences in the one-to-one setting while exploring new ways of relating and expressing themselves in the group setting. Information pertaining to the individual therapy is not divulged in the group, but the patients are told that their therapists will share information from both settings and that it will inform the therapeutic process (Zulueta and Mark 2000).

A time-limited, group-based approach for patients suffering from simple PTSD is proving to be very useful. After an initial period spent getting to know one another, each patient takes it in turn to focus on his or her traumatic experience while the others help by validating the experience, sharing some aspects and challenging the sense of guilt and other negative assumptions. This work can be much more effective than the one-to-one therapeutic experience, but patients need to feel ready to go into a group.

In some chronic cases, the damage perpetrated on the wife and children by the sufferer's irritability and even violence makes it essential to involve the family in treatment. A systemic therapist sees several such families.

Knowing how PTSD can negatively affect people's capacity to express themselves verbally, it is no surprise to find that art therapy can also be extremely helpful in enabling some patients to move on when they appear stuck in one therapeutic modality. Whatever the form of therapy being offered to a patient, the team approach remains central to our service. One of our psychiatrists will see patients in therapy to offer them the possibility of taking medication to help with their symptoms and to address legal issues that arise with this population. In this way the patient has an involvement with at least one other member of staff who can be contacted when the therapist is away. Medication is offered as a 'life jacket' to cope with the difficulties of the therapeutic journey. The most useful types of medication are usually the antidepressants known as serotonin re-uptake inhibitors or SSRIs.

THERAPEUTIC DIFFICULTIES AND HOW WE DEAL WITH THEM

No amount of assessment and careful management will prevent destructive processes appearing in the treatment of patients with complex PTSD, particularly in those who suffer from what is referred to as a borderline personality disorder (Zulueta 1999). An attachment-based approach can help us to understand what may be happening to a patient and enable us to set up remedial action.

Problems around dissociative phenomena

These occur mostly with patients suffering from complex PTSD. They may emerge as a conflict regarding 'who is in control'. Many of these patients have one or more destructive self-states that become very active when treatment appears to threaten the idealised attachment to their abusive caregiver. This can happen, either when patients feel they are becoming dependent on the therapist and, as a result, start to fear a recreation of their earlier abusive relationships, or when the material they bring to the session challenges their idealised view of their abusers. This will elicit the terror of being re-abused or worse, the fear of losing their caregiver altogether. When this takes place, patients may 'act out' by missing sessions, forgetting what took place or by identifying with their abuser and thereby re-enacting early traumatic experiences both in and out of the session. When this threatens the safety of the therapeutic experience, the patient will need to be confronted with what they are doing and offered help in finding alternative means of expressing their fears, anger and pain. Suicide threats are often seen as the ultimate way of taking control by one of the dissociated self-states when faced with the terror of feeling helpless and the potential victim of further abuse.

In the early phases of treatment, the patient is made aware of the function of these dissociative self-states and steps are taken by both the patient and the therapist to minimise their possible sabotage of the treatment process. It is then made quite clear that therapy cannot proceed unless a more positive approach can take place where the patient takes responsibility for his or her actions. This may involve a request for admission to an inpatient unit or more intensive involvement of the community health team or GP who is kept informed of what is taking place.

> *Case* A 40-year-old man from Pakistan with a history of early physical and emotional abuse and high DES scores found himself repeatedly and 'unknowingly' involved in stealing from shops. He was arrested on several occasions and then discovered that if he took antidepressant medication (an SSRI), he could not dissociate enough to steal. However, after a family crisis, he stopped taking his medication and finally ended up in jail. Throughout this period, he remained in touch with the therapist and the group and returned later, requesting further treatment. In the second assessment interview, it was made clear to him that he could not embark on further treatment without taking his medication on a regular basis. He is now receiving group therapy and systemic therapy to deal with his family problems.

Problems around avoidance

Many of our clients are ambivalent about coming in for treatment. They may attempt to avoid any reminders of their traumatic experience either by bringing up different issues and problems in their treatment sessions, by failing to attend sessions, or by not carrying out the tasks they agreed to do. If this avoidance pattern persists, the therapist needs to clarify what may lie behind this behaviour. In some cases, the client clearly believes that the therapeutic journey is too dangerous or too painful and they cannot make a commitment. In these cases, we go with the resistance and advise them to stop treatment for the time being. They are encouraged to return when they feel ready for the journey. Many patients make a stronger commitment at this point. In other cases, their diagnosis of PTSD has clearly given them a role in the system which they do not want to lose, either for legal reasons or for family reasons. In the first case, we advise them to return when their compensation has been resolved and in the second, we offer a systemic family assessment followed in many cases by treatment.

In some cases of therapy, a traumatic re-enactment may take place within the therapy that appears as an insoluble conflict for either the patient and/or the therapist or both. In these cases, the dynamics are often changed by having a third person in the room acting as mediator. This could be the original assessor or the psychiatrist involved with the patient and, in our experience, this form of 'marital therapy' can be extremely helpful for all involved.

Problems associated with ending

The ending of treatment is always a major step in the therapy of patients suffering from complex PTSD. For many, the gains experienced in the treatment may seem to disappear and very child-like wishes to be cared for emerge. The prospect of ending brings back childhood experiences of rejection, loss and abuse that need to be worked through. If rage can be expressed in the therapy this bodes well for these patients who have spent their lives either suppressing their anger or expressing it inappropriately.

Problems relating to the false memory syndrome

The subjective reality of the patient's experience is central to the therapeutic process but we always make it clear that memories may not always reflect what actually took place in the past. Therapists will withhold any ideas they may have about what took place in their patients' lives so as not to influence their patients in any particular direction. They help their patients stay with the experience of not knowing. In the later phases of treatment, the therapists may support patients who wish to seek external confirmation and validation of their abusive experiences. However, the therapists won't endorse such behaviour before they know that their patients are prepared to face the possibility that these abusive experiences may be denied and that they may face rejection and attack. If patients later want to confront their abusers by taking legal action, the therapist will strongly recommend that no such action is taken before corroborative evidence has been obtained by the patient and that he or she has a good lawyer involved in the case.

It is interesting how most of our patients bring up the possibility of suffering from a false memory syndrome as an attempt to deny the horrific abuse they realise has probably taken place. 'Oh, if only it was a false memory', they say as the horror and pain of what they have been through begins to hit home.

TAKING CARE OF THE THERAPIST

There is no doubt that secondary or vicarious traumatisation is a very dangerous aspect of working with this particular group of patients. In order to work
in this field, it is important for therapists to develop other activities and interests both within and outside their professional life.

Group supervision should be provided on a weekly basis and the team members need to feel that they can express themselves freely. They may feel anger
or disgust, frustration and helplessness and, in many cases, doubt as to whether
they are doing the 'right thing'. While supervision does take place in a group
setting, a therapist should feel free to talk to her supervisor about more personal issues that may arise when a patient touches a personal wound in the
therapist. The latter must know that he or she can seek guidance and support,
as well as therapy outside the work context. A few of our cases are potentially
violent and can therefore only be seen in an outpatient department that provides adequate security.

CONCLUSIONS

The treatment of patients suffering from simple or complex PTSD is one of
the most interesting and challenging areas of work in the field of mental
health. We are not only dealing here with a disorder that is only just beginning to be recognised but we are also constantly learning new forms of
treatment – each one of which opens up new perspectives on how the mind
works in relation to a traumatic experience. An attachment perspective helps
to make sense of what takes place in the sufferer of PTSD, both from a psychobiological perspective and in terms of the meaning he or she gives to such
an experience. It also bridges the gap between the experience of the individual and his or her social context: a supportive community can act as external
protective buffer just as an internalised secure attachment can act as an internal protective buffer for the individual who would otherwise develop PTSD
(Zulueta 1993). To the shattered selves of the survivors who land up in our
clinic, we attempt to help them find their own story – one of integration and
hope.

REFERENCES

American Psychiatric Association (1994) *Diagnostic and Statistical Manual of Mental
    Disorders*, 4th edition (DSM-IV). Washington, DC: American Psychiatric
    Association.
Bloom, S. (1997) *Creating Sanctuary: Toward the Evolution of Sane Societies*. London:
    Routledge.

Bremner, J.D., Randall, P., Scott, T.M., Bronen, R.A., Seibyl, J.B., Southwick, S.M., Delaney, R.C., McCarthy, G., Charney, D.S. and Innis, R.B. (1995) 'MRI-based measures of hippocampal volume in Vietnam combat veterans'. *American Journal of Psychiatry* 152: 973–981.

Ehlers, A. and Clark, D.M. (2000) 'A cognitive model of posttraumatic stress disorder'. *Behaviour Research and Therapy* 38: 319–345.

Fairbairn, R. (1952) *Psychoanalytic Study of the Personality*. London: Routledge & Kegan Paul.

Herman, J. (1992) *Trauma and Recovery: The Aftermath of Violence from Domestic Abuse to Political Terror*. New York: Basic Books.

Lindemann, E. (1944) 'Symptomatology and management of acute grief'. *American Journal of Psychiatry* 101: 141–149.

Main, M. and Hesse, E. (1990) 'Parents' unresolved traumatic experiences are related to infant disorganised attachment status: Is frightened and/or frightening behaviour the linking mechanism?' In M.T. Greenberg, D. Cicchetti and E.M. Cummings (eds) *Attachment in the Pre-school Years: Theory, Research and Intervention* (pp. 161–182). Chicago: University of Chicago Press.

Ogawa, J.R., Sroufe, A., Weinfeld, N., Carlson, E.A. and Egeland, B. (1997) 'Development and the fragmented self: Longitudinal study of dissociative symptomatology in a non-clinical sample'. *Development and Psychopathology* 9: 855–879.

Panksepp, J., Siviy, S.M. and Normansell, A. (1985) 'Brain opioids and social emotions'. In N. Reite and T. Field (eds) *The Psychobiology of Attachment and Separation* (pp. 3–44). London: Academic Press.

Pitman, R.K., van der Kolk, B.A., Scott, P.O. and Greenberg, M.S. (1990) 'Naloxone reversible analgesic response to combat related stimuli in post-traumatic stress disorder'. *Archives of General Psychiatry* 47: 541–544.

Rauch, S.L., van der Kolk, B.A., Fisler, R.E., Albert, N.M., Orr, S.P., Savage, C.R., Fischman, A.G., Jenike, M.A. and Pitman, R.K. (1996) 'A symptom provocation study of post-traumatic stress disorder using positron emission tomography and script driven imagery'. *Archives of General Psychiatry* 53: 380–387.

Ryle, A. (1997) 'The structure and development of borderline personality disorder: A proposed model'. *British Journal of Psychiatry* 170: 82–87.

Segal, H. (1975) *Introduction to the Work of Melanie Klein*. London: Hogarth Press/Institute of Psychoanalysis.

Shapiro, F. (1995) *Eye Movement Desensitisation and Reprocessing: Basic Principles, Protocols, and Procedures*. New York: Guilford Press.

Tennes, K. (1982) 'The role of hormones in mother–infant transactions'. In R.N. Emde and R.J. Harmon (eds) *The Development of Attachment and Affiliative Systems* (pp. 75–80). New York: Plenum.

van der Kolk, B.A. (1996) 'The body keeps the score: Approaches to the psychobiology of post traumatic stress disorder'. In B. van der Kolk, A.C. McFarlane and L. Weisaeth (eds) *Traumatic Stress: The Effects of Overwhelming Experiences on Mind, Body and Society* (pp. 214–241). New York: Guilford Press.

Yehuda, R. (1997) 'Sensitisation of the hypothalamic–pituitary–adrenal axis in post traumatic stress disorder'. In R. Yehuda and A.C. McFarlane (eds) *Psychobiology of Post Traumatic Stress Disorder* (pp. 57–82). New York: New York Academy of Sciences.

Zulueta, F. de (1993) *From Pain to Violence: The Traumatic Roots of Destructiveness*. London: Whurr Publishers.

Zulueta, F. de (1999) 'Borderline personality disorder as seen from an attachment perspective'. *Criminal Behaviour and Mental Health* 9: 237–253.

Zulueta, F. de and Mark, P. (2000) 'A combined approach of group and individual therapy to the treatment of patients suffering from a borderline personality disorder'. *Group Analysis* 33: 486–500.

Part II

Attachment focus: theory and research

Labels

I've been to the neurologist,
A male doctor I saw,
He questioned my labels,
He noted them all,
He examined me then,
He hurried his way,
I was a rag-doll and had no say,
I was alone, in the past I stayed,
The tears I cried,
He did not care,
I showed no pain,
For my body he hurt,
He removed my gown,
The blanket the same,
In my underwear I stood in shame
Feeling helpless being abused again
                                        Beverley

My name is Beverley and I am 27 years of age. I am a survivor of ritual abuse. My rights as a human being to medical treatment and justice have been violated because of the labels given to me by professional bodies who never listened or understood. I am currently studying for a degree in psychology and intend to do a PhD on DID.

Beverley's Mother: How I coped as a mum caring for my daughter who had DID would fill a book so I have just chosen the following. Don't be upset by the label. The mind is a wonderful thing and can be your best friend or worst enemy. I am thankful my daughter developed DID. It saved her life. I was 'tested' in every which way and only showed love in return and learnt very quickly when to intervene and when to stay silent.

I also learnt very quickly about triggers and could anticipate and prevent a crisis. When my daughter couldn't talk I suggested she write things down and she did by way of poems and drawings. Always be available when your child wants to talk. Don't ask questions. Focus your child on their own inner strength – it has got them this far. Use what you can for help.

Miki

I am a mother who has DID. I thought that it was important to help my daughter understand our world, in a way that she could understand. My alters got together to make a simple age appropriate book, which Amy calls her 'special book'. Below is the text from that book.

Amy's Mama has DID

Amy has a mama that loves her lots and lots and lots. Amy's mama at times behaves in a different way than Amy's friends' mamas. This is because she has DID.

Amy's mama was hurt when she was a little girl. It made her very sad so she pretended that it was happening to another little girl. This made the hurt and pain go away. Every time Amy's mama got hurt she pretended she was someone else. When she grew to be a big lady she had lots of pretend people. Amy's mama called these pretend people 'inside' people.

Sometimes Amy's mama behaves like a little girl and plays with Amy in a childish way. Amy has fun. When Amy's mama is tired or sad one of her inside friends will come out and look after and play with Amy. Amy knows that her mama has not gone away and that she is there if ever Amy needs her.

Amy's mama talks to a good lady called a therapist about her problems. She listens to her sadness and wants Amy and her mama to be happy.

It is sometimes hard for Amy having a mama with DID. She gets angry with her mama and sometimes gets frightened that her mama has gone away. Amy always talks about how she feels. She talks about her mama being different people. This is good for Amy that she does not have to have secrets.

Amy's mama wants to know how Amy feels and Amy can always talk to her mama about her feeling even if she is angry with her. Amy knows that her mama loves her lots and lots and lots.

Amy's mama is trying to be the best mama to Amy that she can.

Miki

Chapter 4

Multiple voices versus meta-cognition

An attachment theory perspective[1]

Peter Fonagy

Attachment theory concerns the nature of early experiences of children and the impact of these experiences on aspects of later functioning of particular relevance to personality disorder. The question we attempt to address here is how deprivation, in particular early trauma, comes to affect the individual's propensity to manifest multiple selves, to speak with multiple voices in therapy. As part of this question we are naturally also concerned to understand how such adverse consequences may affect the psychotherapeutic process. The key assumption made by the invoking of attachment theory is that individual social behaviour may be understood in terms of generic mental models of social relationships constructed by the individual. These models, although constantly evolving and subject to modification, exist side by side and constitute the structures underlying the multiple voices of therapy. To elaborate on this point I will consider an attachment theory model of the most extreme of such phenomena: multiple selves in states of dissociation. Let us now turn to the details of the theory.

THE NATURE OF THE ATTACHMENT SYSTEM

Attachment theory, developed by John Bowlby (1969, 1973, 1980), postulates a universal human need to form close affectional bonds. It is a normative theory of how the 'attachment system' functions in all humans. Bowlby described attachment as a special type of social relationship, paradigmatically between infant and caregiver, involving an affective bond. More significantly, it may also be seen as the context within which the human infant learns to regulate emotion (Sroufe 1990).

The stability of early childhood attachment patterns is well demonstrated. Mary Ainsworth and her colleagues (Ainsworth 1985; Ainsworth et al. 1978; Ainsworth and Wittig 1969) developed a procedure commonly known as the *strange situation*, which classifies infants and toddlers into one of four attachment categories. *Secure* infants explore readily in the presence of the primary caregiver, are anxious in the presence of the stranger, are distressed by their caregiver's departure and brief absence, rapidly seek contact with the caregiver following a brief period of separation, and are reassured by renewed contact. The recovery from an over-aroused disorganised state is smooth and carried to completion in the sense that the infant returns to exploration and play.

Some infants, who are usually made less anxious by separation, do not automatically seek proximity with the caregiver on her return following separation and may show no preference for the caregiver over the stranger; these infants are designated *anxious/avoidant*. A third category, the *anxious/resistant* infant manifests impoverished exploration and play, tends to be highly distressed by separation from the caregiver, but has great difficulty in settling after reunion, showing struggling, stiffness, continued crying, or fuss in a passive way. The caregiver's presence or attempts at comforting fail to offer reassurance and their anxiety and anger appear to interfere with their attempts to derive comfort through proximity. Both these insecure groups seem to be coping with arousal and ambivalence through a precautious over-control of affect because they appear to be uncertain in their expectation that the caregiver will do his or her part to modulate their emotional arousal (Main and Weston 1981; Sroufe 1990).

A fourth group of infants appear to exhibit a range of seemingly undirected behavioural responses giving the impression of disorganisation and disorientation (Main and Solomon 1990). Infants who manifest freezing, hand-clapping, headbanging, the wish to escape from the situation even in the presence of the caregiver, are referred to as *disorganised/disoriented*. It is generally held that for such infants the caregiver has served both as a source of fear and as a source of reassurance, thus the arousal of the attachment behavioural system produces strong conflicting motivations. Not surprisingly, a history of severe neglect or physical or sexual abuse is often associated with the manifestation of this pattern (Cicchetti and Beeghly 1987; Main and Solomon 1990). It is those infants who will particularly concern us here.

THE CONTINUITY OF PATTERNS OF ATTACHMENT

Bowlby proposed that the quality of childhood relationships with the caregivers results in internal representations or working models of the self and others that provide prototypes for later social relations. Internal working models are mental schemata, where expectations about the behaviour of a particular individual towards the self are aggregated. The expectations are themselves abstractions based on repeated interactions of specific types with that individual. If the child's physical injury is quickly dealt with, sources of unhappiness are rapidly addressed, the child will develop the legitimate expectation that, with that person at least, his or her distress is likely to be met by reassurance and comforting. The internal working model is the result of a natural process of abstraction of the invariant features from diverse social situations with a particular individual (Stern 1994).

Early experiences of flexible access to feelings are regarded as formative by attachment theorists, enabling secure children both to maximise the opportunities presented to them by the environment and to draw on socially supportive relationships. The autonomous sense of self emerges fully from secure parent–infant relationships (Emde 1990; Fonagy et al. 1996; Lieberman and Pawl 1990). The increased control of the secure child permits it to move towards the ownership of inner experience and come to recognise the self as being competent in eliciting regulatory assistance, to develop metacognitive control and to achieve an understanding of self and others as intentional agents whose behaviour is organised by mental states, thoughts, feelings, beliefs and desires (Fonagy et al. 1995; Sroufe in press).

ADULT ATTACHMENT MEASURES

The stability of attachment assessments is dramatically illustrated by longitudinal studies of infants assessed with the 'strange situation' and followed up in adolescence or young adulthood with the Adult Attachment Interview (AAI) (George et al. 1985). The AAI asks subjects about childhood attachment relationships and the meaning that an individual currently gives to attachment experiences. The instrument is rated according to the scoring system developed by Main (Main and Goldwyn in preparation) which classifies individuals into *secure/autonomous*, *insecure/dismissing or avoidant*, *insecure/preoccupied or resistant* or *unresolved/disorganised* categories with respect to loss or trauma, according to the structural qualities of their narratives of early experiences. While *autonomous* individuals clearly value attachment relationships and regard these as formative, *insecure* individuals are poor at integrating memories of experience with their assessment of the meaning of that experience. Those *dismissing* of attachment deny or devalue early relationships. *Preoccupied* individuals tend to be confused and angry or passive in their current relationships with their parents and others. In the coding of patterns of attachment, *coherence of representations* (the absence of multiple voices) is what most clearly marks the secure adult working model of attachment. Two studies (Hamilton 1994; Waters et al. 1995) have shown a 68–75 per cent correspondence between attachment classifications in infancy and classifications in adulthood. This work speaks to the remarkable stability of attachment classifications across the lifespan.

There is further important evidence that attachment relationships may play a key role in the organisation of interpersonal representations. Adults categorised as secure are three or four times more likely to have children who are securely attached to them (van Ijzendoorn 1995). This turns out to be true even in prospective studies where parental attachment is assessed before the birth of the child (Benoit and Parker 1994; Fonagy et al. 1991a; Steele et al. 1996; Ward and Carlson 1995). These findings also emphasise the importance of the quality of parenting in determining the child's attachment classification.

The findings from our lab suggest that parental attachment patterns predict variance in addition to temperament measures or contextual factors, such as experience, social support, marital relationship, psychopathology and personality (Steele et al. in preparation). If attachment is linked to dissociative disorder we may anticipate a substantial overlap between determinants of infant security and predictors of personality disorders, particularly dissociative or identity problems.

Liotti (1992, 1995), and subsequently Main (1995), conceived the disorganised/disoriented pattern of attachment as predisposing the child to dissociation as a defence. Parents with unresolved patterns of attachment, most likely associated with their own backgrounds of recent loss or childhood maltreatment or abuse, present alternating frightened and/or frightening emotional displays to their child. Consequently, the child is likely to develop numerous contradictory self–caregiver constructs. Imagine the child's likely reaction to a frightened caregiver. He/she may see the adult as helpless or distressed and construe him/herself as at times threatening and at other times rescuing. Equally, the child may see the parent as unconcerned and him/herself as unworthy of parental attention. At other times, when the parent is aggressive and frightening, displaying uncontrolled and perhaps uncontrollable emotion, the child has no escape from terror and a pervasive sense of helplessness may be the consequence. Main and Hesse (1990a) pointed out that abusive experiences place the infant into unbearable approach–avoidance conflict. The internal working models of these infants are thus likely to include extreme negative representations of the self (as evil or devilish) as well as manifesting a multiple and incoherent unintegrated structure.

It is not surprising then that, when reunited with the caregiver, such infants display contradictory behaviour patterns towards the attachment figure. Some show signs of disorientation (of attention), glazed facial expressions, mistimed movements, anomalous postures all suggesting a lack of orientation to the present environment (Main and Hesse 1990a). Other children manifest disorganised behaviour, displaying rapidly cycling contradictory behaviour patterns – e.g. proximity-seeking and fighting, avoidance and crying, inappropriate laughter or distress in the caregiver's absence, followed by a complete collapse. In both the disoriented and the disorganised infants the manifest failure to mount coherent behavioural strategies is evident.

Such behaviours are at least analogous to the behaviour of dissociated patients in the therapeutic relationship. For example, they may assume a glazed expression, look as if they were absorbed in a trance-like state; in such states they may express intense affect without being able to report why and, when questioned, they are unable to report a mental event (thought, image, memory) that might relate their observed behaviour to concurrent events. They are clearly split off, or estranged (as Liotti puts it), from the ongoing dialogue with the therapist. The same patients may manifest an extremely rapid succession of different attitudes to their therapist – not simply opposite poles of the same emotional dimension (e.g. love and hate) but a range of attitudes indicating substantial fragmentation (e.g. asking for comforting and attention then wanting to quit; then expressing the hope that they are loved; then feeling they are dangerous for those around them; then angrily accusing the therapist of having damaged them; then showing fear of the therapist, and so on). At this stage they appeal to the therapist/observer as if they spoke with multiple voices.

There is some evidence from Liotti's group that links the disorganised/disoriented childhood attachment pattern to dissociation as a clinical problem. A number of studies (Ainsworth and Eichberg 1991; Fonagy et al. 1991b; Main and Hesse 1990b) have linked this attachment pattern to infants to an unresolved ('U') AAI narrative. Lack of resolution, in normative samples, most commonly involves unmourned loss of a caregiver. Liotti (1991) demonstrated that 62 per cent of 46 dissociative patients but only 13 per cent of 109 patients with other psychiatric diagnoses were the offspring of mothers who had had a significant loss (parent, child, sibling, husband) up to two years before or shortly after the patient's birth.

These findings are consistent with the assumption of a link between disorganised early attachment and dissociation. Liotti (1995) suggests that the internal working models characteristic of disorganised infants in some cases develop into the disorganisation and disorientation of dissociative patients. If the similarity between infantile disorganisation and dissociative adult behaviour is more than superficial, then the key question becomes: 'what characteristics of the internal working model of dissociative patients may be linked to the typical background of children with disorganised patterns of attachment?'

ATTACHMENT AND MENTALISING

To understand why dissociative disorders are likely to be common consequences of caregiving dominated by such unresolved patterns of parenting, we have to explore a further aspect of the transgenerational processes of attachment. A compelling model for the transmission of secure attachment, which has moved the field beyond a simple view of caregiver sensitivity, was suggested by Mary Main (1991) in her seminal chapter on metacognitive monitoring and singular versus multiple models of attachment. Main (1991) showed that the absence of metacognitive capacity, the inability to 'understand the *merely* representational nature of their own (and others') thinking' (p. 128), makes infants and toddlers vulnerable to the inconsistency of the caregiver's behaviour. They are unable to step beyond the immediate reality of experience and grasp the distinction between immediate experience and the mental state which might underpin it. Main drew our attention to the development in the child of the mental state that Dennett (1987) called 'the intentional stance'. Dennett stressed that human beings are perhaps unique in trying to understand each other in terms of mental states – thoughts, feelings, desires, beliefs – in order to make sense of and, even more important, to anticipate each other's actions. It is self-evident that by attributing an emotional or cognitive state to others we make their behaviour explicable to ourselves. If the child is able to attribute a withdrawing, non-responsive mother's apparently rejecting behaviour to her emotional state of depression, rather than to himself as bad and unstimulating, the child is protected from, perhaps permanent, narcissistic injury. Perhaps even more central is the child's reflective capacity, the development of representations of the mental states, emotional and cognitive, which organise his/her behaviour towards the caregiver.

We attempted to operationalise individual differences in adults' metacognitive capacities which we believe might help to fill the 'transmission gap'. We were curious to know if the extent of self-reflective observations about the mental states of self and others in Adult Attachment Interview (AAI) narratives could predict infant security. We chose the term 'reflective function-scale' to underscore that we were concerned about the clarity of the individual's representation of the mental states of others *as well as* the representation of their own mental state.

Consistent with our expectation, reflective function ratings were reliable (intraclass $r = .8$ and above) and provided a good pre-natal prediction of the strange situation behaviour of the child. Both fathers and mothers who were rated to be high in this capacity were three or four times more likely to have secure children than parents whose reflective capacity was poor (Fonagy et al. 1991a).

The capacity for metacognitive control may be particularly important when the child is exposed to unfavourable interaction patterns – in the extreme, abuse or trauma. For example, in the absence of the capacity to represent ideas as ideas, the child is forced to accept the implication of parental rejection, and adopt a negative view of himself. A child who has the capacity to conceive of the mental state of the other can also conceive of the possibility that the parent's rejection of him or her may be based on false beliefs, and therefore is able to moderate the impact of negative experience.

Ten out of 10 of the mothers in the deprived group with high reflective-self ratings had children who were secure with them, whereas only one out of 17 of deprived mothers with low ratings did so. Reflective-self function seemed to be a far less important predictor for the non-deprived group. Our findings imply that the intergenerational replication of early negative experiences may be aborted, the cycle of disadvantage interrupted, if the caregiver acquires a capacity to fully represent and reflect on mental experience (Fonagy et al. 1994).

METACOGNITIVE MONITORING AND THE DEVELOPMENT OF THE SELF

Metacognitive monitoring completes one aspect of the intergenerational cycle. Not only are parents high in reflective capacity more likely to promote secure attachment in the child, particularly if their own childhood experiences were adverse, but also secure attachment may be a key precursor of robust reflective capacity (Fonagy et al. submitted).

We tested 92 5-year-old children for whom we had one year strange situation observations on a mentalisation task (the Harris Belief–Desire TOM task). Of those who passed, 66 per cent were secure at one year with their mother. Of the 29 who failed, only 31 per cent had been secure. There was clear indication that the reflective-self function of the mother was associated with the child's success. Eighty per cent of children whose mothers were above the median in reflective-self function passed, whereas only 40 per cent of those whose mothers were below the median did so.

These results suggest that the parents' capacity to observe the child's mind facilitates the child's general understanding of minds mediated by secure attachment. The availability of a reflective caregiver increases the likelihood of the child's secure attachment which, in turn, facilitates the development of theory of mind. Throughout these studies we assume that a secure attachment relationship provides a congenial context for the child to explore the mind of the caregiver. As the philosopher Hegel (1807) taught us, it is only through getting to know the mind of the other that the child develops full appreciation of the nature of mental states. The process is intersubjective: the child gets to know the caregiver's mind as the caregiver endeavours to understand and contain the mental state of the child.

The child perceives in the caregiver's behaviour not only *her* stance of reflectiveness which he infers in order to account for her behaviour, but also an image of *himself* as mentalising, desiring and believing. He sees that the caregiver represents him as an intentional being. It is this representation which is internalised to form the self. 'I think therefore I am' will not do as a psychodynamic model of the birth of the self; 'She thinks of me as thinking and therefore I exist as a thinker' comes perhaps closer to the truth.

If the caregiver's reflective capacity enabled her accurately to picture the infant's intentional stance, the infant will have the opportunity to 'find itself in the other' as a mentalising individual. If the caregiver's capacity is lacking in this regard, the version of itself that the infant will encounter will be an individual conceived of as thinking in terms of physical reality rather than mental states.

SOME SPECULATIONS ABOUT PATHOLOGICAL DEVELOPMENT BASED ON THE DIALECTIC MODEL

The fundamental need of every infant is to find his mind, his intentional state, in the mind of the object. For the infant, internalisation of this image performs the function of 'containment', which Winnicott has written of as 'giving back to the baby the baby's own self' (Winnicott 1967: 33). Failure of this function leads to a desperate search for alternative ways of containing thoughts and the intense feelings they engender.

The search for alternative ways of mental containment may give rise to many pathological solutions, including taking the mind of the other, with its distorted, absent or malign picture of the child, as part of the child's own sense of identity. Winnicott wrote:

> What does the baby see when he or she looks at the mother's face? . . . ordinarily, the mother is looking at the baby and *what she looks like is related to what she sees there* . . . [but what of] the baby whose mother reflects her own mood or, worse still, the rigidity of her own defences . . . They look and they do not see themselves . . . what is seen is the mother's face.
> (1967: 27)

This picture then becomes the germ of a potentially persecutory voice which is lodged in the self, but is alien and unassimilable. There will be a desperate wish for separation in the hope of establishing an autonomous identity or existence. However, tragically, this identity is centred around a mental state which cannot reflect the changing emotional and cognitive states of the individual, because it is based on an archaic representation of the other, rather than the thinking and feeling self as seen by the other.

Paradoxically, where the child's search for mirroring or containment has failed, the later striving for separation will only produce a movement towards fusion. The more the person attempts to become himself, the closer he moves towards becoming his object, because the latter is part of the self-structure. This in our view accounts for the familiar oscillation of dissociative borderline patients, between the struggle for independence and the terrifying wish for extreme closeness and fantasised union. Developmentally, a crisis arises when the external demand for separateness becomes irresistible, in late adolescence and early adulthood. At this time, self-destructive and (in the extreme) suicidal behaviour is perceived as the only feasible solution to an insoluble dilemma: the freeing of the self from the other through the destruction of the other within the self.

In some individuals, for whom separateness is a chronic problem, we assume that the experience of self-hood can only be achieved through finding a physical other on to whom the other within the self can be projected. Naturally, this increases the individual's need for the physical presence of the other. Thus many such individuals experience considerable difficulty in leaving home and if they finally achieve physical separation, they can only do so by finding an alternative and comparable figure on to whom the other within the self may be projected. If the other dies, or abandons the individual, a pathological mourning process may be initiated whereby the person feels compelled to maintain a live picture of the other, in order to retain the integrity of the self.

If the child finds no alternative interpersonal context where he is conceived of as mentalising, his potential in this regard will not be fulfilled. In the cases of an abusive, hostile or simply totally vacuous relationship with the caregiver, the infant may deliberately turn away from the mentalising object because the contemplation of the object's mind is overwhelming as it harbours frankly hostile intentions toward the infant's self. This may lead to a widespread avoidance of mental states, which further reduces the chance of identifying and establishing intimate links with an understanding object.

As studies of resilient children suggest, even a single secure/understanding relationship may be sufficient for the development of reflective processes and may 'save' the child. Metacognitive monitoring is biologically prepared and will spontaneously emerge unless its development is inhibited by the dual disadvantage of the absence of a safe relationship and the experience of maltreatment in the context of an intimate relationship. We do not anticipate that trauma outside of the context of an attachment bond would have pervasive inhibitory effects on mentalising. It is because the theory of mind or, more broadly, reflective-self function evolves in the context of intense interpersonal relationships, that the fear of the mind of another can have such devastating consequences on the emergence of social understanding.

A TRANSGENERATIONAL MODEL OF DISSOCIATION IN PERSONALITY DISORDER

Although accurate figures are hard to come by and vary across studies, considerable evidence has accumulated to support the contention that child abuse is transmitted across generations (Oliver 1993). Research has documented that a specific link exists between the history of childhood maltreatment and dissociative personality disorder, with sexual abuse being especially implicated. In brief, as infants and children such individuals frequently have caretakers who are themselves within the so-called 'borderline spectrum' of severely personality disordered individuals (Barach 1991; Benjamin and Benjamin 1994). The social inheritance aspect of dissociation may be an important clue in our understanding of the disorder.

We propose that dissociating individuals are those victims of childhood (sexual) abuse who coped by refusing to conceive of the contents of their caregiver's mind and thus successfully avoided having to think about their caregiver's wish to harm them. They go on to defensively disrupt their capacity to depict feelings and thoughts in themselves and in others. This leaves them to operate upon inaccurate and schematic impressions of thoughts and feelings and they are thus immensely vulnerable in all intimate relationships.

The symptom of dissociation itself, the predominance of multiple voices in treatment, may be usefully seen as the converse of mentalisation. In its usual definition, dissociation refers to a disjunction of the association between related mental contents (Ross et al. 1989). Information, whether incoming, stored or outgoing, is not integrated in the normal way. To be more precise, it is the psychological impact of the stimulus which is not conceived of or mentalised. The individual is aware of the presence of the stimulus but is not able to be aware of that awareness. Without such reflection, the normal meaning of the stimulus is lost, the associative context into which that experience may be expected to be couched is unavailable to the individual. In brief, dissociated experience is unmentalised experience. It exists in limbo separate from other aspects of the patient's mental functioning.

Why should such a state of affairs come about? The deactivation of mentalisation is a defence available to the abused child or any individual suffering from trauma where the aim is the reduction of the psychic experience of pain, terror or other overwhelmingly negative affect. Attachment theory suggests that it is precisely such emotional states that call forth the need for the caregiver. If the child learns in infancy that the caregiver is unable to provide the reflective containment necessary to regulate such states and if, consequently, the child only acquires this metacognitive aspect of self-soothing to a limited extent, the likelihood of resorting to this dramatic, but in the short term adaptive, defence is increased.

There are a number of specific symptoms commonly found in dissociative patients which might have a clear link to failures of mentalisation. The switching from one state of consciousness to another – which is accompanied by facial, postural, motor, speech, affective and cognitive changes in dissociative identity disorder – is made possible because no core sense of identity exists to which external and internal experiences are invariably referred. The sense of self incorporates representations which derive from the non-reflective other. They are experienced as part of the self but are not *of* the self. Switching between these representations is likely to occur when the alien other cannot be externalised to another physical body. The individual thus has no option but to switch to that identity. At times the switching is incomplete and the representation of the other is 'heard' and a misdiagnosis of psychosis may be made. The degree of intra-awareness between alters is likely to be a function of the extent of residual metacognitive capacity.

The incomplete structuralisation of the self enables dissociative patients to disavow ownership of both their bodies and their actions upon them. This is of great importance in all patients who control their thinking by harming themselves, since the pain and discomfort is probably only bearable because of the pathological separation of the psychological self-representation from the representation of the physical state. Further, the normal integration of intention and behaviour which generates self-agency requires the presence of a caregiver capable of mentalising the child's intentional state and bringing the external state of affairs in line with his rudimentary action. In the absence of such early experience, the self will feel no true ownership of its acts and thus a further barrier against externally or internally directed violence is lifted.

Childhood maltreatment may or may not have long-term sequelae and the determinants of the outcome are only partially understood. Here we propose that if children are maltreated but they have access to a meaningful attachment relationship which provides the intersubjective bases for the development of mentalising capacity, they will be able to resolve (work through) their experience and the outcome of the abuse will not be one of severe dissociative personality disorder. We do not expect that their reflective processes will protect them from episodic psychiatric disorder, such as depression, and epidemiological data suggests that victims of childhood maltreatment are at an elevated risk for many forms of (Axis-I) disorder.

However, if the maltreated child has no social support of sufficient strength and intensity to enable an attachment bond to develop which could provide the context for the acquisition of a reliable capacity to envisage the psychological state of the other in intense interpersonal relationships, then the experience of abuse will not be reflected on or resolved. Naturally, the unresolved experience of abuse diminishes the likelihood of meaningful relationships which, in a self-perpetuating way, further reduces the likelihood of a satisfactory resolution of the disturbing experience through the use of reflective processes. In fact a pattern may be established whereby suspicion and distrust become generalised and lead to a turning away from the mental state of most significant objects and an apparent 'decoupling' of the 'mentalising module', leaving the person bereft of human contact. This may account for the 'neediness' of these individuals; yet no sooner do they become involved with another than the malfunctioning of their inhibited mentalising capacity leads them into terrifying interpersonal confusion and chaos. Within intense relationships their inadequate mentalising function rapidly fails them, they regress to the intersubjective state of the development of mental representation and they are no longer able to differentiate their own mental representations from those of others and both of these from actuality. These processes combine and they become terrorised by their own thoughts about the other experienced (via projection) *in the other*, particularly their aggressive impulses and fantasies; these become crippling and, most commonly, they reject or arrange to be rejected by their object. Psychoanalysis or psychotherapy can break the vicious cycle by reinforcing reflective capacity.

PSYCHOTHERAPY AND MENTALISING

Psychotherapy inevitably deals with individuals whose past experience has left them vulnerable to current stress and the repetition of adverse early experiences. The treatment imposes a non-pragmatic elaborative, mentalistic stance. This enhances the development of reflective function and may in the long run enhance the psychic resilience of individuals in a generic way, providing them with improved control over their system of representation of relationships. It equips them with a kind of self-righting capacity where, through being able to operate on their representational models, the latter can become an object of review and change. Such gradual and constant adjustments facilitate the development of an internal world where the behaviour of others may be experienced as understandable, meaningful, predictable and characteristically human. This reduces the need for splitting of frightening and incoherent mental representations of mental states, and new experiences of other minds can more readily be integrated into the framework of past relationship representations.

The abused child, evading the mental world, rarely acquires adequate meta-control over the representational world of internal working models. Unhelpful models of relationship patterns emerge frequently and the internal world of the child and adult comes to be dominated by multiple voices. The individual's enhanced suspiciousness of human motives reinforces his/her strategy to forego mentalising, thus further distorting the normal development of a reflective function. Caught in a vicious cycle of paranoid anxiety and exaggerated defensive manoeuvres, the individual becomes inextricably entangled into an internal world dominated by multiple and often dangerous, evil and above all mindless working models of relationships. He has abnegated the very process which could extract him from his predicament, the capacity to reflect on mental states.

Psychotherapeutic treatment in general, compels the patient's mind to focus on the mental state of a benevolent other, that of the therapist. The frequent and consistent labelling, elaboration and interpretation of the mental state of both therapist and patient are then essential, if the inhibition on this aspect of mental function is to be lifted. Over a prolonged time period, diverse interpretations concerning the patients' perceptions of their psychosocial environment, including the therapeutic relationship, would enable them to attempt to create a mental representation both of themselves and of others, as thinking and feeling. This could then form the core of a sense of self, with a capacity to represent ideas and meanings, and create the basis for the bond that ultimately permits independent, coherent and unitary existence.

NOTE

1 Paper given at Society for Psychotherapy Research Annual Meeting 28 June 1997, Geilo, Norway.

REFERENCES

Ainsworth, M.D.S. (1985) 'Attachments across the lifespan'. *Bulletin of the New York Academy of Medicine*, 61: 792–812.

Ainsworth, M.D.S., Blehar, M.C., Waters, E. and Wall, S. (1978) *Patterns of Attachment: A Psychological Study of the Strange Situation*. Hillsdale, NJ: Erlbaum.

Ainsworth, M.D.S. and Eichberg, C. (1991) 'Effects on infant–mother attachment of mother's unresolved loss of an attachment figure or other traumatic experience'. In C.M. Parkes, J. Stevenson-Hinde and P. Marris (eds), *Attachment Across the Life Cycle* (pp. 160–183). London: Tavistock/Routledge.

Ainsworth, M.D.S. and Wittig, B.A. (1969) 'Attachment and exploratory behavior of one-year-olds in a strange situation'. In B.M. Foss (ed.), *Determinants of Infant Behavior* (pp. 113–136). London: Methuen.

Barach, P. (1991) 'Multiple personality disorder as an attachment disorder'. *Dissociation Progress in the Dissociative Disorders*, 4: 117–123.

Benjamin, L. and Benjamin, R. (1994) 'Application of contextual therapy to the treatment of multiple personality disorder'. *Dissociation Progress in the Dissociative Disorders*, 7: 12–22.

Benoit, D. and Parker, K. (1994) 'Stability and transmission of attachment across three generations'. *Child Development*, 65: 1444–1457.

Bowlby, J. (1969) *Attachment and Loss, vol. 1: Attachment*. London: Hogarth Press and the Institute of Psycho-Analysis.

Bowlby, J. (1973) *Attachment and Loss, vol. 2: Separation: Anxiety and Anger*. London: Hogarth Press and Institute of Psycho-Analysis.

Bowlby, J. (1980) *Attachment and Loss, vol. 3: Loss: Sadness and Depression*. London: Hogarth Press and Institute of Psycho-Analysis.

Cicchetti, D. and Beeghly, M. (1987) 'Symbolic development in maltreated youngsters: An organizational perspective'. In D. Cicchetti and M. Beeghly (eds), *Atypical Symbolic Development: New Directions for Child Development* (vol. 36, pp. 5–29). San Francisco: Jossey-Bass.

Dennett, D. (1987) *The Intentional Stance*. Cambridge, MA: MIT Press.

Emde, R.N. (1990) 'Mobilizing fundamental modes of development: Empathic availability and therapeutic action'. *Journal of the American Psychoanalytic Association*, 38: 881–913.

Fonagy, P., Leigh, T., Steele, M., Steele, H., Kennedy, R., Mattoon, G. and Target, M. (1996) 'The relation of attachment status, psychiatric classification, and response to psychotherapy'. *Journal of Consulting and Clinical Psychology*, 64: 22–31.

Fonagy, P., Steele, H., Moran, G., Steele, M. and Higgitt, A. (1991a) 'The capacity for understanding mental states: the reflective self in parent and child and its significance for security of attachment'. *Infant Mental Health Journal*, 13: 200–217.

Fonagy, P., Steele, H. and Steele, M. (1991b) 'Maternal representations of attachment during pregnancy predict the organization of infant–mother attachment at one year of age'. *Child Development*, 62: 891–905.

Fonagy, P., Steele, H., Steele, M. and Holder, J. (submitted) 'Quality of attachment to mother at 1 year predicts belief–desire reasoning at 5 years'. *Child Development* (in press).

Fonagy, P., Steele, M., Steele, H., Higgitt, A. and Target, M. (1994) 'Theory and practice of resilience'. *Journal of Child Psychology and Psychiatry*, 35: 231–257.

Fonagy, P., Steele, M., Steele, H., Leigh, T., Kennedy, R., Mattoon, G. and Target, M. (1995) 'The predictive validity of Mary Main's Adult Attachment Interview: A psychoanalytic and developmental perspective on the transgenerational transmission of attachment and borderline states'. In S. Goldberg, R. Muir and J. Kerr (eds),

Attachment Theory: Social, Developmental and Clinical Perspectives (pp. 233–278). Hillsdale, NJ: The Analytic Press.

George, C., Kaplan, N. and Main, M. (1985) *The Adult Attachment Interview*. Berkeley: Department of Psychology, University of California at Berkeley.

Hamilton, C. (1994) 'Continuity and discontinuity of attachment from infancy through adolescence'. Unpublished doctoral dissertation, UC-Los Angeles, Los Angeles.

Hegel, G. (1807) *The Phenomenology of Spirit*. Oxford: Oxford University Press.

Lieberman, A.F. and Pawl, J.H. (1990) 'Disorders of attachment and secure base behavior in the second year of life: Conceptual issues and clinical intervention'. In M.T. Greenberg, D. Cicchetti and E.M. Cummings (eds), *Attachment in the Preschool Years* (pp. 375–398). Chicago: University of Chicago Press.

Liotti, G. (1991) 'Patterns of attachment and the assessment of interpersonal schemata: Understanding and changing difficult patient–therapist relationships in cognitive psychotherapy'. *Journal of Cognitive Psychotherapy*, 5: 105–114.

Liotti, G. (1992) 'Disorganized/disoriented attachment in the etiology of the dissociative disorders'. *Dissociation*, 5: 196–204.

Liotti, G. (1995) 'Disorganized/disorientated attachment in the psychotherapy of the dissociative disorders'. In S. Goldberg, R. Muir and J. Kerr (eds), *Attachment Theory: Social, Developmental, and Clinical Perspectives* (pp. 343–363). Hillsdale, NJ: Analytic Press.

Main, M. (1991) 'Metacognitive knowledge, metacognitive monitoring, and singular (coherent) vs (incoherent) models of attachment: Findings and directions for future research'. In J.S.P. Harris and C. Parkes (eds), *Attachment Across the Lifecycle*. New York: Routledge.

Main, M. (1995) 'Recent studies in attachment: Overview, with selected implications for clinical work'. In S. Goldberg, R. Muir and J. Kerr (eds), *Attachment Theory: Social, Developmental, and Clinical Perspectives* (pp. 407–474). Hillsdale, NJ: Analytic Press.

Main, M. and Goldwyn, R. (in preparation) 'Adult attachment rating and classification systems'. In M. Main (ed.), *A Typology of Human Attachment Organization Assessed in Discourse, Drawings and Interviews* [Working Title]. New York: Cambridge University Press.

Main, M. and Hesse, E. (1990a) 'Adult lack of resolution of attachment-related trauma related to infant disorganized/disoriented behavior in the Ainsworth strange situation: Linking parental states of mind to infant behavior in a stressful situation'. In M.T. Greenberg, D. Cicchetti and M. Cummings (eds), *Attachment in the Preschool Years: Theory, Research and Intervention* (pp. 339–426). Chicago, IL: University of Chicago Press.

Main, M. and Hesse, E. (1990b) 'Parents' unresolved traumatic experiences are related to infant disorganized attachment status: Is frightened and/or frightening parental behavior the linking mechanism?' In D.C.M. Greenberg and E.M. Cummings (eds), *Attachment in the Preschool Years: Theory, Research and Intervention* (pp. 161–182). Chicago: University of Chicago Press.

Main, M. and Solomon, J. (1990) 'Procedures for identifying infants as disorganized/disoriented during the Ainsworth Strange Situation'. In D.C.M. Greenberg and E.M. Cummings (eds), *Attachment in the Preschool Years: Theory, Research and Intervention* (pp. 121–160). Chicago: University of Chicago Press.

Main, M. and Weston, D. (1981) 'The quality of the toddler's relationship to mother and to father: Related to conflict behavior and the readiness to establish new relationships'. *Child Development*, 52: 932–940.

Oliver, J.E. (1993) 'Intergenerational transmission of child abuse: Rates, research, and clinical implications'. *American Journal of Psychiatry*, 150: 1315–1324.

Ross, C., Norton, G. and Fraser, G. (1989) 'Evidence against the iatrogenesis of multiple personality disorder'. *Dissociation Progress in the Dissociative Disorders*, 2: 61–65.

Sroufe, L.A. (1990) 'An organizational perspective on the self'. In D. Cicchetti and M. Beeghly (eds), *The Self in Transition: Infancy to Childhood* (pp. 281–307). Chicago: University of Chicago Press.

Sroufe, L.A. (in press) *Emotional Development*. New York: Cambridge University Press.

Steele, H., Steele, M. and Fonagy, P. (1996) 'Associations among attachment classifications of mothers, fathers, and their infants: Evidence for a relationship-specific perspective'. *Child Development*, 67: 541–555.

Steele, H., Steele, M. and Fonagy, P. (in preparation) 'A path-analytic model of determinants of infant–parent attachment: limited rather than multiple pathways'.

Stern, D.J. (1994) 'One way to build a clinically relevant baby'. *Infant Mental Health Journal*, 15: 36–54.

van Ijzendoorn, M.H. (1995) 'Adult attachment representations, parental responsiveness, and infant attachment: A meta-analysis on the predictive validity of the Adult Attachment Interview'. *Psychological Bulletin*, 117: 387–403.

Ward, M.J. and Carlson, E.A. (1995) 'Associations among Adult Attachment representations, maternal sensitivity, and infant–mother attachment in a sample of adolescent mothers'. *Child Development*, 66: 69–79.

Waters, E., Merrick, S., Albersheim, L., Treboux, D. and Crowell, J. (1995) 'From the strange situation to the Adult Attachment Interview: A 20-year longitudinal study of attachment security in infancy and early adulthood'. Paper presented at the Society for Research in Child Development, Indianapolis, May 1995.

Winnicott, D.W. (1967) 'Mirror-role of the mother and family in child development'. In P. Lomas (ed.), *The Predicament of the Family: A Psycho-Analytical Symposium*. London: Hogarth.

Chapter 5

A theoretical framework for understanding multiplicity and dissociation

John Southgate

INTRODUCTION

In this chapter I will describe a theoretical framework for understanding multiplicity and dissociation which I have been developing for the past twelve years. The framework is divided into two parts; the first outlines a structural model to aid our overall understanding and the second is a set of dynamic working models which can be applied to clinical work.

A conversation with John Bowlby circa 1988

I took the lift at the Tavistock and at the fourth floor turned along the corridor, to be welcomed by my supervisor John Bowlby. On that day I showed him lots of drawings of little children being abused and telling me their stories of unbelievable horrors. My patient was a middle-aged woman who could not understand why I could not understand these children. John mused and thought, looking away and thinking as he often did and said 'I think this woman is a multiple personality'. And I said – a what? He said there is a lot of work in the USA on dissociation and proposed that I should talk to these children and listen to the story they were trying to tell me.

All I have to say today is a continuation of that conversation about listening to the children within us (see Southgate 1996).

What I have learned over the ensuing 12 years is:

1 The considerable creative potential of many dissociators.
2 That one must distinguish that group from those who have psychotic selves who are often but not always abusers.
3 That a therapist who has primarily worked with those labelled as neurotic will need to adapt her or his approach when working with dissociators.
4 That the overall goal in any therapy can be described as helping the person become what I have called an 'Associating Multiple Person'.

Before describing the framework in detail we need to reflect on a more funda-mental question about the nature of self.

On the multiple nature of the Self

My own view, and that of many contemporary philosophers and relational psy-choanalysts in the post-modern tradition is that the Self is always in relationship to an Other, sometimes described as selfother, and is multiple from the beginning. Putnam (1989) writes

> We are not born into this world with a single unified personality. Rather the infant research data indicate that we come organised as a basic set of behavioural states with the capacity to generate new states and develop and modify complex sequences of behavioural state . . . Two of the funda-mental developmental tasks facing a young child are the integration of a more continuous sense of self across discrete behavioural states and the development of self-modulation of behavioural states.

Bromberg (1996) states that

> Psychological integration does not lead to a single real you or true self . . . it is the ability to stand in the spaces between realities without losing any of them . . . the capacity to feel oneself while being many [and] What is required is that the multiple realities being held by different self states find opportunity for linkage . . . through narrative.

With a similar argument Pizer (1996: 499) in an article entitled 'The Distributed Self' discusses the evolving contemporary model of a post-modern Self as 'decentred and disunified': in short a normative multiple self.

Val Bucknall (1999) writes that among writers it is almost taken for granted that people have many selves and operate on many levels. It is a sine qua non for writing fiction. (Similar views have been expressed by Doris Lessing (1998).)

In a very complex analysis of the way in which the concept of individual is privileged over the concept of group, Farhad Dalal (1998: 94) also argues:

> There is a Sufi saying 'we are in this world, but not of it'. The thesis of this book is the polar opposite of that — it is saying we are completely of this world from our molecules, to our thoughts, to our feelings, to our aspira-tions. To counter the Sufi saying, let me indulge in inventing an elliptic epigram: The I is We.

In one of his lectures he has substituted Wego for Ego! Later he says:

Once again whilst in broad agreement with the proposition that the more complex society becomes the more layers there are, the point I would take issue with is the fantasy that there has ever been a time of singularity. As we saw in the chapter on biology, the division of labour and the multiple roles that imposes on one, is as old as existence itself.

As psychotherapists we need models of the Self and Other that cover a multiple of continua to guide our clinical practice. It is my view that the dissociative response of the multiple self to trauma is fundamentally creative and for survival. In attachment terms summarised as *the essence of disorganised attachment is fright without a solution* (Hesse and Main in press; van Ijzendoorn et al. 1999: 225–249).

In the next section I argue that you cannot separate the Self from the group dynamics within the individual and the social context.

On the need for a group dynamics theory when working with dissociation

The therapist gets involved not only in the dynamics of a pair but of a group when working with dissociators. One has to remember that there is an internal group within the patient modelled on the family or group systems (White 1999). Group dynamics are also relevant to our subject because ritual abuse and other abusive family systems take place in groups. The most appropriate group theory is, in my view, that of Wilfred Bion.

Bion's group dynamic theory in individual and group settings

Bion (1961) proposed that in any group, organisation, ethnic clan or nation state which fears that its existence is threatened (realistically or otherwise), two emotional and usually unconscious processes arise, one creative and the other destructive.

The *creative* group is called the work group (w-group), which manages and controls the destructive process and tries to pull in a creative developmental direction. The *destructive* one he called a 'basic assumption group' in which the group acts or cycles between three *assumptions*. As we are descended from group animals Bion assumed this to be programmed into the individual by evolution (a view which both Bowlby and Freud would endorse). The three assumptions are:

1   The basic assumption of fight–flight (shorthand baFF) where the group acts as though it must fight or flee;
2   The basic assumption of dependency (shorthand baD) where the group acts as if it must seek a leader to be utterly dependent upon;

3   The basic assumption of pairing (shorthand baP) where the group acts as if it must seek a pair whose sexual activity will produce an idealised family.

I have divided Bion's basic assumption groups into two categories. One is 'normal', found in everyday life, and can arise in any organisation, group or pair. In therapy it is illustrated by the complaints some patients make about the annual family gatherings where people do not actually murder or rape each other but experience very painful and difficult dynamics. I have named the more extreme version a *primitive basic assumption group*.

The primitive basic assumption of fight–flight is important in this context because it affects large-scale, small-scale and pair relationships so I will expand a little about it. Bion rudely but accurately said that the leader who is unconsciously 'chosen' by this group is the most psychiatrically sick member of the group. Neither leaders nor members can think creatively or developmentally – the unconscious goal is to preserve some earlier cultural or emotional state.

Large-scale examples of this are Hitler in Nazi Germany (see Alice Miller 1983), and some religious sects (see Greven 1990). In contemporary terms one can see it in Milosevic in Kosovo or any of the ethnic conflicts around the world (sadly all too common in what Eric Hobsbawm (1994) called 'the most murderous Century in human history'). Bion had personal experience of this situation as a young tank commander in the First World War and was one of very few to survive in this role (Bion 1982).

Having explored the need for therapists of dissociators to understand groups, there are two alternative ways of reading the rest of this chapter. Some people are mainly visual thinkers and relate well to charts and diagrams. In this case a reader might turn to the composite diagram at the end of the chapter (see Figure 5.6). On the other hand, if you are more a verbal thinker then it might be easier to read straight through.

On working models

I use the term 'working model' which is taken from the work of John Bowlby (1979: 117). In his view, working models, derived from his interest in systems theory, can be open or closed. The open working model allows for extension and change. The closed working model does not. It is intended that all the working models here except for one, are 'open' and the test of this is whether the reader can apply them creatively to working therapeutically with people.

I will use four archetypes about people as a fundamental basis derived from the notion that 'Everybody's multiple, in their own way'. These are:

1   *The associating multiple person* i.e. relatively good emotional health;
2   *The repressed multiple person* i.e. ordinary neurosis;

3   *The dissociating multiple person* who blames the Self but has no psychotic selves;
4   *The dissociating multiple person* who blames the Other and has psychotic selves.

One of the difficulties in writing about human interaction, both internal and external, is its immense complexity. We need to be able to hold thoughts and ideas at multiple levels

Please have a preliminary look at Figure 5.1. I hope it is not too complicated but it is the best way I can find of holding a complex set of factors in a succinct way. The reader will need to hold in mind the matrix below dialectically while I describe the framework linearly.

Reading the columns downwards, the four archetypes are as follows.

Archetype 1: the associating multiple person

At the end of a successful therapy, or if you are lucky to have had good-enough parenting, then you will be healthy in the sense of being able to choose which self-states are appropriate at particular moments in time. Looking down column 1:

- You would be securely attached to those close to you and able to let selected Others be secure with you.
- You would also be able to give and take in the arena of primary erotic attachment which is modelled on the infant–carer relationship (and includes men as well as women).
- You would enjoy love and the creative orgasmic cycle.
- You could take part in creative play and improvisation.
- You would not avoid conflict and would be able to make management decisions.
- You would have a capacity for creative and reflective thinking.
- You would take part and assist a group to be creative.

Now this all sounds too good to be true and to some degree it is so. More realistically you can tend towards being an associating multiple person but still have parts of yourself that are repressed or dissociated, though you would be able to relate to others in terms of secure attachment.

Archetype 2: the repressed multiple person

We are speaking here of ordinary neurosis which has been studied by psychoanalysts for a long time. On the surface, such a person may seem singular rather than multiple. But, like everyone else, when dreaming the multiple selves of the unconscious are present. The goal of therapy is to move from being a repressed

Four archetypes

Goal corrected instinctual systems originating in the proto-mental system	Associating Multiple person	Repressed multiple person	Dissociating multiple person who blames self (no psychotic selves)	Dissociating multiple person who blames other (psychotic selves)
Attachment innate system	Secure attachment. Primary erotic attachment	Anxious resistant & anxious avoidant attachment	Anxious disorganised attachment	Primitive punishing attachment & brainwashing
Erotic & sexual innate system	Primary erotic attachment. Love and creative orgasmic cycle. Orgasmic rituals	Anxious resistant & avoidant sexual relating	Masochistic sexual relating to please other	Sado-masochism. Rape, sexualised cruelty. Castration
Exploration & play innate system	Creative play & development Improvisation.	Mixture of creative and trivial pursuits	Play to help or please other. Unable to play	Cruel rituals and humiliating games
Fight/flight innate system	Creative conflict and management	Anxious forms of fight/flight	Forms of flight e.g. fugue and self-harm	Murder and torture where fight predominates to harm Other
Group dynamics	W-group Creative orgasmic group	Basic assumption group	Basic assumption group	Primitive basic assumption group
Thinking (k)	k = creative thinking	K and ~k Some creative, some not so	K and ~k Creative but in the service of the Other	~k × 100 no developmental thinking at all

Notes

I have taken Bion's (1961) proto-mental system and Bowlby's (1988) goal corrected instinctual systems and made a synthesis. The proto-mental system is the fundamental set of systems with which we come into this world. A goal corrected instinctual system is one whereby the animal concerned makes changes in behaviour in the pursuit of a goal, for example acquiring food. The four main goals can be summarised as the desire for attachment, erotic and sexual relating, exploration and play (cf. Winnicott 1974) and the desire to survive which, when under threat, activates the fight–flight system.

Figure 5.1 Everybody's multiple in their own way

multiple person to an associating multiple person. There is so much literature accumulated on this sort of therapy that it is included here only to complete the picture and to contrast with other self states. A brief summary is:

- anxious resistant and/or avoidant attachment relating;
- anxious resistant and/or anxious avoidant sexual relating;
- able to play sometimes, sometimes not and sometimes only able to engage in trivial pursuits;
- prone to anxious forms of fight/flight;

- sometimes can think creatively and sometimes not;
- prone to the basic assumption group dynamic.

It is usual in working with such a person to use transference and counter-transference, interpretation, the analysis of dreams, etc. as major tools. This works well with neurosis because the psyche is split *horizontally* and working with the unconscious has to be indirect because the unconscious selves are not available directly. But it is important to be aware that such methods are not always effective when working with the dissociating multiple persons described below because the split of the psyche is *vertical*, so to speak, with each self able to speak directly about the past experiences. In using transference and counter-transference there is a danger of treating the reliving of real experience as imaginary or symbolic. There is value in the child's use of the imaginary for survival both then and now which must not be misinterpreted.

A crucial clinical distinction for those who work with dissociators is between archetypes 3 and 4.

Archetype 3: the dissociating multiple person who blames Self; no psychotic selves

This person will readily come for psychotherapy, though it may take, in my experience, 8–10 years work at two or three times per week or more. Sometimes sessions need to be longer than 50 minutes. The long-term prognosis is very good. The key factor is that this person blames themselves rather than the Other. To summarise:

- Because of early life traumas, has anxious disorganised attachment and has used the defence of dissociating in order to survive.
- Tends to have the repetition of choosing unhealthy partners and may act masochistically in a sexual relationship to please the Other. Despite the history, the person may be a more than good enough parent.
- In play and exploration, tends to please the Other and sometimes unable to play.
- Can easily get in to forms of flight (rather than fight) – for example fugue and self-harm.
- Can be very creative but often in the service of the Other.
- Prone towards the basic assumption group but can work co-operatively with others.

Archetype 4: the dissociating multiple person who blames the Other and has psychotic selves

This person rarely comes voluntarily for therapy and is often, but not always, an abuser of some kind. A part of the person's system may have been programmed, through destructive early relationships, to destroy. The prognosis for cure is very poor indeed. Usually, if therapy is undertaken it does not last for very long as the patient runs away or wears out one therapist after another. The person may have paranoid and suicidal selves. The summary is:

- Prone to take part in punishing attachment and brainwashing.
- The erotic and sexual system may be infused with sado-masochism, rape, sexualised cruelty and desires for castrating the Other.
- Play tends towards cruel rituals and humiliating games.
- Extreme fight systems can lead to murder, and torture where the desire is to harm the Other.
- In the primitive fight–flight group there is, as Bion originally pointed out, no developmental thinking at all. He also points out that this is not only in groups but programmed by evolution into the individual as a group animal.
- Tends to join or lead a primitive basic assumption group acting as a leader or follower who must fight or flee.

Reading across the rows

If you read across the categories then you can see changes over the four archetypes.

- The attachment innate system goes from secure, to anxious avoidant, to anxious resistant, to anxious disorganised and the primitive punishing attachment where the person has been controlled and brainwashed by carers.
- Erotic and sexual innate systems go from primary erotic attachment; the creative orgasmic cycle and orgasmic rituals (e.g. dancing), to masochistic sexual relating to please the Other and finally to sado-masochism, rape, sexualised cruelty and castration.
- The innate system for exploration and play moves from the creative, to a mixture of creative and trivial pursuits, to play which is designed to help or please the Other and finally to cruel rituals and humiliating games.
- The fight/flight innate system goes from creative conflict and management, to sublimated competitive games and anxious forms of fight/flight. The dissociating multiple person who is self-blaming engages predominantly in forms of flight such as fugue and self-harm. Finally, murder and torture where fight predominates to harm the Other is the characteristic, in this analysis, of the dissociating multiple person who blames the Other, i.e. archetype 4. (Incidentally, some schools in psychoanalysis privilege a part of the fight/flight system such as innate greed and envy. I think this is a mistaken emphasis since we are born with the *five innate systems intact*.)

- The group dynamic innate system goes from the creative work group to the basic assumption group and finally to the primitive basic assumption group.
- The last row is about thinking (Bion's K, i.e. 'knowing'). Reading across, it starts with linking creative thinking to secure attachment, then goes to some creative thinking and continues to some not so creative thought, often in the service of the Other. These latter categories are associated with forms of insecure avoidant and resistant attachment. Finally 'no developmental thinking at all' is linked to chaotic attachment.

Clearly there are far more variations in multiplicity than the above would indicate. Some persons may have aspects of all four and everyone has their own unique way of relating. However, it is important to distinguish between archetypes 3 and 4.

Work with archetype 3, the dissociating multiple person who blames the Self, can be very rewarding indeed and this is the kind of person who my own organisation has most experience of working with therapeutically. Some of these persons can become excellent therapists themselves.

Work with archetype 4, the dissociating multiple person who blames the Other, is very difficult, and sometimes dangerous. Looking back over 30 years of clinical practice and doing supervision, the score or so persons who fit this category bear out this statement.

Real persons are not archetypes

In reality few patients are 'pure' examples. The archetypes can be seen as stages of therapy. The same person moves through archetypes, with archetype 1 having the best possible outcome of the therapy.

Having discussed structural frameworks I now move on to dynamic working models.

DYNAMIC WORKING MODELS

The problem and joy of working in ways derived from psychoanalysis is that you never know in advance what the person will say, do or feel from one moment to another. Structural tools help with overall understanding, diagnosis and supervision but do not solve the problem that confronts the clinician, i.e. dynamic tools that help you to think from one moment to the next in a session.

Perhaps the first impression that a therapist or other helper should expect in working with a dissociator has been described by a therapist reviewing early meetings with dissociators. She was surprised at 'the extreme speed that the emotions can alter – whether of happiness, sadness or whatever. I always wonder how did we get to this place so quickly?' (Michael 1999).

In working with neurosis (the repressed multiple person) there are plenty of dynamic concepts developed over the last 100 years, many of them by Freud himself. The dynamic unconscious, dream analysis, transference and counter-transference are just a few examples. However, when working with dissociation you also need fluid concepts that help in moment-to-moment interaction.

Moments in movement – the microscopic aspects of the therapy process

The structural models presented in Figure 5.1 illustrate the macro, long-term processes and are a general guide for practitioners. But in any one session between therapist and patient, what is happening is a series of 'moments'. Moment 1, for example, could be opening the door; we look at each other (or don't look), smile or remain impassive, speak or do not speak and follow whatever routine has been evolved in the therapy. The inexperienced therapist may rely on received wisdom and do the same routine with each patient – for example to look impassive, make no comment in ancient psychoanalytic terms or engage in an immediate bear-hug in ancient humanistic terms. The important factor is to be empathic to what is happening in this *specific* now moment and for both parties, patient and therapist, to be aware of their lived experience at *this* moment in time.

The four archetypes of multiple persons can also be seen as moments rather than rigid structures, for example,

- Secure moments – attachment, erotic relating, love, creative play, creative conflict, creative group dynamics and creative thinking.
- Insecure moments – of anxious resistant and avoidant attachment, and sexual relating, play, fight–flight, basic assumption in group dynamics, some creative forms of thinking.
- Moments of psychosis and destruction, punitive attachment, sado-masochistic sexuality, cruel rituals and humiliating games, murder and rape, primitive basic assumption group dynamics, and primitive forms of not thinking or developing.

The mourning cycle and the creative orgasmic cycle

The mourning cycle is a core therapeutic process. It is most simply understood in the case of bereavement yet it applies to any kind of trauma (Southgate 1989). It does not have to be learned but has been 'wired in' by evolution. Bowlby called it 'nature's cure for trauma'. Over a year or so the mourner goes through phases, or sometimes gets stuck in one of them.

However, in the case of dissociation, each phase of the mourning cycle may be divided between different selves. For example, one self may be in the

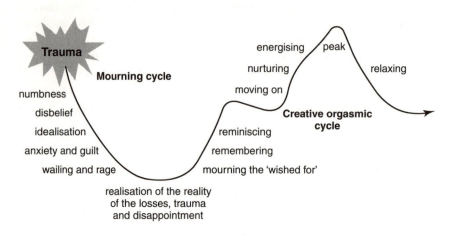

Figure 5.2 The mourning cycle and the creative orgasmic cycle

'then-now' re-experiencing the trauma in the form of a 'flashback'. Another is simply numb. Another expresses disbelief in what has happened. Another may idealise the abuser, yet another handles anxiety and guilt, another wailing and rage, and so on. Yet with each self the mourning cycle will need to be worked through over time in what I have called the 'attachment space'. I have described this (Southgate 1996) as bringing each self on to the *attachment space* created between the therapist and patient:

> We have to have a space on which our attachments take place, which is why attachment is a spatial theory. As you read this or hear me speak, there is a space on which we both exist whether on the written page or this lecture hall. There is such a space inside and outside both of us, but it is not always very obvious.

This concept has similarities to Mollon's 'global workspace' (1996: 186):

> The therapist's own mind, which is part of the therapeutic setting, provides an enlarged Global Workspace within which various dissociated parts of the patient's mind can communicate . . . The patient can draw upon this enhanced Global Workspace and make it his/her own.

The managing self of the patient may create a working alliance with the therapist where they both act as a parent to the younger selves and advocate for the older ones (cf. Davies and Frawley 1994).

So what essentially happens on the attachment space? It is here that one must consider the dynamics of any creative process. The creative orgasmic cycle (Figure 5.2) was derived by Southgate and Randall (1976) from the work of Reich and Bion. The essential argument is that any creative activity whether it be erotic, sexual, intellectual, craft, science or art goes through a discernible cycle. This is where there is a *nurturing phase* where ideas or practices are prepared, an *energising phase* where these are put into operation, an *orgasmic peak*, and a phase of *relaxing and celebrating*. In our work on co-operative and group dynamics (Southgate and Randall 1981) examples were shown of a co-operative organisation going through such a process. To return to this process in a psychological frame, one of the outcomes of successful mourning in therapy is to help a person to express their creativity. At a micro level, moments of meeting (see below) could be seen as the work of the orgasmic cycle.

The working alliance is important here to help the different selves to partake in the creative cycle. I have noticed for a long time that many dissociators are extremely imaginative in arts and sciences, and may draw, write poetry, dance, sing or play music. In fact the therapy relationship can be very enriching for all participants and helps us to endure the consequences of terrible trauma.

However, in 'pure' versions of archetype 4, the dissociating multiple person who blames the Other, it is difficult, and sometimes impossible, to go through either the mourning or the creative cycle successfully.

Moments in movement, time and reconstruction

This dynamic working model tries to deal with the micro movements in time and reconstruction.

Stern (1998), in examining the successful moments leading to creative change in the process of psychoanalysis, discovered that these were characterised as 'moments of meeting' where (a) both participants have an experience of enlightenment; (b) they have a greater sense of attachment to each other; and (c) they are in an implicit mode of relational knowing. This is something that everyone knows, but not even psychoanalysts have given it the importance it deserves – although they know about it, they have not given it a name. It is the emotional non-verbal communication that underpins discourse. For example, if you taped and typed up the conversations in a pub or restaurant they would largely be banal. But in fact people do not go to 'talk' but to relate emotionally. Watching and listening to the 'music' behind the words one sees messages of love, hate, fear, seduction, etc. Psychotherapy takes place very much in this implicit mode.

Figure 5.3 is an extension of the ideas in Stern (1998). It is a stylised map of important moments in time that are part of a relationship. It uses words like moving along, now, then, new, old, wow!, emerging, core, intersubjective, verbal, dissociating, depression, mania, paranoia and splitting. What they have in common is that they are various *states-of-being-with-the-Other*.

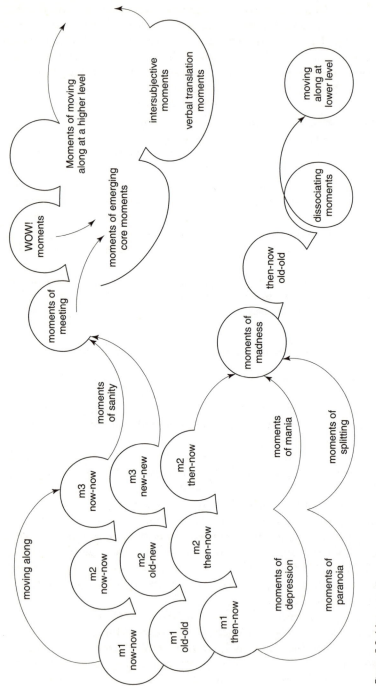

Figure 5.3 Moments in movement

This schematic diagram tries to show visually various pathways constructed of moments in time. The definitions and origins will follow later:

- Now-now, then-now and was-then (Kitsen)
- Moments of meeting, moving along (Dan Stern)
- Schemas of being with (Dan Stern)
- Old-old, old-new, new-new (Shane, Shane and Gales)
- Wow! moments (London)
- Moments of emerging (Stern–Southgate)
- Core moments (Stern–Southgate)
- Inter-subjective moments (Stern–Southgate)
- Verbal translation moments (Stern–Southgate)
- Moments of madness; moments of mania
- Moments of paranoia; dissociating moments
- Moments of sanity; moments of depression.

These moments can move to a higher level or to a lower one.

Moments in movement derives from the work of Stern (1998). The study group of psychoanalysts and infant developmental theorists were exploring the complex interaction in therapy and what could be identified as producing therapeutic change. They were linking it to their observations of the infant carer relationship. An important part of clinical work is what Stern describes as the *implicit mode of relational being*.

Then-now, was-then and now-now were coined by Kitsen (1999). *Then-now* experiences are when a self is experiencing what Bowlby (1988) called 'a real event displaced in time'. *Was-then* is simply a memory of something recalled from the past and stored in the preconscious. The *now-now* is when both patient and therapist are fully in the present relating in now moments and sometimes Wow! moments (see below). When therapist and patient are familiar with this schema the therapist, for example, in helping a person prepare for the end of a session can say something like, 'You are in the then-now but if you come with me into the now-now they [abusers] will not exist'.

The concepts of old-old, old-new and new-new were coined by Shane et al. (1997) to describe three configurations in the patient–therapist relationship. Old-old is dealing with repressed material in both participants. Old-new is where one partner, either therapist or patient, is into old material and the other into the new. Moments of madness, moments of sanity (which even the very mad usually have), moments of paranoia, moments of depression, moments of mania, and moments of splitting speak for themselves.

In explaining the Wow! moments London (1999) writes:

> A wow! moment comes at a point in time just after the peak of the Creative-orgasmic cycle. It is a significant Moment of Meeting (Stern 1998) that is very moving and special.

Wow! is perhaps the first word spoken between you after you have mutually shared an intense emotional experience. Together you share this moment of exhilaration and pleasure at its peak. Although a Wow! moment can be experienced alone, there is perhaps always the desire somewhere to share the revelation with a person you are close to. The whole experience including the Wow! moments takes place in the new-new (Shane et al. 1997). It is fresh, lived emotionally in the present, built of many now-moments-of-being with (Stern 1995) and uses the implicit relational mode as its primary means of communication. The experience may be mainly nonverbal, but is not without form or structure which has within it many familiar schemas-of-being-with (Stern 1995) and also improvised creative play that is full of joy and anticipation. With the familiar and the improvised, a sense of pleasurable anticipation builds throughout the experience until the peak has been reached. As well, there are smaller waves, anticipation–joy–surprise, rising and falling with their own interweaving rhythms and phrases which help to build the total symphony, gestalt, or experience. It is just after the peak has been reached, when the whole experience has been seen and felt together that you stand back with awe and amazement, wonder, joy and surprise. This is a wow! moment. Afterwards you relax and begin to digest the total experience, still feeling the afterglow of joy and surprise at the same time (cf. Theodore Reik's 'Aha! and Surprise' 1949).

So what does the therapist *do* with these lived moments? My metaphor would be like two tailors making a complex tapestry (cf. *The Tailor of Gloucester*, Beatrix Potter 1903). The moments are eventually stitched or woven together until the therapist and patient can jointly see a pattern and verbalise what it is. This can be a Wow! moment, or a moment of inspiration and joint realisation of a truth known at the real, imaginary and symbolic levels. The process of reaching such a point may have taken years or a decade. It is very exhilarating when it happens. It is not an everyday happening but when it does it justifies celebrating and relaxing.

Figure 5.4 is a visual summary of the process by Bob Miller (1999).

The real, the imaginary and the symbolic registers

Working traditionally with transference and counter-transference often does not help and sometimes is correctly resisted by the dissociating patient. Most helpful in my experience are Lacan's terms 'the real', 'the imaginary' and 'the symbolic' and although most obscure when you read Lacan (1966) I find that many patients can intuitively grasp these notions without much definition (see Figure 5.5).

For example, when talking to a young self (within the person) I might note that in the 'real' register (in the musical sense of registers in an orchestra) I am aware at this moment of the real events displaced in time as they are unfolding in front of me (cf. Bowlby 1988). The young person is using the imaginary to recreate now (i.e. a 'then-now') the feelings and dissociations. In the 'sym-

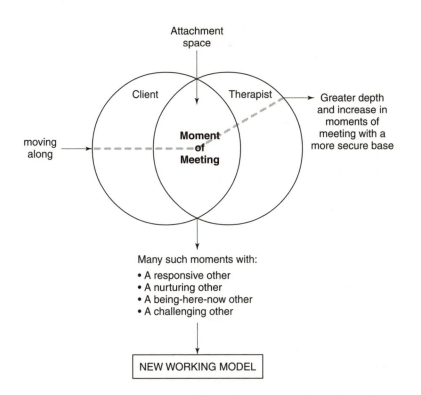

Figure 5.4 Moments in movement between therapist and client. Source: Bob Miller (1999).

bolic' register the young person uses language to tell me in words what is happening or I may have to ask another Self to explain to me if the person concerned has not reached the verbal stage. The real, imaginary and symbolic concept allows a much wider lens on an interaction than those terms useful in the treatment of neurosis.

Working with pre-verbal selves

In working with dissociating multiple persons the therapist often needs to relate to pre-verbal children or babies. The natural way to relate is nonverbally in the implicit mode. An infant or child may want to be held physically or sit on your knee. The therapist can get an internal adult or mothering self to hold the baby. Sometimes the dissociator may use teddy bears and the like. Sometimes only real holding of some kind will do, at other times imaginary and symbolic holding is sufficient. The patient can cradle a toy, or the therapist might be given a toy to hold.

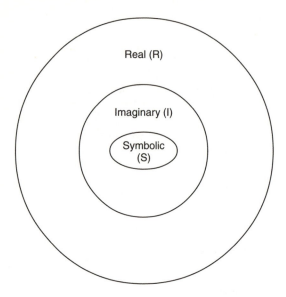

Figure 5.5 The real, the imaginary and the symbolic

Nevertheless, real holding by the therapist should, in my experience, be undertaken only with great caution. Quite often the kind of symbolic or imaginary holding that therapists use is sufficient. The archetype 3, the dissociated multiple person who has no psychotic selves may be held if there is no managing self or others who can tell you what the infant or child is feeling. It is dangerous to hold psychotic selves and this should be avoided at all costs. Phil Mollon (1996) recounts how he was being bullied to hold a woman who threatened in his presence to fatally inject if he did not do so. He decided that he would rather have a live patient than a dead one and reluctantly agreed.

Another aspect of the infant–carer relationship is to recognise and understand that for both partners there is what I have called 'primary erotic attachment' where the attachment and sexual systems are undifferentiated. It is also the underlying working model for successful adult sexual relating. This was pointed out as long ago as 1939 by Alice Balint (in Michael Balint 1952).

When working with a dissociated person one may re-experience in the real, imaginary and symbolic registers this relationship between infant and carer (whatever the gender of those concerned). It is especially important where the original relationship between the patient and his or her mother was either chaotic or altogether absent.

Finally a contribution to our understanding from neuroscience

Finally we have to think in a non-linear multiple-causation manner because that is how the psyche, the soma and the natural world are organised. Our brains work as multi-modular interacting systems (see Moore 1998). Our bodies operate as an impossibly complicated multi-determined entity and the natural world is a mass of interacting non-linear systems. We have to simplify this mass of information in order to think at all. The clinician needs multiple and flexible working models that can guide us both consciously, pre-consciously and unconsciously as we try to operate in our 'impossible profession' (Malcolm 1982).

TECHNICAL NOTES

Technical note 1

The most well known kind of dissociation I would describe as 'explosive', i.e. the person experiences selves as exploding out into the sky, so to speak. In referral interviews questions like fugue states (lost and not knowing where or who you are), loss of time, changing style of clothes, seeing the self from the outside and having more than one self are answered in the affirmative. However I have discovered another general form which I call 'implosive'. Such a person will answer no to all but the last question 'have you more than one self'. One man said he had hundreds. The person seems to have self-other states that have gone deep inside rather than outside and uses imagery like deep caverns where selves reside. It is often the outcome of torture where the child cannot get 'out there' and so goes 'deep down'.

There are times when both the explosive and implosive mode is used. The clinical practice remains the same for both explosive and implosive structures.

Technical note 2

A state of the art discussion of the relationship between psychoanalytic schools and attachment clinical approaches can be found in Fonagy (1999), and discussion of current developments and future problems in attachment research can be found in Main (1999).

Figure 5.6 presents a composite picture of the dynamic working models described in this chapter.

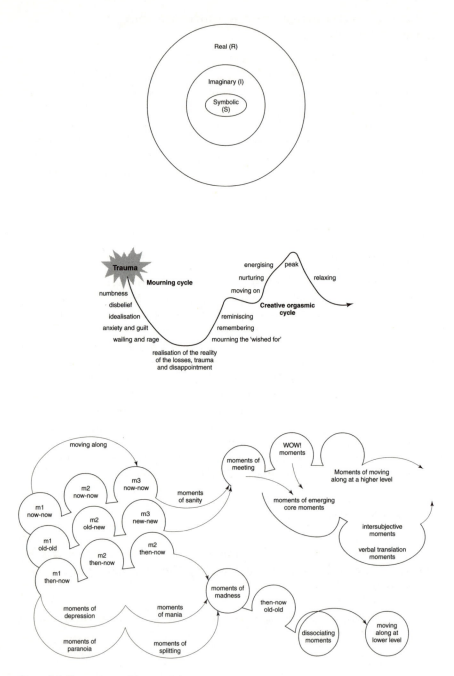

Figure 5.6 Dynamic working models

BIBLIOGRAPHY

Balint, Alice (1939) in *Primary Love and Psycho-analytic technique*, Michael Balint (1952) London: Maresfield Library.

Bion, W.R. (1961) *Experiences in Groups*. London: Tavistock/Routledge.

Bion, W.R. (1982) *The Long Week-end*. London: Karnac Books.

Bowlby, John (1979) *The Making and Breaking of Affectional Bonds*. London: Tavistock.

Bowlby, John (1988) Personal communication.

Bromberg, P. (1996) 'Standing in the spaces: The multiplicity of self and the psycho-analytic relationship'. *Contemporary Psychoanalysis* 32(4): 509–535.

Bucknall, Val (1999) Personal communication.

Dalal, Farhad (1998) *Taking the Group Seriously*. London: Jessica Kingsley.

Davies, J.M. and Frawley, M.G. (1994) *Treating the Adult Survivors of Childhood Sexual Abuse*. New York: HarperCollins.

Fonagy, P. (1999) 'Psychoanalytic theory from the viewpoint of attachment theory and research', in *Handbook of Attachment, Theory Research & Clinical Applications*, ed. J. Cassidy and P. Shaver. New York: Guilford Press.

Fonagy, P., Steele, M.B.G., Steele, H. and Higgitt, A.C. (1991) 'The capacity for understanding mental states: The reflective self in parent and child and its significance for security of attachment'. *Infant Mental Health Journal* 13: 200–216.

Greven, P. (1990) *Spare the Child: The Religious Roots of Punishments and the Psychological Impact of Physical Abuse*. New York: Knopf.

Herman, J. (1992) *From Trauma to Recovery*. New York: Basic Books.

Hesse, E. and Main, M. (in press) 'Frightened behaviour in traumatised but not mal-treating parents: Previously unexamined risk factor for offspring'. *Psychoanalytic Inquiry*.

Hobsbawm, Eric (1994) *Age of Extremes 1914–1991*. London: Michael Joseph.

Kitsen, J. (1999) 'Time and multiplicity', paper first presented at International Society for the Study of Dissociation Conference, Manchester, 1998.

Lacan, J. (1966) *Ecrits. A Selection*. (1977 edition, London: Routledge.)

Lessing, D. (1998) *Under My Skin*. London: HarperCollins.

London, E. (1999) 'Wow! moments', unpublished MS.

Lyons-Ruth, K. et al. (1998) 'Interventions that effect change in psychotherapy: A model based on infant research'. *Infant Mental Health Journal* 19(3).

Main, M. (1999) 'Epilogue. Attachment theory: Eighteen points with suggestions for future studies', in *Handbook of Attachment*, ed. J. Cassidy and P. Shaver. New York: Guilford Press.

Malcolm, J. (1982) *Psychoanalysis. The Impossible Profession*. London: Pan Books.

Michael, Jess (1999) Personal communication.

Miller, Alice (1983) *For Your Own Good: The Roots of Violence in Child-rearing*. London: Virago Press.

Miller, Bob (1999) Unpublished MS.

Mollon, P. (1996) *Multiple Selves, Multiple Voices*. Chichester: Wiley

Moore, S.M. (1998) 'How can we remember but be unable to recall? The complex functions of multi-modular memory', in *Memory in Dispute*, ed. V. Sinason. London: Karnac Books.

Pizer, S.A. (1996) 'The distributed self: Introduction to symposium on The Multiplicity of Self and Analytic Technique'. *Contemporary Psychoanalysis* 32(4): 499–507.

Potter, Beatrix (1903) *The Tailor of Gloucester*. London: Fred Wayne & Co. Ltd.

Putnam, F.W. (1989) *Diagnosis and Treatment of Multiple Personality Disorder*. New York: Guilford Press.

Reich, W. (1973) *The Function of the Orgasm*. New York: Farrar, Strauss and Giroux.

Reik, T. (1949) *Listening with the Third Ear*. New York: Farrar, Strauss and Giroux.

Shane, M., Shane, E. and Gales, M. (1997) *Intimate Attachments*. New York: Guilford Press.

Southgate, J.P. (1989) 'The hidden child within', pp. 277–233 in *Child Abuse and Neglect*, ed. Stainton Rogers. Buckingham: Open University Press.

Southgate, J.P. (1996) 'An attachment approach to dissociation and multiplicity', paper presented at the Third John Bowlby Memorial Lecture, Centre for Attachment-based Psychoanalytic Psychotherapy, London.

Southgate, J.P. and Randall, R. (1976) *The Barefoot Psychoanalyst*. London: Barefoot Books.

Southgate, J.P. and Randall, R. (1981) *Co-operative and Community Group Dynamics*. London: Barefoot Books.

Stern, D. (1995) *The Motherhood Constellation*. New York: Basic Books.

Stern, D. (1998) 'The process of therapeutic change involving implicit knowledge'. *Infant Mental Health Journal* 19(3).

van Ijzendoorn, M.J., Schuengel, C. and Bakermans-Kranenburg, M.J. (1999) 'Disorganized attachment in early childhood: Meta-analysis of precursors, concomitants, and sequelae'. *Development and Psychopathology* 11: 225–249.

White, Kate (1999) Personal communication.

Winnicott, D. (1974) *Playing and Reality*. London: Penguin.

Chapter 6

Multiple dissociation in the context of the Adult Attachment Interview

Observations from interviewing individuals with Dissociative Identity Disorder

Howard Steele

This chapter reports on the experience of working as an attachment research consultant to the Clinic for Dissociative Studies in London (Director: V. Sinason), interviewing several individuals, with confirmed or suspected Dissociative Identity Disorder, early in their therapeutic consultations with the clinic. The resulting profiles emerging from these Adult Attachment Interviews (AAIs) are remarkably similar in that, when the patients engage with the challenge of describing and evaluating their attachment history, severe evidence of distress emerges with clear signs of dissociation in the interview context itself. When the adult listener/speaker is addressed, it is not long until the interview elicits other voices, personalities or alters whose origin and viewpoint depends on a particular mode of experiencing and responding to extreme, organised and repeated abuse perpetrated by attachment caregivers throughout childhood. This chapter provides examples from, and comments upon, from an attachment perspective, the Adult Attachment Interviews collected from a number of these adult survivors of ritualised abuse.

The chapter will first provide an overview of the normative findings utilising the AAI and the recent extension of the interview to clinical and forensic psychiatric populations, before moving on to the central focus upon current and pronounced dissociation in the context of the AAI when administered to individuals suffering from Dissociative Identity Disorder. While previous research has highlighted associations between evidence of unresolved mourning in the context of the Adult Attachment Interview with external assessments of proneness to dissociation (Hesse and van Ijzendoorn 1999), and mild signs of dissociation in the interview itself, e.g. current absorption in details regarding past loss or trauma (Main and Goldwyn in press; Main and Morgan 1996), this is the first report of administration of the Adult Attachment Interview to a sample of adults suffering from Dissociative Identity Disorder or Multiple Personality Disorder. An attachment-based perspective on this compelling phenomenon has recently been advanced by Liotti

(1999). Liotti sees dissociative identity disturbances as a reflection of the human individual's ongoing species-specific need to achieve a personal synthesis or integration of meaning structures deriving from one's experience of the environment. The present report shares this perspective, assuming that the adult with a dissociated identity has failed to develop a singular coherent self on account of extreme and repeated violence perpetrated by the very person or people a child naturally turns to for support, understanding and survival – one's caregivers (after Bowlby 1969).

In the course of normal development, it is the cumulative quality of one's interactions with caregivers over the first many months of life which inform the child's evolving internal working model of the self and attachment figure(s). This sense of self with others guides the selection and interpretation of information relevant to attachment, qua survival. Much subsequent research has detailed the longitudinal behavioural and internal implications of early attachment experiences (see Cassidy and Shaver 1999; Sroufe 1988). Out of these early interactions with the caregiver are formed the child's evolving personal synthesis of meaning structures. When experiences are more or less sensible or coherent the child will develop an organised and coherent sense of self and others that is oriented toward trust and hope (the well-known secure pattern) or toward mistrust and despair (the insecure avoidant or resistant patterns). With respect to the tendency toward avoidance or resistance, personal integration is skewed toward under- (avoidant) or over- (resistant) awareness of negative experiences and emotions (see Main 1990).

Crucially, caregiving factors, not child temperament factors, are identified in multiple research investigations as the primary determinants of early infant–caregiver patterns of attachment (see Vaughn and Bost 1999). In other words, a well-cared for child, *whatever his or her initial temperament*, will develop a secure attachment – though it is admittedly particularly challenging to care for a baby who is *initially* a highly irritable child. The word 'initially' is written in italics on account of the consistent evidence that babies with negative emotional profiles in the first few months may come to develop a more positive emotional outlook by the end of the first year. For example, if cared for by parents who themselves have a co-operative marriage and/or other sources of social and emotional support available to them, 'irritable' infants may develop a more agreeable emotional profile by 9 months (e.g. Belsky et al. 1991), and a secure infant–mother attachment at 12 months (e.g. Crockenberg 1981; van dem Boom 1994).

When infants' experiences of their caregiving environment are nonsensical, such as being abused by the parent who alternately provides care, the possibility of arriving at a coherent internal synthesis of the meaning of the attachment relationship is fundamentally compromised (Lyons-Ruth and Jacobvitz 1999). The insecurity arising in the child's attachment to an abusive caregiver goes beyond the 'normal' insecurities known as avoidance or resistance (see Boris and Zeanah 1999). The term given to describe the abused baby's internal experience is the very same term Bowlby used to describe the adult's normal response to the loss of a loved one, i.e. disorganisation and disorientation – the loss of a sense of place and time – not knowing where one is or where one is going (Main and Hesse 1990; Solomon and George 1999). These considerations are especially relevant to the current chapter as the early and ongoing childhood experiences of persons with Dissociative Identity Disorder invariably involve abuse. But before detailing the picture of these individuals' experiences which emerges from interviewing them with the Adult Attachment Interview (George et al. 1985), the chapter first provides a review of this interview-based assessment in terms of its origins, normative and clinical findings.

ORIGINS AND NORMATIVE RESEARCH FINDINGS BASED ON THE ADULT ATTACHMENT INTERVIEW

Origins and evidence of intergenerational patterns

The Adult Attachment Interview was developed and first tested in the context of the Berkeley longitudinal study of attachment patterns (George et al. 1985; Main et al. 1985). The Berkeley-based group of developmental psychologists reported that when parents of 6-year-olds were interviewed in a standard way about the nature of their childhood relations with caregivers, and their current thoughts and feelings about these relationships, the tape-recorded narratives (transcribed verbatim for subsequent study) could be classified into secure (free–autonomous) or insecure (dismissing or preoccupied) groups. Furthermore, in the pioneering Berkeley study, these adult interview classifications were reported to map on to the well-known infant patterns of attachment available for their children from prior assessments made of these children's attachment relationships with mother (at 12 months) and with father (at 18 months). Great excitement surrounded and followed the report of these results because of what were already robust findings concerning the long-term social, emotional and cognitive consequences of infant patterns of attachment such that, in terms of both short- and long-term developmental outcomes, secure attachments during infancy predict optimal patterns of peer relations and adjustment in the preschool years, high levels of academic achievement in the school years, and adaptive coping in the adolescent years (see Cassidy and Shaver 1999). In the original Berkeley work, mothers' interviews were uniquely related to the previously observed infant–mother relationship and fathers' interviews were similarly predictive of the infant–father relationship. This suggested a remarkable level of cross-generational consistency, and relationship specificity, in the social and emotional meaning young children derive from their interactions with parents. These findings were confirmed in a prospective design, involving attachment interviews with expectant mothers and fathers and subsequent assessments of the infant–mother and infant–father attachment quality (Steele et al. 1996) and replicated widely across diverse linguistic and cultural barriers (van Ijzendoorn 1995).

Notably, the Adult Attachment Interview is classified in a way that assumes a singular coherent orientation toward attachment. This contrasts with the solid research-based understanding that attachment during infancy is a relationship-specific construct, i.e. infant–mother, infant–father, or infant–other/caregiver phenomenon where agreement across infant–caregiver relationships may or may not exist. Thus, developmental questions arise concerning the processes by which infant–mother and infant–father attachments come to be integrated in the mind of the developing child and adolescent. Does one parent have precedence in influencing the path of self development and extent of integration achieved within the mind of the developing individual? When is such integration ordinarily achieved? These questions are the subject of much ongoing research, but one thing is certain with respect to the present chapter, that is, the adult with a Dissociative Identity Disorder has failed to develop an integrated state of mind concerning attachment.

The capacity for arriving at, and expressing, an integrated state of mind concerning attachment

The use of the Adult Attachment Interview with non-clinical samples has clearly indicated that by the mid/late adolescent years (e.g. 17 or 18 years) if not sooner, the individual has developed a well-functioning capacity to report, monitor and evaluate their possibly very different types of early attachment experiences, e.g. with mother, father and others (e.g. Kobak and Sceery 1988). Further, Main (1990, 1991) has suggested that by 10 years of age, children who have benefited from a secure early attachment to mother are more likely to demonstrate metacognitive awareness in response to probing questions exploring the nature of mind and knowledge. Relatedly, it has also been shown that children as young as 6 years can understand mixed emotions arising within the same person in response to pictured dilemmas *but* such understanding is most likely to be present if the child was securely attached to mother at 1 year, and if the mother was herself autonomous-secure and *integrated* in response to the Adult Attachment Interview (Steele et al. 1999).

The Adult Attachment Interview may be seen to both permit and, at times, demand evidence of an integrated coherent evaluation of attachment experiences within the normal and atypical range. The questions fall into three types: (1) questions that ask about negative experiences and related emotions which are part of *everyone's* childhood experiences, including emotional upset, physical hurt, illness and separations from parents; (2) questions that ask about negative experiences and related emotions that are part of *some people's* childhood experiences, including loss and abuse; and (3) questions that demand of a speaker the expression of thoughts about the possible meaning and influence upon adult personality of childhood attachment experiences, including requests that the speaker provide an account of why parents behaved as they did during childhood. Because the adult's childhood experiences with specific caregivers (e.g. mother, father, others) are probed in detail, the interview provides a fertile ground for assessing the extent to which attachment experiences are integrated in the mind of the speaker into an autonomous point of view concerning the balance an adult needs to seek between depending on important and valued others – and having such others feel that one is dependable. Drawing on a non-clinical example from the Steele et al. (1996) study, one expectant father, when asked about his hopes for his unborn child 20 years on, stated his awareness of this integrative balancing act as follows:

> When I think about my child's future, well I hope he or she will be strong enough to follow their interests and passions . . . and that I will be able to make them feel that I am still there for them . . . not too busy or cut off, like I too often felt from my own father . . . that they can count on me for guidance without undue interference . . . and most importantly I'm sure, that they find with another the range of feelings I share with their mother – I don't think it will be easy for them – or I – but I am looking forward to it!

Approximately 65 per cent of the normal population conveys in one way or another a valuing of attachment, and a respect for exploration, which leads raters to assign their attachment interviews to the category 'autonomous– secure'.

Failures at integration

The remainder of interviews from non-clinical samples show evidence of difficulties with integrating past negative attachment experiences into a current and balanced state of mind concerning attachment, erring on the side of minimising or dismissing past difficulties with one or both parents (about 25 per cent of the non-clinical population) or erring on the side of maximising and becoming preoccupied with past attachment difficulties (about 10 per cent of the non-clinical population). These two alternates to the free–autonomous group are termed insecure–dismissing and insecure–preoccupied respectively. In the former 'dismissing' case, the speaker seems inexorably focused *consciously* on positive or normal aspects of experience, to the exclusion of what is probably (*unconsciously recognised as*) a much more mixed and negative set of actual experiences. In the latter 'preoccupied' case, the speaker seems angrily or passively gripped by past relationship difficulties that intrude upon current thoughts about relationships and are accompanied by confusing and difficult to control negative feelings. While this pattern is observed only about 15 per cent of the time in non-clinical samples (van Ijzendoorn 1995), the proportion of interview responses fitting this preoccupied pattern swells to over 50 per cent when clinical psychiatric populations have been assessed.

The disruptive influence of loss and/or trauma: resolution vs lack of resolution

A further important consideration when rating and classifying attachment interviews concerns past loss and trauma. When there is clear evidence of a significant loss or trauma (physical and/or sexual abuse) the rater or judge follows a number of specified guidelines (Main and Goldwyn in press) for assessing the extent to which the past trauma is resolved. In sum, this comes down to determining the extent to which the overwhelmingly negative experiences are (a) identified as such and (b) spoken about in such a way as to indicate that they have acquired the characteristics of belonging to the past without lapses in the monitoring of reason or discourse when discussing the past loss and/or trauma (after Main and Goldwyn in press). For example, where loss has occurred, it is important for the speaker to demonstrate full awareness of the permanence of this loss. And, where abuse has occurred in speakers' childhood experiences, it is important for speakers to at once acknowledge the abuse, and also show that they understand they are not responsible for the maltreatment they suffered. Important clues as to the extent of resolution in the speaker's mind follow from careful study of the narrative for a logical and temporally sequenced account of the trauma which is neither too brief, suggesting an attempt to minimise the significance of the trauma, nor too detailed, suggesting ongoing absorption.

Interestingly, in a study of 140 college students, Hesse and van Ijzendoorn (1999) report that speakers whose attachment interviews were judged unresolved with respect to past loss were statistically more likely than speakers who were judged resolved (or those who had suffered no significant losses) to score highly on Tellegen's Absorption Scale. Thus, in a non-clinical sample, brief lapses in the monitoring of discourse or reason when discussing loss in the context of the AAI have been associated with the propensity toward absorption, measured by agreement to questionnaire items such as 'At times I feel the presence of someone who is not physically there'.

Unresolved loss and/or trauma is observed in approximately 10 to 15 per cent of non-clinical interviews, which are also assigned to one of the three main groups, autonomous, dismissing or preoccupied – any of which may be assigned in the context of references to loss and/or abuse that qualify as unresolved. An interviewee who is autonomous (integrated and valuing of attachment) throughout an AAI, save for when speaking of a past loss in an unresolved manner, may not represent the same risk factor for child development (i.e. leading to disorganised infant attachments) as unresolved/insecure interviews (Schuengel et al. 1999). Perhaps resolution of loss is more easily arrived at if the individual who suffers the loss has a basically autonomous and valuing attachment orientation to 'fall back on'.

It is a similarly positive sign when a speaker demonstrates that past trauma has been resolved. Indeed, in the non-clinical population, where childhood experiences involved trauma it is not uncommonly the case that the speaker conveys a sense of moving beyond the fear they felt so often as a child, and is capable in the present of going some way toward understanding, though not necessarily forgiving, the caregiving figures who perpetrated abuse. In these circumstances, the interview often reveals a robust sense of self, interpersonal awareness and valuing of attachment so that one can say the adult who was abused is not likely to become an abuser. Such resilience invariably emerges out of the individual discovering one or more secure bases or refuges beyond the abusive relationship, such as may be provided by an extended family member, spouse or therapist.

CLINICAL FINDINGS BASED ON THE ADULT ATTACHMENT INTERVIEW

Applying the standard categorical scoring system to non-standard experiences and conditions

Early efforts to apply the Adult Attachment Interview in clinical contexts have revealed that loss and trauma experiences are highly common in psychiatric samples. With respect to specific (sometimes comorbid) diagnostic groups, borderline personality disorder has been associated with high prevalence of unresolved and insecure–preoccupied interviews (Patrick et al. 1994; Fonagy et al. 1996); eating disorder disturbances have been linked to unresolved and insecure–dismissing interviews (Fonagy et al. 1996); and suicidality has been associated with unresolved and 'disorganised' interviews (Adam et al. 1996). There have been two forensic studies reporting on the administration of AAIs to prisoners incarcerated for crimes against people and/or property (van Ijzendoorn et al. 1997; Levinson and Fonagy 1998). These Dutch and British studies provide convergent evidence that the prison population is likely to include individuals who have been physically abused in early life, who are prone to deny the significance of these experiences, and who present with an overall dismissing stance toward attachment.

Emerging recognition of profound threats to self-integration and organisation of feelings and thoughts concerning attachment

As Adam et al.'s use of the word 'disorganised' suggests, what the standard scoring system takes for granted – i.e. a primary, integrated and more or less organised mental and emotional stance toward attachment – may be fundamentally lacking in some speakers. This was a phenomenon noted by one of the individuals closely involved with the development of the interview coding system who has also studied a great number of interviews from clinical populations (Hesse 1996). Hesse's (1996) brief report suggested that a likely conclusion from considering some interviews, particularly those from clinical samples, is that they should be assigned to a 'cannot classify' category because they contain deeply divided states of mind concerning attachment. For example, a speaker may be insecure–dismissing with respect to a physically abusive father, e.g. speaking of him in a cool, non-feeling and uncaring manner, while being insecure–preoccupied with respect to an occasionally very caring mother who failed miserably at protecting the child, e.g. speaking of her in a heated, angry and involving manner. This is but one of many pathways that may lead to an attachment interview that is impossible to classify in a singular way. Such severe failures at personal integration are thought to derive from overwhelming adverse childhood experiences which compromise the mind's ability to make sense of them. It was expected then, that the attachment interviews collected from patients being seen at the London Clinic for Dissociative Studies would be impossible to classify in any straightforward way.

OBSERVATIONS FROM ADMINISTERING THE ADULT ATTACHMENT INTERVIEW TO INDIVIDUALS WITH DISSOCIATIVE IDENTITY DISORDER

Some technical considerations when administering the AAI to an individual with Dissociative Identity Disorder

Presented with the opportunity of interviewing people with DID, I had first to consider whether I would address each personality in turn, or challenge the speaker to provide a singular account of past attachment experiences and current appraisals. I favoured the latter strategy, believing that to follow the former could be judged as colluding with the presumed multiple personality structure, and what guarantee would I have that 'all' personalities would be available to be interviewed? I therefore began each interview by telling the interviewee that the questions I would raise followed an established procedure for learning about the possible effects of early family experience upon adults' thinking, feeling and behaviour. I further pointed out that the interview is in wide use throughout the world's universities and research centres. Finally, I would state that I was interested in the extent to which listeners can call on one voice from within to tell the story of the different things that have happened with parents and other caregivers during childhood, as well as telling how one currently thinks and feels about all that has happened in one's early family experience. Notably, for the beginning of every interview – always including my above-mentioned introduction – the individual's therapist was present. After a few minutes, and well before the question concerning 'please provide five adjectives that describe your childhood relationship with your mother' was asked, the therapist asked the interviewee if s/he felt comfortable with the interviewer, and thereafter took his or her leave. Occasionally, where the safety of the interviewee and those around her was judged to be at risk, accompaniment was provided by chaperones (often nurses). On one particular occasion when the interviewee suddenly shifted into an ominous 'alter' threatening violence, I was grateful for the restraining presence of these chaperones. Because the interviewees are all in therapy before and after the administration of the AAI, there is the possibility of allowing the interview to inform the therapy and for the interviewer to be informed by the therapist about the interviewee's experience of being interviewed. To date, at the Dissociative Disorders Clinic in London the AAI informs the course of therapy only insofar as the individual patient may refer to it. Interestingly, interviewees have often reported to their therapists that the stance of the interviewer[1] was experienced as a threat, i.e. insofar as he assumed there might be *only one* voice which could be relied on to tell the story of one's early family experiences. None the less, all patients so far asked to be interviewed have agreed.

Multiple dissociation in the context of the Adult Attachment Interview

The interviews have ranged from narratives which are produced by multiple identifiable personalities who each speak for a time before retreating and giving 'the floor' to another voice, to discrete personality organisation, often with an identifiable origin in the speaker's gravely troubled childhood history. Curiously, when different 'alters' appear in the same interview they predictably correspond to different attachment patterns, serving distinctive functions. A gloss on the matter which has been suggested to me from interviews conducted so far points to the following associations between attachment patterns and inner self-representations stemming from extreme and repeated abuse from caregivers: secure patterns are typical of observer and survivor personalities, dismissing patterns indicate persecutor and/or protector personalities, while preoccupied patterns seem to be a common vehicle for victim personalities to express themselves.

For example, one woman presented with a surface personality that was pleasant, polite, and valuing of attachment (she was in fact engaged to be married). Yet this same speaker was also troubled by what she described as a distant and difficult relationship she has with her mother who rejected, abused and abandoned her (suggestive of a mildly preoccupied and resentful type of hard-earned security/autonomy). But as the interview progressed, a series of different attachment patterns were represented by a series of distinct voices/personalities. Curiously, at no point in the interview did I deliberately seek to elicit another voice/person with a different view from the one being expressed by the 'current' speaker. Staying with the present example, a marked shift was introduced by a question about who cared for her after her mother abandoned her at age 5. A different, more hostile, voice emerged to tell me 'care means chronically abused and ruined emotionally'. This was now a male voice, not a female one, who had a tough observer 'big brother' status in the interviewee's life. He spoke with severe disapproval of any attempt by the surface personality to repair relations with her mother, saying 'I think she should tell her mother to fuck off after all she's done to her . . . make her face up to reality, make her listen to what we went through'. The content of what 'we' endured includes ongoing ritualised abuse over many years perpetrated and maintained within the context of being in the care of governmental social services. Interestingly, beyond the horrendously abusive experiences suffered within the context of services set up to protect children, what was perhaps the strongest source of ongoing suffering for this interviewee (in all her persona) was the abandonment by her own mother. This relates to a theme uniting many of the narratives provided by individuals suffering from DID, i.e. that it is often not the abuse per se, but the betrayals by trusted caregivers and family members which appear to have the most profoundly disruptive influences upon the developing child's attempts to maintain an integrated sense of self.

Adult Attachment Interview questions concerning memories of being upset and hurt are often the impetus to a different personality appearing as one alter sees the opportunity to rush to the aid of another incapable of giving words to the details of pain experienced during childhood as in 'she can't answer that 'cause she doesn't want to know but *I* can tell you what we went through'. For these individuals who dissociate within the context of the Adult Attachment Interview, showing evidence of (some of) their different personalities, the dissociated identity disturbance seems to be very much ego-syntonic (to borrow from a psychoanalytic lexicon) or accepted as the only working solution to severe relationship problems. Other attachment interviews with this same population do not yield such clear evidence of dissociation.

For example, one interview began with the female speaker confessing how desperately anxious she was at facing the task of telling the story of her childhood experiences with caregivers. An hour and a half later when the interview ended, she confessed how very hard it was to hold herself together free of a severe anxiety (panic) attack. This she indicated was only managed by fixating her attention on the next task she has to execute, e.g. walking to the bus stop, then waiting for the bus, then paying the bus driver and so on. Were she to let her mind wander from the task at hand, an overwhelming flood of fearful anxieties awaited her. When the speaker alluded to 'other personalities' in her interview; namely, others who could convey the unintegrated details of the trauma she has suffered, she did not 'split' and assume another voice/personality as has been my experience when interviewing other individuals with suspected or confirmed DID. Thus what I observed was a woman struggling to achieve a sense of integration and coherence with respect to an extraordinarily painful childhood history, including ritual abuse and the painful experience of being betrayed by her older brother. This was an older brother who had helped her to survive the concentration camp style persecutions that both of them were made to suffer. Thus the devastating blow to her was when he fully identified with and joined the cult rather than resist as the 'speaker' did.

With respect to the diverse range of attachment patterns which appear in these routinely 'can't classify,' 'unresolved,' and 'multiply insecure' interviews obtained from individuals suffering from DID, there appears to be a preponderance of dismissing (persecutor) patterns. This is consistent with Liotti's (1999) suggestion that the initial (childhood) response to abuse is deactivation of the attachment system (at the expense of loss of cohesion in the sense of self). The corresponding behavioural strategy adopted by the developing child, or one or more of the developing child's non-integrated selves, is identification with the aggressor (after Freud 1936/1946). Thus, infants with disorganised attachments (correlated with abusive caregiving) are prone to develop antisocial and aggressive behavioural profiles in the later childhood and adolescent years, as well as (though perhaps less readily observed) a tendency toward dissociation (Carlson 1998).

On the possibility of resolving ritual abuse

It must be emphasised that, when speaking of unresolved loss and trauma in this population, when these speakers refer to painful past happenings they are in the domain of almost unthinkable events and interactions, on the order of the most horrific examples of severe racial and/or ethnic violence. For the victims of ritual abuse I have interviewed, the difference stems from the fact that the abuse is unremitting and perpetrated by attachment figures, thus profoundly disfiguring the developing mind of the child. Consider the following account provided by one interviewee in response to the standard AAI question about past losses:

INTERVIEWER The interview moves on now to ask you about loss. What would you say was your first experience of the loss of a loved one?
INTERVIEWEE Yeah . . . I don't think I loved anybody. But there was somebody I cared about . . . Erm, actually no I take that back there was one person I did love . . . and it is a memory that I have dealt with and the personality has integrated it into me, so I remember it properly. Her name was Shelly and she was locked up in the cellar and she was a secret friend, or an attic, I was allowed to have. This was before the age, I must have been about six, and . . . I don't know how much you know about ritual abuse but you are starved and all that, but I was allowed to sneak food to her, I mean, now looking back it's obvious that they must have known I was doing it, but they let me do it and they let me get very close to her . . . we were sometimes allowed to play freely in the fields by the lake . . . then . . . they said that we had talked, I can't remember but my fault – somebody

did talk, we'd done something really bad, like we'd spoken to somebody, we'd talked, somebody knew about her being in the attic – so she had to die. So Shelly was tied to a chair, erm . . . and . . . put on erm top of a large row boat. I was made to sit in the boat with my grandfather who was the chief power and dictator in the family, if you can call it that. He was the whole time telling me that if I moved too much in one direction or the other Shelly and the chair would fall in the deep water. I can still hear Shelly's sobs, and terrified face. Neither of us could swim very well, so I was completely horrified and helpless . . . Sure enough the chair did fall in and as I heard Shelly's scream before she hit the water, he insisted it was all my fault, adding, 'go in after her . . . try and reach her, see if you can untie her from the chair!' I was faced with the choice of drowning too, or living (as I have done) with the burden of guilt for Shelly's death . . . So, I've always blamed myself for her dying . . . and she was my best friend, she was my only friend, after that . . . I never . . . got near anyone, I never did. That's one memory I've dealt with . . . and Alter M was the personality that dealt with that for me at the time when I couldn't, and that has now been integrated – and I think Shelly would be proud to know of how I've worked toward survival and integration.

This passage illustrates well the sense of resistance to horror, and affirmation of the value of close relationships, which has been a common thread through all of the attachment interviews I have collected through the London Clinic for Dissociative Studies. This feature of the interviews speaks for the elemental power of the primary strategy, inherent in each human being, for a secure attachment (Main 1990), which has the potential to survive despite repeated attempts by twisted attachment figures to extinguish it. The interviewees have all shown an impressive loyalty to the goals of integration, and a valuing of attachment, just as their behaviour in the interviews has also provided clear and compelling evidence of dissociation. That the dissociation occurs so vividly in the context of being interviewed about past attachments is a clear reflection of the severity and frequency of the ritual abuse these speakers have suffered. Effectively and completely deprived of childhood and any prospect for a normative adult life, these individuals are often prone to despair and self-harm. Yet as one interviewee put it, in response to the final AAI question: 'What three wishes might you have for the future of your own children (i.e. if you had children)?' The response was tragic yet hopeful,

I can't have kids, because we don't know how much damage has been done [i.e. from the invasive attacks on her female organs] and I know I can't adopt because I've been sectioned [i.e. forcibly detained in a Psychiatric Unit] . . . but if I did have children, it would be that they would go through nothing that we ever went through and have completely the opposite kind of life.

In conclusion, some thought should be given to the possibility of resolving loss and trauma on the scale reliably identified in these interviews. I believe resolution would be achieved if and when the overwhelmingly terrifying past situations acquire the characteristics of belonging to the speaker's past, where the speaker is free to speak of them or not. This is the hoped for outcome from the process of mourning which is inevitably a long one. But is there a foreseeable end? Therapy research, with respect to severely and repeatedly traumatised individuals such as those we are discussing, has yet to conclude whether this process may be ever completed, or is necessarily an ongoing lifelong process. Two important stumbling blocks in the recovery process may be detected from the attachment interviews I have so far collected. First, there is the issue of loyalty to the abusive parent(s) and/or grandparent(s) for, as Bowlby said, it is difficult for a child to think of mother in any terms other than good ones (after Bretherton 1998). Second, there are the perverse and deep connections in the minds of these victims of incest, which tie together the experiences of sexual excitement, submission, awe of power, pain and attachment. Quite how the abusive attachment figure can be acknowledged for what s/he was, and a more normative pattern of intimacy with a benign loved other may be established and maintained, must be among the chief questions of any therapeutic endeavour with these remarkable survivors of ritual abuse.

NOTE

1 The interviewer was the author of this chapter, who has administered the Adult Attachment Interview (AAI) more than 200 times, and has rated and classified more than 700 interview-transcriptions, from a range of clinical and non-clinical populations. He was trained to high levels of reliability by Drs Mary Main and Erik Hesse.

REFERENCES

Adam, K.S., Sheldon-Keller, A.E. and West, M. (1996) 'Attachment Organisation and History of Suicidal Behaviour in Clinical Adolescents'. *Journal of Clinical and Consulting Psychology*, 64: 264–272.

Belsky, J., Fish, M. and Isabella, R. (1991) 'Continuity and Discontinuity in Infant Negative and Positive Emotionality: Family Antecedents and Attachment Consequences'. *Developmental Psychology*, 27: 421–431.

Boris, N.W. and Zeanah, C.H. (1999) 'Disturbances and Disorders of Attachment in Infancy: An Overview'. *Infant Mental Health Journal*, 20: 1–9.

Bowlby, J. (1969) *Attachment and Loss, vol. 1: Attachment*. London: Hogarth Press and Institute of Psycho-Analysis.

Bretherton, I. (1998) 'Commentary on Steele and Steele: Attachment and Psychoanalysis: A Reunion in Progress'. *Social Development*, 7: 132–136.

Carlson, E. (1998) 'A Prospective Longitudinal Study of Attachment Disorganization/ Disorientation'. *Child Development*, 69: 1107–1128.

Cassidy, J. and Shaver, P. (eds) (1999) *Handbook of Attachment*. London: The Guilford Press.

Crockenberg, S. (1981) 'Infant Irritability, Mother Responsiveness, and Social Support Influences on the Security of Infant–Mother Attachment'. *Child Development*, 52: 857–865.

Fonagy, P., Leigh, T., Steele, M., Steele, H., Kennedy, R., Mattoon, G., Target, M. and Gerber, A. (1996) 'The Relation of Attachment Status, Psychiatric Classification, and Response to Psychotherapy'. *Journal of Consulting and Clinical Psychology*, 64: 22–31.

Freud, A. (1946) *The Ego and the Mechanisms of Defence*. New York: International Universities Press (originally published 1936).

George, C., Kaplan, N. and Main, M. (1985) 'Adult Attachment Interview (2nd edn)'. Unpublished manuscript, University of California at Berkeley.

Hesse, E. (1996) 'Discourse, Memory and the Adult Attachment Interview: A Note with Emphasis on the Emerging Cannot Classify Category'. *Infant Mental Health Journal*, 17: 4–11.

Hesse, E. and van Ijzendoorn (1999) 'Propensities to Absorption Are Related to Lapses in the Monitoring of Reasoning or Discourse during the Adult Attachment Interview: A Preliminary Investigation'. *Attachment and Human Development*, 1: 67–91.

Kobak, R.R. and Sceery, A. (1988) 'Attachment in Late Adolescence: Working Models, Affect Regulation, and Representations of Self and Others'. *Child Development*, 59: 135–146.

Levinson, A. and Fonagy, P. (1998) 'Criminality and Attachment: The Relationship between Interpersonal Awareness and Offending in a Prison Population'. (Submitted manuscript).

Liotti, G. (1999) 'Disorganization of Attachment as a Model for Understanding Dissociative Psychopathology'. In J. Solomon and C. George (eds) *Attachment Disorganization*, pp. 291–317. New York/London: Guilford Press.

Lyons-Ruth, K. and Jacobvitz, D. (1999) 'Attachment Disorganization: Unresolved Loss, Relational Violence, and Lapses in Behavioral and Attentional Strategies'. In J. Cassidy and P. Shaver (eds), *Handbook of Attachment*, pp. 520–554. London: The Guilford Press.

Main, M. (1990) 'Cross-cultural Studies of Attachment Organization: Recent Studies, Changing Methodologies, and the Concept of Conditional Strategies'. *Human Development*, 33: 48–61.

Main, M. (1991) 'Metacognitive Knowledge, Metacognitive Monitoring, and Singular (Coherent) vs. Multiple (Incoherent) Models of Attachment: Findings and Directions for Future Research'. In C.M. Parkes, J. Stevenson-Hinde and P. Marris (eds), *Attachment Across the Life Cycle*, pp. 127–159. London: Routledge.

Main, M. and Goldwyn, R. (in press) 'Adult Attachment Classification System'. In M. Main (ed.) *Behavior and the Development of Representational Models of Attachment: Five Methods of Assessment*. Cambridge University Press.

Main, M. and Hesse, E. (1990) 'Parents' Unresolved Traumatic Experiences are Related to Infant Disorganized Attachment Status: Is Frightened and/or Frightening Parental Behaviour the Linking Mechanism?'. In M.T. Greenberg, D. Cicchetti and E.M. Cummings (eds), *Attachment in the Preschool Years: Theory, Research and Intervention*, pp. 161–182. Chicago: University of Chicago Press.

Main, M., Kaplan, N. and Cassidy, J. (1985) 'Security in Infancy, Childhood and Adulthood: A Move to the Level of Representation'. In I. Bretherton and E. Waters (eds), *Growing Points in Attachment Theory and Research*, pp. 66–104. Monographs of the Society for Research in Child Development, 50, Serial No. 209.

Main, M. and Morgan, H. (1996) 'Disorganization and Disorientation in Infant Strange Situation Behavior: Phenotypic Resemblance to Dissociative States'. In L.K. Michelson and W.J. Ray (eds), *Handbook of Dissociation: Theoretical, Empirical, and Clinical Perspectives*, pp. 107–138. New York: Plenum.

Patrick, M., Hobson, R.P., Castle, D. and Maughan, B. (1994) 'Personality Disorder and the Mental Representation of Early Social Experience'. *Development and Psychopathology*, 6: 375–388.

Schuengel, C., Bakermans-Kranenburg, M.J. and van Ijzendoorn, M.H. (1999) 'Frightening Maternal Behavior Linking Unresolved Loss and Disorganized Infant Attachment'. *Journal of Consulting and Clinical Psychology*, 67: 54–63.

Solomon, J. and George, C. (eds) (1999) *Attachment Disorganization*. New York/London: Guilford Press.

Sroufe, L.A. (1988) 'The Role of Infant–Caregiver Attachment in Development'. In J. Belsky and T. Nezworski (eds), *Clinical Implications of Attachment*, pp. 18–38. Hillsdale, NJ: Erlbaum.

Steele, H., Steele, M., Croft, C. and Fonagy, P. (1999) 'Infant–Mother Attachment at One Year Predicts Children's Understanding of Mixed Emotions at Six Years'. *Social Development*, 8: 161–178.

Steele, H., Steele, M. and Fonagy, P. (1996) 'Associations Among Attachment Classifications of Mothers, Fathers, and Their Infants: Evidence for a Relationship-Specific Perspective'. *Child Development*, 67: 541–555.

van den Boom, D.C. (1994) 'The Influence of Temperament and Mothering on Attachment and Exploration: An Experimental Manipulation of Sensitive Responsiveness among Lower-class Mothers with Irritable Infants'. *Child Development*, 65: 1457–1477.

van Ijzendoorn, M.H. (1995) 'Adult Attachment Representations, Parental Responsiveness and Infant Attachment: A Meta-analysis on the Predictive Validity of the Adult Attachment Interview'. *Psychological Bulletin*, 117: 382–403.

van Ijzendoorn, M.H., Feldbrugge, J., Derks, F., de Ruiter, C., Verhagen, M., Phillipse, M., van der Staak, C. and Riksen-Walraven, J. (1997) 'Attachment Representations of Personality Disordered Criminal Offenders'. *American Journal of Orthopsychiatry*, 67: 449–459.

Vaughn, B.E. and Bost, K. (1999) 'Redundant, Independent, or Interacting Influences on Interpersonal Adaptation and Personality Development?'. In J. Cassidy and P. Shaver (eds), *Handbook of Attachment*, pp. 497–519. London: The Guilford Press.

Part III

Psychoanalytically orientated clinical work

Halloween

Please don't turn your head and walk away
Have you the strength inside to stay?
I know it's hard to face the fact
That human beings can do such violent acts

Open your eyes and see what I can see
Stretch up tall and look between the trees
A fire alight in the dead of night
And a little girl whose froze in sheer fright

I'm not asking for you to take her place
Just hold out your hand and help her face
The horrific torture and pain
Her little body had to embrace

Open your ears, don't just listen but hear
As she tells you of those lonely childhood years
Please believe her that's all I can ask
To help her cope with her horrific past

Reach out your hand and hold her tight
Stand by her side throughout her fight
As she tells of the humiliation, violent torture
And pain she went through
Her hate for herself she'll believe you will feel too!

Teach her to feel safe, secure and a love that's true
Hold her gently as her teardrops flow through
The barriers that she built to help her fight
To survive through all those horrific nights

Hearing her story will be hard to do
Her pain inside will hurt you too!

Just believe in yourself as others believe in you
And you will help this little girl pull through

Please don't turn and walk away
You have got the strength to stay
I know it's hard to face the facts
But human beings REALLY can do such violent acts

Toisin

Chapter 7

The shoemaker and the elves
Working with multiplicity

Valerie Sinason

Almost a hundred years after Freud's first work on trauma there was a conference entitled 'Women Overcoming Violence' at Logan Hall, London. The auditorium, which held a maximum of 1000, was completely packed and several hundred people were turned away. Compared with the usual 50–200 members at clinical conferences I was startled by the numbers and wondered what it meant. I soon found out.

A significant number of those present were abuse survivors, advocates, refuge workers, trauma workers and volunteers. Present were those whose abusive histories and their emotional sequelae had not previously met with courtesy or adequate treatment in the mainstream mental health services. Also present were the huge army of front-line workers who form the main 'care in the community' for those whose problems fall into an abyss of mainstream practice or conceptualisations. They were attending this conference because they knew most of the speakers acknowledged the existence of sexual abuse, ring abuse, ritual abuse and Dissociative Identity Disorder. I was handed several envelopes by would-be clients who had read some of my work and had come to assess me at this meeting to see if they felt they could trust me enough to seek a referral.

I will present an initial meeting with one young woman. I have chosen one in which the unbearable nature of the ritualistic torture she has suffered since earliest childhood is only briefly mentioned. This is so that the complex technical issues of DID can be considered without passing on a vicarious secondary traumatisation. However, even the brief amount that is mentioned is likely to have an impact.

One letter came from a young woman who I will call Anna. I will give you the first session so we are all facing the initial encounter together. I have the permission of Anna and all the self-states/alters that share her body to write this chapter. I must also preface it, at one alter's request (who wishes to be called Rowan) that Anna's multiplicity was only revealed to me so speedily in a first session because I was trusted. 'We would never normally show ourselves on a first meeting', she insisted. Everyone in Anna also wished to make clear that they gave permission for me to write this chapter for publication and for open debate, with background disguises, because 'after all, we only knew about you because you were willing to talk and write books'.

Anna was 22 years old. She had just gained a first class arts degree and was a highly regarded artist. Her tutor and lecturers predicted a brilliant career. However, her mental state was deteriorating. From her O-levels onwards (nine starred 'A' grades) through to A-levels (four 'A' grades) and during her degree she had experienced weeks of inpatient treatment which had provided a range of diagnoses from schizophrenia to paranoid psychosis to border-line to manic depression. The anti-psychotic medication did not help her and her self-injury, wrist cutting and thigh slashing increased.

A friend tried to persuade her to go to her GP again but Anna was unwilling to undergo yet again what to her were abusive experiences of being in hospital. When Anna had heard of this Conference and saw that I was speaking she asked her friend to accompany her and hand me this letter should she decide I could be trusted enough to have an initial meeting. Like many other such patients she had a sensible amount of paranoia that allowed her to raise the disturbing hypothesis that I might only be doing this work in order to gain control of their secrets and betray them.

The letter had an answering machine number and I decided to ring in the first instance. I have found with many traumatised patients that the formal experience of writing in and waiting for a reply is intolerable. When I dialled the number a BT kind of voice announced 'Please give your name and message – your call is being screened'. Once I said it was Valerie the phone was lifted up and a very scared young voice asked 'Yes?' I said my name was Valerie and I would like to speak to Anna. I do not give a surname on these machines in case it is not the patient's home or in case it identifies the patient's call to a clinician.

> 'Yes', said the childish voice.
> 'Is she there?'
> 'She will be in a minute. Would you please hold on a minute.'
> There was a pause and then an older voice came to the phone.
> 'Hello. This is Anna.'
> 'This is Valerie.'
> 'Valerie?'
> 'Valerie Sinason.'
> 'Hold on.'
> A pause.
> A slightly different voice returned to the phone.
> 'Thank you for calling, Valerie.'
> I felt quite bemused.
> 'Is that Anna?'
> 'You could say so.'

I felt very awkward and said as I had not met her before I could not really say so as I did not know who was Anna or not.

'OK', said a tired voice, 'Anna will do for the moment.'

Pause.

'It's all of us.'

'All of you?'

'Yes. We think we are all here.'

'Well – I am phoning about your letter and I wonder if you would like to come and talk to me' (and I realised that the word 'you' could stand for plural too).

'Yes', said the childish voice.

'It was you who answered the phone wasn't it?' I asked.

'Yes', said the child voice proudly. 'Mummy says I am very good at answering the phone. And I say please and thank you very much too.'

'That's very good', I said. What else could I say?

'Thank you', she said.

'Who do I speak to to make a time.'

'Make a time? You can't make a time. It's on watches. It goes by itself', said the child voice.

'I mean, who do I speak to for us to make an appointment. Do you know what an appointment is?'

'Yes. I have to go to the doctors – ouch – don't hurt me!'

She started crying, terrible little child cries.

'What's happened?' I asked in alarm.

'She's hurting me.'

'Who?'

'The lady. She says I am not to talk about doctors' appointments. Ouch! My arms! My back! Oh no.'

There was a terrible child scream that chilled me. I felt it as coming from an abused 5- or 6-year-old trapped in a moment of time in which she was being recurringly abused ad infinitem.

'Now stop hurting her', I said firmly, feeling rather mad. 'No one is allowed to hurt anyone at all.'

There was a silence.

The older voice returned.

'Thank you', said the Anna voice. 'The children have gone away now and you stopped them being hurt.'

'Good', I said. 'Can we make an appointment?'

'Yes. But I am scared of being seen. There are lots of people after me. You know what I mean. They don't want me in treatment in case I tell. But you are my last chance.'

I said that sounded very difficult.

I offered her a time and place and said I hoped it would be manageable to come. (I was unsure at this point whether to say I hope you can all come.)

On the day of the appointment, Tuesday at 10am, my secretary received a call from someone called Lily. 'Tell Valerie I am not coming today'. For a while I struggled with that name. Had I forgotten a colleague coming for supervision or a consultation? At 10am there was no Anna. The receptionist and secretary wondered if Lily could be an 'alter' of Anna.

If Lily was linked to Anna, what was I to do about internal resistance that was being acted out in this concrete way by a named other person? At 10.50am with perfect analytic timing the phone went for me. It was Anna. She was utterly distraught. 'I don't know where I am. Lily took the car at 9am this morning although it was my turn. I've only just come out. I don't know what to do. I don't know where I am.' Her voice was getting more desperate.

I said how horrible to not know where she was and not know where her car was and to have missed her session. As I spoke, the breathing at the other end of the phone changed and a little child voice said, 'Hello, it's all right. I'm a happy girl and I will cheer Anna up.' 'Where is she?' I asked. 'She is crying in the corner. And – ouch – stop it Lily.' The child voice was in great pain and Lily was apparently internally attacking her.

> As on the telephone before I said 'Lily, stop hurting the child. I would like to talk to you by yourself. Will you come to the phone? You phoned me earlier and I did not know who you were – I am sorry – please speak to me now.'
>
> Silence.
>
> Anna's voice suddenly reappeared. 'That's better. Little Lillian always cheers me up – she is so sweet.'
>
> I said I had been trying to speak to Lily.
>
> 'She's listening', said Anna.
>
> 'Lily, it would be really helpful if you could tell Anna where the car is because I am free at 6pm today and if you were able to get her in the car I would be able to talk to you and anyone else that wanted to come'.
>
> Pause.
>
> 'Oh – that's better', said Anna, 'Now I know where I am.'

There are many complicated technical issues just in this tiny extract. I have had a policy based on experience with abused adolescents and adults that their phone calls are urgent communications and require a response as soon as possible. Leslie Sohn (personal communication 1996) saw psychotic patients in analysis every day of the week including weekends because he saw that time had no meaning for them. A baby is not being greedy or attention-seeking when it wants something urgently *now* in the present, and I think many formal treatment centres fail these patients when they try to apply useful boundaries that work with less traumatised patients. There is also the issue of courtesy and calling alters or states – whatever you think they are – by their names. Clinicians who refuse to accept the alters and only address the host personality are behaving like Pavlovians – offering conditional responses only according to approved states.

At 6pm a late adolescent in a wheelchair arrived. She had long plaits, a long black skirt and top and wheeled her wheelchair in with great physical difficulty, breathing hard. I did not know how she would get up the stairs. After I said 'hello' a different voice replied – this was Anita. I mentioned the problem of the stairs. 'That's all right', said Anna. 'No. I'll do it', said a 6-year-old girl – who we will call Lillian. 'I'll go up the stairs for you. I am good at climbing and I can go up two stairs at a time.' 'All right', said Anna. And suddenly, before my eyes, a little girl climbed off the wheelchair, skipped after me and walked speedily up the stairs, two at a time.

Once inside the room, a ferocious young woman stared aggressively at me and walked round the room punching the walls and the pictures. This was Lily.

> 'Hah – look at that couch. You probably don't even know it is a special colour – typical and you think you might know something about us. Look at that picture. The pattern. So this is your room. I should have guessed.'

I thanked her for coming and said perhaps she was annoyed I was disappointing to meet. She laughed. 'I don't mind. It means they won't have to be worried about you. I can tell them what you're like.'

'Them?' I asked.

'The temple', she replied.

'Inside you or outside?' I asked.

'Oh – outside – stupid. You can't have a temple inside. You ought to know that. Call yourself an expert.'

I said I didn't, but she was, and in order to say how stupid I was. She laughed in a more relaxed way.

> 'Well, I brought stupid Anna here but she is asleep. She sleeps most of the time and she is not much use to anyone anyway. And I didn't need Anita – getting a wheelchair folded up is a drag – stupid cripple. She thinks she can take torture but just look at her. Stuck in a fucking wheelchair. I can take it. I take it for the whole bloody lot of them and they don't thank me either.'

I said that must be really hard, really lonely, to be taking the torture for all of them and not being thanked and, right here in the room, she was taking the appointment for everyone and perhaps that was hard too. I was very careful not to call the session torture. Only clinicians who have not worked with real torture victims use such terms to describe sadomasochistic practices in the transference and counter-transference.

As if reading my mind Lily burst out laughing. 'Oh – isn't she clever. She knows we have been really hurt.' She walked round the room fingering her plaits. 'These aren't my plaits. They are Lillian's. Soppy little kid – always in the way. But I am in my clothes. Eve thought she could get up first but she never can. Not for work, not for exams. It has always been me.' She pulled the elastic band off the plaits and undid them aggressively, combing them out. She looked very different then. She opened her bag and made up her eyes with large black spider lashes.

'Is it you that got everyone through school and university?'

'Course it is. They are all a load of snivelling cowards. Oh – it hurts! I try to toughen them up, get them used to it, they ought to be able to cope by now. I am sick of always being the one to take it. But me and Peter do the paintings. I have got a wonderful studio for us and that is one reward for everything I put up with'. She sat down, looked at me and then burst out laughing.

'The crazy thing is that Anna, Anita and Annette didn't even know until the day before your conference that Peter and I do the paintings and Iris and I do the exams. I don't know if it sunk in. I don't know all of them. Well – Iris did the A-levels and we shared the degree. The As wouldn't have got the lowest grade GCSE. As for Lillian – she is stupid – she can't even read yet.'

Lily's face suddenly flushed and distorted and then Lillian was sitting there.

'I am not stupid', she said.

I said she had managed to help everyone come up the stairs.

She smiled. 'I do help. I try very hard but I am not allowed to go to school. I have to stay at home all the time so nobody teaches me anything.'

I said that was really horrible.

She felt her hair and started crying. 'Where's my twirlies?'

'Twirlies?' I asked.

'For my hair – bobbles – for my plaits. They've gone and I will be beaten again for losing them.' Her cries grew in intensity. 'Ouch. No. Don't. You are hurting me.'

I said 'Stop it! There are only two rules in here. You can't hurt me and you can't hurt anyone else. Stop.'

Lillian wiped her eyes and then disappeared. A very tired Anna appeared.

'Thank you', she said. 'I hate it when Lillian is crying. She is such a good little girl and she tries so hard and some of them are so cruel to her'.

I agreed. 'What is she doing now?' I asked.

'Oh, she is playing with the other children.'

'Other children?'

'Oh yes – there are quite a few. I don't know all of them and there is the baby too but he is rather sickly.'

I took a deep breath. I asked if she had heard my conversation with Lily. 'Well – I was asleep for some of it.' Pause. 'I suppose you want to know why we came.' I said that would be helpful.

Taking a deep breath Anna said, 'Well, I wanted to see you because I didn't properly admit to myself that I was multiple until very recently. I had always known about some of the others but because no one took them seriously I just decided it was easiest to call myself mad. I've been an inpatient in psychiatric hospitals several times. Just before my A-levels, after I got my degree results and really I was mad almost all through my degree. I have been called border-line, schizophrenic, manic-depressive, anti-social personality – you name it. When I said, when I tried to say about voices I was just laughed at and told I was mad. I went to a therapist when I was 12. I got a scholarship to X school and I could not understand it because I knew I was not clever and then all my paintings were winning awards and everyone was telling me I was a good artist. I knew it wasn't me. I just felt mad.

'I tried my first overdose then. School got worried and really forced my parents to let me go to a therapist. I tried to tell her about Lillian and Anita and she just spoke about baby parts of the self and different states and said I should try not to call them names. The child psychiatrist was the same. He said it was like having imaginary friends and you grew out of it and my poor parents were so fucking worried about me'. (There was a sudden flash of Lily when she swore.) 'I gave up then and decided if they were all sure I was mad I just better keep quiet about it.

'Then when it came to A-levels I was asleep nearly all the time. I went on to drugs. I was in a terrible state. Heard voices and then I got really good results and all my teachers said it was what they expected and how pleased they were and I felt even worse because I had no idea how to do those subjects or how to paint. And it went on like that and after my degree – when I got a first – and my paintings were doing so well I just wanted to die. I got all the paracetamol. And then Lily said hello – and then Anita . . .'

There was a jolt and her face changed and little Lillian was there.

'No thank you very much. I am a polite girl. I am not being rude but I was there after Lily. I said hello second. Second. That's where I was. I know first, second, third even though I can't read'. I agreed and she beamed.

She disappeared and Anita appeared. 'She only met me a few weeks ago. I don't think they like me – because I am a cripple – me and little Annette. Sometimes Peter says I need to go to the doctor's and he rings for me or sometimes one of the children helps.'

I asked if Peter would like to speak. Anita said it was hard for him because he could not get a proper voice out of us and he had to cope with not getting the outside body that was right either but inside her had a proper male body. I asked if he would like to say hello through someone else's voice.

There was a flush and a face change and a shy looking male faced me. I said hello and Peter said he would just say hello for a moment to look at me more clearly and then go back inside because he liked to spend his time thinking of painting. Then he disappeared and Anita reappeared.

'He is back painting again. What was I saying? Oh yes. Anna can't really bear it or Lily. You see I took the physical pain. Lily takes the mental pain from it. But she goes to the cult – have they told you yet – it's our family. They have been Satanists for several generations and we've been in it since we were babies. I tried to run away for us when we were only 6.'

Suddenly her face changed and there was the little child invalid, Annette, in the room, holding on to the sides of the chair tightly and clearly in pain. 'They carried us in. We were very cold. We didn't have any clothes on and there were lots of people in the room and they didn't have any clothes on except for these long black things round them but you could see all their rude bits. It wasn't polite.' Her face changed and Lillian appeared.

'I am a good polite girl and I always wear all my clothes and I don't take them off in public.' She then disappeared and little Annette reappeared. 'And they passed me around and people touched me and hurt me. And they stuck things up me and I cried and Mummy said I would be shut up in a box and never let out if I cried – and then they put me down and then – and then . . .'

She disappeared and Lily came. 'Fuck all this – it was a simple ceremony. I was to be made Satan's daughter. I deserved to be. I had learned it all and that stupid little one has to suddenly take over just when the goat's horn was being shoved up my bum. Big deal.'

Little Annette reappeared. 'So I ran and Daddy kicked me and said I wasn't worth using.' She disappeared and terrible child screaming came out of a blank face.

'Stop it!' I called. 'Whoever is doing that, leave her.'

Anita appeared. 'So they hurt me – they trampled on me – they broke my back. I had to go to a school for the physically handicapped. The others did not help.' I asked why. 'I suppose they were glad I had been crippled because then they were safe.'

'So Lily has to take the ceremonies for everyone because she feels she can be the child of Satan properly and you took the physical pain and have stayed there and Peter and Lily and Iris do the art and the exams. So that must be hard – whoever does something for everyone must feel a bit lonely then.' I found I was making systemic group interpretations.

I asked who was screaming before.

'That was little Annette – she thought she was being tortured again and her back was being broken.' I found myself wondering about the awful science fiction idea of an alter having separate flashbacks.

Silence.

Anna continued. 'Can you imagine? I would find myself in my school art class when I hated art and was no good at it. I would feel ill and then I would come to in front of a wonderful painting and find my teacher congratulating me. I thought it was like my family. It was all a set-up to humiliate me. I said I had not done it and my teacher said sometimes really good creative people went into trance states when they did work so it did not feel like their own and that did help a bit, but with my A-levels I had no idea of how I got that. Can you imagine getting such good grades? And at degree level? Everyone offered me further degree places but how I could I do that when I did not know who it was.'

I asked if she knew the story of the shoemaker and the elves. The poor shoemaker is poverty-stricken and he is down to his last bits of leather and because he is so hardworking he works even on the last night before he is to be evicted when he will lose everything. He sets out the shapes at night ready to make two pairs of shoes. In the morning, to his shock, there are two perfectly made pairs of shoes. They catch the eyes of a rich customer and the money paid allows the shoemaker to buy leather for four pairs of shoes. These two appear perfectly made in the morning, are sold and bring in money for eight pairs of shoes. It carries on and on with the elves completing whatever the shoemaker leaves out for them.

He is shocked at first but then grateful and finally decides to stay up to meet his benefactors. When he spies the elves, who don't see him, he sees they are in rags and poorly fed. He and his wife then make lovely sets of clothes and shoes for them all and leave out food and, as they can see he is now rich and successful, the elves happily go away. He carries on making his excellent shoes.

There was a long silence and the shared body was wracked with tears. Lily came out and was crying too. I said the point of the story was that the shoemaker did know how to make good shoes so it was not fake – his success – and he was able to acknowledge the secret night-time help he got. Perhaps they would be able to be happy at some point with the shared gifts they had and that would help them deal with the terrible memories.

Suddenly there was a terrible little child's cry and I could hear little Annette. Anna held out her hands and closed her eyes. 'Little Annette – come here – come to me – I want you here with me.' There was an electrified tension in the room. Suddenly Anna hugged herself and looked transfixed with joy. 'I got her. She is with me and they can't hurt her any more.' 'That's wonderful', I said. 'Congratulations everybody.'

As therapy progressed, Anna was able to make clear that little Lillian was born at the same time as little Annette to split the terrible experience of physical and sexual abuse in the initiation ceremony. Eventually the children were able to be incorporated into helpful internal adults so that they did not have to keep repeating forever the terrible nowness of the abuse they had all experienced. Anna and Anita were able to link with Iris but Lily and Peter and several others resisted joining up. Additionally, several other alters came forward who allegedly still took part in the ritual abuse.

Anna was able to make a recovery and move on in a life successful in personal relationships as well as work.

The shoemaker and the elves can be understood from many different points of view. It could be seen as a reversal of the child's envy of the parental couple able to make babies at night. In this scenario it is the elderly couple who are saved by what the babies make at night! However, in the context of multiplicity, the fairytale offers a moving account of acknowledgement of the night-time work done by others and the importance of knowing who the others are. Jean Goodwin (see Chapter 8) also writes of the use of fairytale in understanding this work.

TECHNICAL AND ETHICAL ISSUES

The issue of consent and confidentiality is complex when writing about a person whose 16–20 alters also need to be disguised. While I gained consent to write this from Anna, Annette, Anita, Lily, and others, there are some whom I have never met who therefore could not give permission.

Indeed, the subject is beset with ethical difficulties. In several cases there was the issue of whether one personality who was in real danger could be sectioned, although it was not 'out', and what the consequences would be to the host personality and the others who could then feel misplaced in a psychiatric unit.

Where one personality – as with Lily – has allegedly committed murder and other offences what is the legal responsibility of the clinician in terms of the other personalities? When a police officer, such as Detective Inspector Clive Driscoll, tried to interview Lily on the crimes she had continued to speak about she would disappear and someone else would be there who was genuinely innocent. Indeed, perhaps my most significant finding in relation to the police is the need for joint training in this subject to avoid enormous wastage of police time when they are misled by alters/self-states trying to protect family attachments in cults.

Freud ('The ego and the id' 1923: 30) endeavoured to understand the psychic structure:

> we cannot avoid giving our attention for a moment longer to the ego's object-identifications. If they obtain the upper hand and become too numerous, unduly powerful and incompatible with one another, a pathological outcome will not be far off. It may come to a disruption of the ego in consequence of the different identifications becoming cut off from one another by resistances; perhaps the secret of the cases of what is described

as 'multiple personality' is that the different identifications seize hold of consciousness in turn. The host Anna can be seen to be filled with fleshed-out object-cathexes, moments of trauma, familial abusive identifications, fixations.

It is worth considering whether Fräulein Anna O was a multiple. When she was 'at her best and most free she talked French and Italian. There was complete amnesia between these times and those at which she talked English. At this point too, her squint began to diminish and made its appearance only at moments of great excitement' (Freud 1893–4: 25). A little while later she only spoke in English and 'could not understand what was said to her in German'.

Coleridge wrote of a young woman of 24 or 25 who 'could neither read nor write, was seized with a nervous fever during which she continued incessantly talking Latin, Greek and Hebrew'. In her 'first' state she recognised her surroundings and was relatively normal but in her 'second' state she hallucinated, was abusive and 'naughty'. She saw her hair as black snakes. She complained 'of having two selves, a real one and an evil one which forced her to behave badly'. The 'second' personality or alter in MPD is usually more vivacious and 'naughty' than the primary host (Hacking 1995).

Klein (1935) underpinned the concepts of vertical and horizontal splitting as a primitive defence. By horizontal splitting the mind is divided in two, with each separate relationship co-existing, whereas vertical splitting is a process whereby repression moves one part of the mind into the unconscious without destroying it. Later (1952) she comments on how repression does not normally result in the disintegration of the self because it comes at a later stage, but that splitting processes in the first few months of life can vitally affect later use of repression. The concept of splitting was Freud's development of the older concept of dissociation but as we move into Kleinian theory the richness of theoretical underpinning nevertheless moves further away from traumatic aetiology. It is useful to explore Klein when thinking of traumatic sadistic abuse in that the splitting of the ego and the fragmenting attack on the object are there, but from parent to child rather than the other way round.

Fairbairn (1931, 1944) is one of the few psychoanalysts to try to develop Freud's concepts of multiplicity further. In both 'Features in the analysis of a patient with a physical genital abnormality' and 'Endopsychic structure considered in terms of object relations' he returns to Freud's first attempt to reveal the structure of multiple personality. He comments that Freud found himself compelled to postulate the existence of a structure capable of instigating repression – i.e. the super-ego. He said

It is therefore only another step in the same direction to postulate the existence of structures which are repressed . . . repressed 'impulses' are inseparable from an ego structure with a definite pattern. The correctness of this assumption is confirmed by the phenomena of multiple personality in which the linkage of repressed 'impulses' with a submerged ego structure is beyond question; but such a linkage may also be detected in the less extensive forms of dissociation which are so characteristic of the hysteric individual. In order to account for repression, we thus appear to be driven to the necessity of assuming a certain multiplicity of egos.

(Fairbairn 1944: 90)

Brearley (1986: 151–67) speaks of

the stranger within: the form of life within each of us that is to some degree alien to that lived by our conscious selves. Such splits are most glaring in multiple personalities . . . These splits are also striking in the perversions where people who for the most part lead rational and sober lives find themselves compelled to enact in some corner of their lives sexual fantasies which strike themselves as utterly bizarre and incomprehensible.

However, he does not provide contemporary case material for MPD.

Not surprisingly it is to the American psychoanalytic literature we need to look for help with this subject. Just as sexual abuse and ritual abuse were represented in the American journals 10 years before England, dissociative disorders have also been well researched there, although the lack of a real engagement with theory has been noted.

In a ground-breaking issue of *Psychoanalytic Inquiry* (Volume 12 1992) devoted to Multiple Personality Disorder, leading psychoanalysts struggled to deal adequately with this subject. Kluft (1992: 139–72) accounts for some of the difficulties in that he feels the subject brings a challenge to prevailing paradigms of mental function. Using Kuhn's work he argues that when an older paradigm cannot account adequately for a subject, the psychoanalytic clinicians find it 'profoundly jarring'. Without help from existing psychoanalytic models the analyst can go 'into strange waters, where a difficult and strange definitely non psychoanalytic literature . . . awaits'.

Kluft (1992) also importantly draws attention to the common error of psychoanalytic clinicians that Anna herself referred to – to take a suppressive role in insisting that all alters talk as one or that only the alter with the legal name should be validated: 'Such stances are commonly associated with therapeutic failure'. He emphasises that, because MPD often results when children were not protected, silence, 'neutrality' and blandness 'Will be perceived as uncaring and rejecting and make the traumatic transference more difficult to address . . . In general trauma victims do not tolerate a neutral therapist . . . Taking a warmer and more active stance and interrupting stances is helpful'. This is also true for working with patients with learning disability, abused children (Sinason 1993) and autistic children (Alvarez 1992).

Training analyst Sheldon Roth (1992: 112–24) helps us into the emotional world of DID by reminding us that each night in dreams we experience that world and in the morning, 'Like the host personality of a multiple we have partial or total amnesia for our complex nocturnal alter activities.' He reminds us of the terrible depth of the trauma these patients have experienced and the way the dissociated experiences 'symbolised by alters, howl about the multiple personality like mysterious family ghosts, seeking a proper transference figure to bring surcease through revenge and grief. Alters, like dream symbols, disguise unbearable affects.' He reminds us too of the developmental points that are frozen in child alters and that 'Adult pain can never cease until some accommodation is made with the pains of childhood.'

At this stage of work it is hard to bring together analytic theories and the processes that other clinicians have identified in America. For example, I am deeply indebted to David Neswald's basic mind-control program reassociation procedure. A psychotherapist in California specialising in PTSD, he found that many MPD/DID patients had been programmed to make certain responses. For example, the mention of a doctor's appointment in Annette caused an internal attack. David Neswald is keen to get alters together to share their memory fragments so that the programming for self-punishment (among others) can be defused. I have been deeply shocked at the layers of quite formal brainwashing in certain patients but will not be able to write about that until the research project is over. However, as psychoanalytic psychotherapists we find we are light years behind the military in understanding how to work with military indoctrination, torture, brainwashing and programming and we need to be theoretically and clinically capable of coming to grips with these subjects.

Certain ideas have been more fruitful for me than others. Southgate (1996) makes clear that all of us move fluidly from different emotional and chronological states in a day. For example, we can be involved in a 2-year-old tantrum. However, if a real child came in we would hopefully become an adult again. In other words we are associating multiples. However, through trauma, these patients have become fixated (as Janet says), pinned like butterflies to the moment of terror, so that they are not free to move into a different state.

Time is not a continuous narrative. Each alter is confined to its own cell, its own torture room. The terrible cognitive and emotional impingements have destroyed faith in the continuity of developments. Just as a crying baby feeling near death does not know its mother will come back in time, each alter does not know there will ever be safety. The locked room is always there. A scream resounds forever. Can we bear to hear? If we can, and if we are supported in creating a holding situation (in the absence of adequate facilities for DID/MPD patients in the UK), then slowly, very slowly, the terrible memories that the dissociation succeeded in fragmenting can come together again and some integration and hope can take place. To do this we need to appreciate the courage of the host and the alters and the tasks they have borne and the way they have carried them out.

ACKNOWLEDGEMENTS

With thanks to David Leevers, Joan Coleman, Peter Fonagy, Mervin Glasser, Sarah Gordon, Rob Hale, Brett Kahr, Carole Mallard, Phil Mollon, John Morton, Susie Orbach, John and Kate Southgate, Joe Schwarz, Ainsley Gray, Pearl King, Tina Carlile, Mario Marrone, Nicola Diamond, Liz Campbell, Patsy and Eduardo Pitchon, Claire Usiskin.

REFERENCES

Alvarez, A. (1992) *Live Company*. London: Routledge.

Brearley, M. (1986) 'Psychoanalysis: A form of life?', talk given at the J.R. Jones Memorial Lecture at the University College of Swansea, October 1986. Reprinted in A. Phillips Griffiths (ed.) (1991) *Wittgenstein Centenary Essays*, pp. 151–67. Cambridge: Cambridge University Press.

Fairbairn, W.R.D. (1931) 'Features in the analysis of a patient with a physical genital abnormality', in *Psychoanalytic Studies of the Personality* (1992) London: Tavistock.

Fairbairn, W.R.D. (1944) 'Endopsychic structure considered in terms of object relations', in *Psychoanalytic Studies of the Personality* (1992) London. Tavistock.

Freud, S. (1893–4) 'Studies on hysteria', in *The Standard Edition of the Complete Psychological Works of Sigmund Freud*, vol. 2. London: Hogarth Press.

Freud, S. (1923) 'The ego and the id', in *The Standard Edition of the Complete Psychological Works of Sigmund Freud*, vol. 19, pp. 30–1. London: Hogarth Press.

Hacking, I. (1995) *Rewriting the Soul: Multiple Personality and the Sciences of Memory*. London: Princeton University Press.

Klein, M. (1935) 'A contribution to the psychogenesis of manic depressive states', *The Writings of Melanie Klein*, vol. 1, pp. 262–89. London: Hogarth Press.

Klein, M. (1952) 'Some theoretical conclusions regarding the emotional life of the infant', *The Writings of Melanie Klein*, vol. 3, pp. 61–93. London: Hogarth Press.

Kluft, R. (1992) 'A specialist's perspective on multiple personality disorder', *Psychoanalytic Inquiry* 12(1): 139–72.

Roth, Sheldon (1992) 'A psychoanalyst's perspective on multiple personality disorder', *Psychoanalytic Inquiry* 12(1): 112–24.

Sinason, M. (1993) 'Who is the mad voice inside?' *Psychoanalytic Psychotherapy* 7: 207–21.

Southgate, J. (1996) 'An attachment approach to dissociation and multiplicity', paper presented at the Third John Bowlby Memorial Lecture, Centre for Attachment-based Psychoanalytic Psychotherapy, London.

Chapter 8

Snow White and the seven diagnoses

Jean Goodwin

This chapter is the result of a prolonged quest, a quest for the fairy tale that best illustrates and encapsulates major dissociative disorders – their clinical picture, their developmental origins, and their natural history, especially the trajectory toward healing when this can occur.

Experience taught me the utility of finding the right fairy tale. A generation ago in the 1970s when I first began to treat incest victims, I was fortunate to encounter the long-suppressed Grimms' fairytale, 'Thousandfurs' (Grimm and Grimm 1977). This is the story of a princess whose mother dies and whose father turns to the daughter in his loneliness, finally insisting that she become his wife. The girl refuses, objects, bargains, asking for gifts so impossible that she is certain her demands will defeat the father's forbidden imperative. To her horror, the father persists, producing each fantastic gift in turn, including the cloak made of the furs of a thousand animals, the gift she had believed utterly beyond the reach even of a king. However, being a flexible and resourceful princess, she realizes at once that she has now exhausted the possibilities for negotiation; so she dons the cloak of a thousand furs and flees to the forest, thereby assuming the identity of 'Thousandfurs', an uncharted species that combines wildness and sophistication, the beast and the princess. The remainder of the story concerns the careful empathic, reparative work done by the prince who discovers her in the forest and persuades her to resume her human identity. Step by step he confounds her expectations that he will be as self-centred, intrusive, unempathic, oblivious and exploitative as was her father. This prince sees and appreciates her hidden treasures of goodness, beauty and wholeness. He keeps trying to connect with her no matter how many times she eludes and escapes, outwitting his efforts to penetrate her disguises. At last she feels safe and supported enough to resume her rightful place as his beautiful and beloved princess. This map for the healing journey out of the wilderness of childhood sexual abuse has never led me astray and often has set me back on the right track in moments of empathic failure or impasse.

I was doubly fortunate, next, to discover a second fairy tale, 'Manekine' (Goodwin 1982), in the 1980s just as I was beginning to work with women whose symptoms and childhood trauma were more frightening and disabling and whose frustrating patterns of self-harm, chronic anger and treatment resistance often had been labeled borderline. Once again, the right fairy tale, this time obscure and Hungarian, found in a moldering Victorian tome in a musty corner of Harvard's Widener Library, answered my most pressing clinical questions. 'Manekine' grows up in a more violent and disturbed family than does 'Thousandfurs'. Her father suffers a severe clinical depression after mother's death. His incest proposal is couched in the language of physical threat, not bribes. Both father and daughter threaten suicide and self-harm. Like 'Thousandfurs', 'Manekine' manages to get away at last, but not with all her parts intact; she has lost the power of speech and her right arm. Also, the prince who finds Manekine is a far cry from the consummately sensitive character we met in 'Thousandfurs'. His family is as abusive as hers and he compounds this stress by going off to war; so 'Manekine's' violence victimization continues into adulthood. This lifetime of violence and running away culminates in the neglect and eventual death of her own beloved child. Finally, just as Manekine – isolated, homeless, non-functioning – reaches the absolute nadir of her multi-problem life journey, the fairy tale amazingly finds her a way out. In a holy city, in the presence of a healing fountain, she overhears both father and husband as they acknowledge their violations of her and their readiness to make amends. Suddenly, her severed arm reappears in the flow of the fountain and reconnects to her body just as her dead baby comes splashing toward her alive and happy, reaching up to embrace her. So 'Manekine', no longer a mannequin but once again a real person, finds her voice and reclaims her roles as princess daughter and queenly wife.

Once again, I found this tale to be an unerring guide to the childhood situation, the frustrating clinical course, the tasks of therapy in this more troubled group of survivors. Of course, it is a more difficult map (Goodwin 1990), one which asks us essentially for miracles. It may require many voices – family therapy, group therapy, therapists working in a team – to persuade this princess that violence is the problem and that what happened in childhood was not her fault. It requires similarly heroic therapeutic efforts to convince such a survivor of the miraculous healing powers of her own tears (the fountain) and of the aliveness and richness that still survive beneath the disguises – the numbing and mutilation of the self – that have so long been her protection from attack (Attias and Goodwin 1999). I recall one such survivor saying, 'I thought there was nothing left of me. I thought they had taken everything. But they hadn't quite.' Only when she is convinced that the body self that remains is really her own living self, not just a mannequin, do ideas about self-care and safety have any meaning.

So far, so good, except that the exigencies of my clinical practice continued to escalate. By the late 1980s I was caring for women who described all the problems of 'Thousandfurs', all the brutalities of 'Manekine's' life story and more. Like 'Thousandfurs' they had run away and were still running, certain they were beastly and monstrous in some way and beyond the pale of the princely. Like

'Manekine' they self-mutilated and had been re-abused in adulthood and feared for the fate of their children. Some functions seemed lost forever. But this new group of survivors in addition displayed multiple self-states in a way that went far beyond the princess–beast or princess–mannequin dichotomies I had worked with before. Some of these identities seemed like children, others like critical and cruel incarnations of abusers. At times these patients fell into deep sleep-like trances and became mute; seizures and catatonia had often been diagnostic worries. There were too many diagnoses of all kinds and too many different specialists with too many different ideas about what was wrong. The body was treated at times as an irrelevant appendage; huge swathes of sensory experience and autobiographical history might similarly be relegated suddenly to a place of banishment outside conscious awareness. There was so much immersion in fantasy, often fantasy about actual traumatic incidents, that often we could no longer discern which images described actual narratives of trauma – early or recent – and which represented intrusive recollections or brooding elaborations of past hurts. Episodes that seemed at first to be narratives of re-abuse might turn out to be experiences of psychotic flashbacks, so vivid that the survivor believed the trauma was actually happening again. It was as if in the process of running, the self had whirled itself into so many pieces, now so alienated from each other, that it was impossible to gather them all up in a single space and time – a place like the sacred fountain that 'Manekine' found; so in these cases the necessary miracle of restoration could not take place.

Thus began my quest for a third fairy tale. 'Beauty and the Beast' came close to what I was looking for. The 'Beauty' self and the 'Beast' body find themselves somehow at war. Only when 'Beauty' becomes able to see 'Beast' when she looks into the mirror does she come to embrace the magnificence of her own body, to be grateful for its devotion to her and to honour its need that she care deeply for it in return. This story centres us in the somatic problems of dissociation. But what about the alternate identities? The derealization, amnesia and trancing? The comorbidities? I kept on searching.

Then a few weeks ago in the same week two patients, both with Dissociative Identity Disorder, told me the names of alters I had not yet befriended; one was 'Sleepy', the other 'Sneezy'. So I went back and re-read my first favourite fairy tale and it turns out this is the one for which I had been looking all along.

SNOW WHITE AND THE SEVEN DIAGNOSES

Once I looked with enlightened eyes at this story, I saw a familiar situation. An extremely attractive and appealing young woman is fleeing from a murderously abusive childhood situation ('I will run off through the wild woods and never come home again'). She feels helped by childlike identities who seem to be accessible mostly at night (the dwarfs, we are told, stay down in the deep unconscious of the mines all day). She feels hounded and murderously stalked by a persecutor entity, the wicked Queen. Several adult male entities (the huntsman and the Prince) seem to contain the strength she needs to combat the Queen and extricate herself from perpetual entrapment in victim–persecutor interactions. But Snow White is not certain she can trust these men and flees from them as well. The protective dwarfs try, with varying levels of success, to keep Snow White safe from the murderous Queen. They also introduce her to the delights of ordinary daily living, outside the world of abuse. There are clues that even the Queen might have some insight that she herself belongs, as the dwarfs do, to Snow White's inner system. 'Snow White must die', says the Queen, 'even if it costs me my own life'. Unfortunately, this insight does not deter the Queen from proceeding to deploy all her powers in the all-out effort to destroy Snow White. However, in psychotherapy, this would be a major step – to help the persecutory alter realize that the death of the body would mean that all the alters would die, including the persecutor herself. As it is, all these self-states live in perpetual warfare, which in turn leads to self-isolation, angry outbursts, mood shifts, constant fears and hyperalertness, dissociative flights, and self-destructive acts. Snow White experiences many other common dissociative symptoms: the need to reconstruct her day from the position of objects in the house, mirrors that give unexpected and upsetting feedback, trance states so deep as to simulate death and dissociative episodes in which she loses her breath, falls into a dead faint, punctures herself and ingests toxic substances.

The symptoms are so numerous that long ago I developed a mnemonic to help me remember them (Goodwin et al. 1990). The acronym BAD FEARS reminds me to screen for Borderline personality disorder, Affective disorders, Dissociative symptoms, Fears and anxiety disorders including post-traumatic anxiety, Eating disorders, Alcoholism and substance abuse, Re-abuse, Suicidality and Somatization. I was intrigued to find that the Disney Studios' names for the dwarfs fit rather nicely into the BAD FEARS table sketched below. The dwarfs must be supplemented by the other ego-state characters – Snow White, the Poison Apple and the Wicked Queen – whose interplay provides much of the self-destructive action in the plot. However, it was pleasing that the Disney version of the story provides its own new set of mnemonics for the comorbidities in Dissociative Disorders.

Problem list	*Disney character*
Borderline personality	Grumpy
Affective disorder	Happy
Dissociative symptoms	Sleepy, Snow White
Fears and anxiety	Bashful
Eating disorder	The Poison Apple (Queen/Snow White/Prince)
Alcoholism/substance abuse	Dopey
Re-abuse, suicidality	The wicked Queen
Somatization	Sneezy, Doc, The mirror

It is not fashionable to cite Disney versions when applying fairy tales to clinical questions. However, it seems likely that the people in the Disney Studios possess an unconscious, too. It seems possible that the Disney unconscious may be even closer to our own than those of the storytellers who spoke with the brothers Grimm. So when the Disney version becomes overly intrigued by the dwarfs and overly punishing of the Queen, we perhaps should worry that these may presage our own countertransference tendencies at the present sociocultural moment.

Personally, I am grateful for any clinical clues, no matter where I find them, and the Disney version of the BAD FEARS mnemonic seems apt in many ways. 'Grumpy' recalls the intense irritability in these patients often secondary to the exhausting effort to keep all the parts satisfied and contained. 'Happy' reminds me that undiagnosed bipolar mood disorder – an excess of 'happy' at times – can be the cause of continuing severe symptoms and treatment unresponsiveness in some cases (Wills and Goodwin 1996). Both 'Sleepy' and Snow White display the shifting levels of consciousness and awareness that characterize dissociation. 'Bashful' is a reminder that in some patients the post-traumatic anxiety will present as social phobia; this fear of being with people relates both to the fragmented self-image and to fears that alters will appear without warning. The odd eating problem in Snow White illustrates the involvement of several alters which is the usual pattern in dissociation (Goodwin and Attias 1993). The Queen prepares the pathological food, Snow White ingests it, and the Prince arranges for it to be disgorged. In a clinical case, one finds one alter shopping for binge foods, another ambivalently undertaking the binge, and yet another handling the purge aspect of the cycle. When something even more toxic is ingested, as in an overdose, the pattern again involves several different alters. The protective dwarf alter who finally brings the system to the emergency room may have only a sketchy notion of what was planned or what was actually done to the body. Sometimes the ambulance ride proves to be a false alarm; at others something even more grave may have been done to the body than the protective alters suspect. Uncomplaining (and mute) 'Dopey' is the most loveable dwarf of all, reminding us that when love has come seldom, the ingestion of massive disabling quantities of toxins may seem a small price to pay for this scarce and precious commodity. Finally, the trio of 'Sneezy', 'Doc', and the mirror sketches accurately the confusing situation that may develop when a dissociative patient comes to the doctor for help. The target symptom may prove to be localized in only one alter; 'Sneezy' may sneeze constantly regardless of treatment; if other alters are asked about the symptom they may be oblivious (nineteenth-century observers called this 'la belle indifference'). 'Doc' will usually handle doctor visits with great enthusiasm. However, unless the care provider takes into account that 'Doc' is only one-tenth of the system (if that), that provider is at risk of overestimating the patient's investment in the treatment and likelihood of compliance. Psychotherapists have conceptualized this 'Doc' alter as an internal self helper (the 'ISH') which can be of critical use in treatment but whose particular viewpoint and limitations must be understood (Comstock 1991). The mirror problems in dissociation mean that 'Doc' may not be able to see 'Sneezy' in either an actual mirror or a subjective, sensory mirror. When the doctor asks whether the symptom is better or worse, 'Doc' may have no idea.

PRECURSORS TO THE SEVEN CHILD ALTERS: DEATH FEARS, CRUEL PARENTING AND THE MIXED UP ATTACHMENT MIRROR

Our best data on the antecedents of major dissociative disorders suggest physical abuse, sexual abuse and attachment difficulties as the most significant environmental precursors (Draijer and Langeland 1999). I have posited (Goodwin 1985) that for a child to flee as far as Snow White fled – to the outer limits of the self – the threat probably encompasses bodily death. I have also wondered whether active sadistic cruelty (Goodwin 1993a, b) must be added to the traumatic disruption of bodily attack in the absence of a holding environment in order to prevent the traumatized child from recapturing and reassembling the goodness and permanence of the self.

Snow White adds flesh to these statistics and theories. Both 'Thousandfurs' and 'Manekine' must flee their families because of threats and physical attack, and, like Snow White, both have dead mothers. But only in Snow White is the abusive parent cruel enough to pursue the fleeing daughter, stalking and deliberately trying to destroy her. We have here not only neglect but also a malignant over-involvement (Gelinas 1993). Like other sadistic perpetrators the wicked Queen acquires accomplices (the mirror, the huntsman) and vents her ire on any dwarfs who presume to assist her victim; she threatens mutilation and cannibalism (cutting out the lungs and liver and stewing and eating them). She is also adept at elevating her sadistic aims to a moral agenda; when the mirror claims the Wicked Queen as 'fairest' we hear both meanings of the adjective; the Queen doesn't look like a villain and the 'right-thinking' mirror has somehow claimed justice and fairness for her side; it is her victims and their allies whose motives are more likely to be questioned.

Snow White's attachment problems are another consequence of this malignant narcissism. We are told at the beginning that the pinnacle of this child's parenting occurred before her birth when her 'good mother' narcissistically and dissociatively fantasized an aesthetically perfect baby while at the same time self-mutilating by pricking her pregnant body with a needle. This was as good as it ever got for Snow White. The 'bad mother' seems unable to see the child at all except for the clues she gleans from looking at herself in the mirror. It is not clear that anyone has ever looked at this girl with delighted love, cherishing her real body and the self that inhabits it. Perhaps this is why the dwarfs have such trouble teaching Snow White to keep that body safe and why the glass casket – which allows her to be seen in all three dimensions – is such a healing antidote to the mirror with its rigid, binary good–bad judgments.

None of this contradicts the traditional Oedipal interpretations of the inter-personal difficulties between Snow White and the wicked Queen (Bettelheim 1975). It's just that Oedipal problems become particularly insoluble (Horney 1945) when one begins with a mixed-up attachment situation, adds a parent who has the unresolved greed and envy of a 5-year-old, tosses in actual bodily attack with threats of killing or mutilation and throws in for good measure deliberate sadistic cruelty. No wonder this parent imago ends up as a persecu-tory alter rather than a core identificatory figure that could stabilize Snow White's gender identity and sexual aims. No wonder it is the child's feminin-ity that is so vulnerable to attack – with corsets, with combs, with food. No wonder she is too frightened to allow herself to become attached to anyone at all, much less the Prince. No wonder it requires the voices of all seven dwarfs to help her superego cleave to what is right for her and stay away from what is wrong and hurtful.

SNOW WHITE AND THE SEVEN THERAPISTS

The dwarfs' cottage in the forest can be seen as an ideal kind of therapeutic community for patients who dissociate. The surroundings are wild and intri-cate, frightening at first but ultimately proof that nature persists despite human evil (Goodwin and Talwar 1989) and champions and weeps for hurt human children as do the owl, the raven and the dove in this story. At first glance Snow White sees that this is a space designed for people to sleep, eat, drink, be with one another – in contrast to the castle where the furnishings seem limited to judgmental mirrors. There are dwarfs enough, perspectives enough, so that Snow White can find someone, depending her ego state, that 'suits' her, like the bed that feels 'just right'. These therapists do not hover; they are off on their own mining the unconscious for many hours each day. But they are there when Snow White needs them which is mostly at night; they work in shifts so that one is awake at all times just in case she needs company. In contrast to the Queen who cannot see Snow White at all, the dwarfs notice everything. They can tell from the depredations to their larder, from the repositioning of objects that she has been there even before she trusts them enough to show herself, even before she trusts them enough to speak.

What do these model psychotherapists say? They ask her name and how she came to them. They give her some rules and healing activities ('wash and sew and knit') and insist that she keep order. They understand about the return of the repressed and about repetition compulsions and ask Snow White to watch out for intrusions from her traumatic past ('Watch out for your stepmother. She'll soon find out you are here') even in the sanctuary they have created together (Bloom 1999). In the beginning, almost all their interventions deal with safety (van der Kolk and van der Hart 1989; Herman 1992). We hear them warning Snow White not only about the dangers of her own internalized persecutors but also about her difficulties recognizing the new, re-enacting abusers who may appear in the present day external world and against whom she is remarkably helpless. Beyond the helplessness they seem also to appreciate Snow White's deep attachment to sadomasochistic violence; 'anyone who saw it would want it, but anyone who ate even the teeniest bit of it would die'; the addictive qualities of this pattern are acknowledged but so are the dreadful risks. Another familiar quality I find in these therapists is how much time they must spend waking Snow White up. It seems that every time they make a comment she nods off. These are active therapists, jolting her, washing her, making sure she is not dead. Finally, as the most murderous moments with the wicked Queen are reconstructed, 'all seven sat down beside her and mourned and they wept for three whole days'. 'Manekine' had been able at last to produce her own tears, but Snow White is too numbed, too depersonalized, too amnestic and fragmented to grieve what has been done to her. The seven therapists are the first to see the horror, to tally up all that has been lost. The final reconstructions rediscover and reframe what was positive in her past. If the huntsman is any measure of how protective the better parent was, this was desperately slight protection ('not having to kill her was a great weight off his mind'). None the less, these dwarfs believe that even this tiny bit counts and write in gold on the coffin, 'She was a king's daughter'. These kernels of golden love now become part of all that is visible and beautiful about Snow White. At some point the therapists start looking better, also – more like princes than like dwarfs. Reconstruction continues up to the moment of integration (the wedding), as they continue to 'stumble over roots' in ways that jolt Snow White into greater awareness. Always the relationship is the orienting polestar of the work. 'Where am I?' asks Snow White. 'With me!' the prince answers joyfully.

The Grimms' story ends with a powerful image of integration. Not even the wicked Queen can keep herself away from the integration festivities, the wedding, that crowns Snow White's recovery. The Queen is too curious, and also too integrated already to keep herself separate. We know at some level that it is the partial integration of the Queen's aggressive and sexual powers that has allowed Snow White to come this far, to declare herself queen in her own right. But how to achieve a final integration of this entity, so caught up in persecutory fantasy, so averse to empathy and co-operation? Couldn't this self-state simply perish or vanish or go somewhere far away? The fairy tale gives us a Delphic answer to these questions; the Queen is simultaneously banished, punished and integrated. The problem is that the Queen lacks the fundamental skill necessary for integration, the capacity to step into someone else's shoes. The story tells us this by giving her iron shoes that have been heated to incandescence in the fire. As the Queen tries to enter the dance, the impossibility of the task consumes and melts her; so it is a melted Queen who is integrated at the end, all her impurities dissolved away in the therapeutic forge of integration.

CONCLUSION

Snow White is a girl with shifting states of consciousness, who is preoccupied with imaginary persons and who describes herself as fleeing from murderous child abuse. The seven dwarfs can be understood variously as representing: (1) her multiple psychiatric diagnoses; (2) the multiple child alters that grow out of her efforts to deal with childhood trauma that included bodily attacks, death threats and disrupted attachments; and/or (3) the multi-therapist, multi-modal treatment team approach that is most likely to be successful in these cases. Multiple therapists – whether in a residential or outpatient team setting – function helpfully at many levels: to provide the manpower to address the multiple problems; to interact optimally with the multiple alters; to stave off therapeutic exhaustion and burnout; to respond to vast unmet needs for mirroring and nurture; to combat jointly the patient's intense temptations to return to a world of sadomasochistic violence; and to confront the dissociative defenses actively and consistently enough to keep the patient awake and able to remember and integrate the therapeutic work. Not only is the multiplicity of therapists – their seven-ness – helpful to Snow White, it is also crucial to the dwarfs' own well-being and continued functioning. This is most clear when they support each other in their grieving at a point when Snow White cannot possibly share the feeling; she is too disconnected from her own cognitive, emotional and sensory experience to understand that there is anything to grieve. This need is also apparent at those moments when the dwarfs share with each other the burden of trying to keep Snow White alive. A lone therapist might succumb to discouragement in the face of Snow White's convincing simulation of death for 'years and years'. The seven dwarfs remind each other that she is not really dead at all. All that is just an illusion. And they work cheerfully on.

REFERENCES

Attias, R. and Goodwin, J. (1999) 'A place to begin: Images of the body in transformation'. In: J. Goodwin and R. Attias (eds), *Splintered Reflections: Images of the Body in Trauma* (pp. 287–304). New York: Basic Books.

Bettelheim, B. (1975) *The Uses of Enchantment: The Meaning and Importance of Fairy Tales*. New York: Knopf.

Bloom, S. (1999) *Creating Sanctuary: Toward the Evolution of Sane Societies*. New York: Routledge.

Comstock, C. (1991) 'The Inner Self Helper and concepts of inner guidance: Historical antecedents, role within dissociation, and clinical utilization'. *Dissociation*, 4: 165–177.

Draijer, N. and Langeland, W. (1999) 'Childhood trauma and perceived parental dysfunction in the etiology of dissociative symptoms in psychiatric inpatients'. *American Journal of Psychiatry*, 156: 379–385.

Gelinas, D. (1993) 'Relational patterns in incestuous families, malevolent variations, and specific interventions with the adult survivors'. In: P. Paddison (ed.), *Treatment of Adult Survivors of Incest* (pp. 1–36). Washington, DC: American Psychiatric Press.

Goodwin, J. (1982) *Sexual Abuse: Incest Victims and Their Families*. Littleton, MA: Wright/PSG.

Goodwin, J. (1985) 'Post-traumatic symptoms in incest victims'. In: S. Eth and R. Pynoos (eds), *Post-Traumatic Stress Disorder in Children* (pp. 157–168). Washington, DC: American Psychiatric Press.

Goodwin, J. (1990) 'Applying to adult incest victims what we have learned from victimized children'. In: R. Kluft (ed.), *Incest Related Syndromes of Psychopathology* (pp. 55–74). Washington, DC: American Psychiatric Press.

Goodwin, J. (1993a) *Rediscovering Childhood Trauma: Historical Casebook and Clinical Applications*. Washington, DC: American Psychiatric Press.

Goodwin, J. (1993b) 'Sadistic abuse: Recognition, definition, and treatment'. *Dissociation*, 6: 181–187.

Goodwin, J. and Attias, R. (1993) 'Eating disorders in survivors of multimodal child abuse'. In: R. Kluft and C. Fine (eds), *Clinical Perspectives on Multiple Personality Disorder* (pp. 327–341). Washington, DC: American Psychiatric Press.

Goodwin, J., Cheeves, K. and Connell, V. (1990) 'Borderline and other severe symptoms in adult survivors of incestuous abuse'. *Psychiatric Annals*, 20: 22–32.

Goodwin, J. and Talwar, N. (1989) 'Group psychotherapy for incest victims'. *Psychiatric Clinics of North America*, 12: 279–293.

Grimm, J. and Grimm, W. (1819/1977) *Grimms' Tales for Young and Old: The Complete Stories*. New York: Doubleday.

Herman, J. (1992) *Trauma and Recovery*. New York: Basic Books.

Horney, K. (1945) *Our Inner Conflicts*. New York: W.W. Norton.

van der Kolk, B. and van der Hart, O. (1989) 'Pierre Janet and the breakdown of adaptation in psychological trauma'. *American Journal of Psychiatry*, 146: 1530–1539.

Wills, S. and Goodwin, J. (1996) 'Recognizing Bipolar Illness in patients with Dissociative Identity Disorder'. *Dissociation*, 9: 104–109.

Chapter 9

Will you sit by her side?

An attachment-based approach to work with dissociative conditions

Sue Richardson

> Do you see? Do you hear?
> Look at that little creature cowering there
> in a corner of my soul,
> shivering and wailing like the lost dead,
> moaning her misery and pain.
> In vain I call her to come
> into the shelter of my love.
> Long, long ago, she learned not to trust,
> fearing the trembling must turn to
> such severe shaking
> the vibration would dissolve her entirely,
> scattering her being irrevocably wide.
>
> Will you go to her? Will you sit by her side?
> Will you touch her,
> holding fast when she flinches,
> expecting pain again?
> Will you patiently sit,
> waiting till she hears your breathing,
> feels your body warmth, hears your song?
>
> Gently now! She moves
> 　　　　　　　　　Constance Nightingale 1988

In my work with traumatised adults, I have found Constance Nightingale's poem a useful template from which to understand dissociation. Frequently, it is the 'little creature' within the traumatised adult who is in need of containing contact. Where that is successfully accomplished, there is a process of emergence, captured so vividly in the poem.

Through the poem I am exploring the following questions:

- what is the nature of the self described in the poem as the 'little creature'?
- what are its origins?

- what is the purpose of its existence ?
- how can it be recognised ?
- how can it be contacted and communicated with?
- how can its existence be transformed and brought into a relationship as part of a whole?

It is interesting that there is no consistent term used to denote this kind of self. In the poem, this self is described as a 'little creature'. One person has called it a 'secret self'. Alice Miller (1986) refers to a 'nearly autistic being'. It has been termed by one contemporary clinician as the 'sacred self' (Nijenhuis 1998) and by another as a 'core personality' (Bryant et al. 1992). It corresponds to Guntrip's (1968) 'withdrawn self' and to Winnicott's (1965) 'true self in cold storage'.

The absence of consistent terminology may be symptomatic of the nature of this kind of self: his or her fear of being known and a need for extensive concealment through expecting pain again. There may be a lack of connection with the world of language, and a profound depth of isolation. This self may be what Guntrip (1968) refers to as the patient's deepest 'withdrawness' and the essence of what he suggests needs to be reached to get at the real roots of his trouble.

I have found that the little creature described in the poem can best be understood and worked with by bringing together developments in knowledge and research in the field of attachment and the field of dissociation.

THE ORIGINS OF THE LITTLE CREATURE: THE PROCESS OF DISSOCIATION FROM AN ATTACHMENT PERSPECTIVE

Psychological trauma has been defined as 'The sudden uncontrollable loss of affiliative bonds' (Lindemann 1944, quoted in Zulueta 1993). The experience of overwhelming fear with no safe place to go activates the attachment system and proximity seeking but without a termination point being reached.

Bowlby (1980) describes how the persistent arousal of the attachment system and failure to respond to it, especially when accompanied by actively damaging responses from caregivers, can result in the de-activation of systems mediating attachment behaviour. He discusses the defensive exclusion of information from processing as an adaptive response to certain types of painful experience. He also considers that adult disconfirmation of unbearable childhood experience can be accompanied by the formation of multiple working models of the self and attachment figures (Bowlby 1988).

There is an interesting trend in the dissociation literature to view dissociative conditions as a disorder of attachment. Barach (1991) focuses on Bowlby's construct of detachment as the foundation of DID while Liotti (1992) favours disorganised patterns of attachment as the antecedent of adult dissociation. The authors' shared view that dissociation can be understood as a way of resolving the dilemma of attachment to an abusive caregiver is developed by others such as Blizard (1997a, b), Blizard and Bluhm (1994), Howell (1997) and Ross (1997).

The little creature can thus be understood as a dissociated part of the self. It is most often seen in individuals who have suffered abuse from a caregiver, which they have had to learn to endure in order to maintain their attachment to the abuser.

THE NATURE OF THE LITTLE CREATURE AS A DISSOCIATED PART OF THE SELF

I want to distinguish between two groups of children on the spectrum of dissociation. First, there are those whose model of self and other is based on reasonably secure attachment or at least a basic quality of primary caregiving before suffering trauma. This first group can be broken down into two subgroups:

1 Those who are subsequently protected, supported and enabled to process the experience. Dissociation is not the inevitable outcome for this group (Richardson and Bacon 1991).
2 Those who are left unprotected and unsupported thus laying the foundations for a dissociative condition. This group may vary in their place on the spectrum of dissociation.

The second group consists of those who have never known good enough attachment and who have been traumatised at an early age. This group may end up at the most severe end of the spectrum of dissociation.

The latter are illustrated in the poem. They are the little creatures who are the most deeply buried and the most hard to find. Guntrip (1968) gives a vivid description of: 'an utterly isolated being, too denuded of experience to be able to feel like a person, unable to communicate with others and never reached by others'.

This kind of experience has been described as a 'developmental void' (Messler Davies 1997) in which the 'dissociated core' of the self has been characterised as 'an absence, rather than genuine psychic content' (Fonagy 1999). With the possible exception of children such as Romanian orphans whose brains have been seriously damaged by maternal privation, this concept is challenged by the presence of the little creature. The void can be regarded as a gap in consciousness and in the void is a dissociative self with the capacity for agency.

AN ATTACHMENT-BASED VIEW OF THE KEY FEATURES OF THE LITTLE CREATURE AS A DISSOCIATED SELF

He or she belongs to a goal-directed system

Goal-directed behaviour to reach the goal of careseeking has to address constant discrepancies and incompatible data emanating from caregivers whose behaviour is abusive or who are failing to provide protection.

The goal-directed behaviour of the system containing the little creature is therefore geared towards two conflicting sets of needs. First, both to maintain a safe distance from and avoid proximity to untrustworthy caregivers and to parts of the self which threaten internal chaos. The latter can include

- the little creature as the part which contains the memory of the trauma and fears becoming disorganised: 'fearing the vibration would dissolve her entirely, scattering her being irrevocably wide'.
- parts of the self who reduce their feelings of anxiety and fear of internal chaos and maintain competency by avoiding the little creature
- parts of the self whose working model is based on the behaviour and beliefs of the abuser and can appear persecutory.

Second, behaviour needs to be directed towards the goal of maintaining attachment to a caregiver even though they may be untrustworthy. Ross (1997) identifies the child's need to keep the attachment system up and running and to remain attached to the perpetrator as the 'primary driver' of dissociative responses to abuse.

The little creature is part of a system that can be looked on as disorganised in that it cannot easily be categorised. However, in the context of reconciling these conflicting needs it can be regarded as highly organised. This is consistent with Herman's (1992) view of fragmentation in response to trauma as: 'not merely a defensive adaptation but the fundamental principle of personality organisation'.

On the spectrum of dissociation, the fragments may or may not develop into separate personality states. They contain discrepant internal memories of experiences in relationships (IMERs) (Heard and Lake 1997). This produces an identity predicament of the kind the latter refer to in individuals whose IMERs cannot 'easily be generalised into one overall coherent model of the self'.

Liotti (1992) and Fonagy (1998) discuss the way in which abusive experiences place the child in an impossible approach/avoidance conflict when faced with a frightened or frightening parent. The child has to construct schema to deal with all conflicting eventualities and ends up with multiple, incompatible, incoherent representational models of the self.

The little creature has an ineffective inner supportive environment

What exists is a mutual state of avoidance and negative empathy for and between parts of the self seen in patterns of avoidant attachment. Added to the child's original experience of abandonment, central to the process of abuse, is a psychic abandonment of the self that holds the memory of the trauma.

The little creature is part of a system which has suffered a loss of narrative context

Stern (1997) comments that adults who have dissociated from their experiences of childhood trauma:

> may be left with only dim, vague, unformulated shards of something there may not even be any words for, because there were none at the time. These fragments of meaning, having no narrative context may or may not be constructible into a viable memory. They may not be assimilable by the victim's 'inner schemata' of the relation of self and the world.

It is a creature whose capacities for metacognitive processing have been disrupted

Main (1991) sees the capacity for metacognition as particularly important in moderating the impact of negative experience. Fonagy (1998) considers that 'the symptom of dissociation itself [may] be usefully seen as the converse of mentalisation . . . dissociating individuals are those victims of childhood (sexual) abuse who coped by refusing to conceive of the contents of their caregiver's mind and thus successfully avoiding having to think about their caregiver's wish to harm them'.

Fonagy (1998, 1999) and Fonagy et al. (1995) explore the effect of an abusive interpersonal context when contemplation of the caregiver's mind is 'overwhelming, as it harbours frankly hostile or dangerously indifferent intentions towards the self – leading to widespread disavowal of mental states' (Fonagy et al. 1995). He is of the opinion that trauma, in the context of an attachment bond, has 'pervasive inhibitory effects on mentalising (to avoid having to think about the caregiver's wish to harm them)' and can lead to an apparent 'decoupling' of the 'mentalising module'.

It is interesting to observe what appear to be the highly developed metacognitive capacities of some fragments. Fonagy's opinion is that some alters have a residual metacognitive capacity which explains awareness between alters.

My hypothesis is that the little creature may well represent the mentalising module which became decoupled. He or she *has* a theory of mind which understands only too well the murderous intention of the caregiver. However, the little creature exists alongside other constructs which have other theories of mind, not only about past caregivers, but also parts of the self in the present whose mental states can be seen as dangerous and therefore can't be recognised. As a result, mentalising capacities may be cordoned off and multiple theories of mind may develop.

The little creature lives in a state of vigilant quiescence

'Vigilant quiescence' (Heard and Lake 1997) is a term used to describe the state of goal-corrected systems until activated by a specific signal. An over-vigilant focus is kept on anything that might activate the attachment system and arouse careseeking behaviour.

The little creature is part of a system which has suffered and is continuing to suffer massive chemical onslaught on the brain

There is a growing body of research evidence of the neurophysiological changes which result from trauma (e.g. Perry 1998; Hartman and Burgess 1993; van de Kolk et al. 1996).

Hartman and Burgess (1993) explore the alterations in the sense of self on a sensory, perceptual, cognitive, behavioural and interpersonal level which result from what they term 'trauma learning'. Their model of information processing of trauma considers the wider context. This context includes all the individual, socio-economic, developmental and other variables such as the quality of the child's attachments. They draw on the language of attachment to categorise different outcomes: integrated, anxious, avoidant, delinquent and disorganised. 'The disorganised outcome is the child who appears fragmented and sometimes bizarre' (Hartman and Burgess 1993).

It is relevant to consider the awareness of attachment shown by some abusers. For example, paedophiles are known to deliberately target insecurely attached children and to manipulate the child's needs for attachment to groom them for abuse. If the abuser is not a primary attachment figure, the threat of the loss of the primary caregiver is often used to enforce silence.

Cult abuse is the most marked example of the deliberate exploitation of attachment needs by abusers. Adult survivors report that, in order to control them, children born into cults receive highly unpredictable caregiving with no real love or affection. Anything the child does gets attached to, such as pets, is taken away or replaced by something obnoxious (Coleman 1994).

In summary, dissociation serves a highly adaptive function in response to the paradox of maintaining attachment to an abusive, exploitative or neglectful caregiver. Dissociation maintains a developmental pathway by minimising the impact of traumatic experiences on the goal-corrected behavioural systems identified by Heard and Lake (1997). These systems are responsible for self-care and self-management. The systems are enabled to function, but not as an integrated whole and homeostasis is maintained via separateness. The inter-personal system for self-defence (Heard and Lake 1997) appears to overdevelop while those responsible for caregiving and careseeking are de-activated.

THE THERAPEUTIC TASK

The therapeutic task rests on the concept of an internalised caregiving system (Heard and Lake 1997). Therapy needs to provide the means of transforming ineffective or non-existent internal caregiving into an internal supportive envi-ronment. It involves recognising, contacting and communicating not only with the little creature but also all parts of the system as a whole. The aim is to create a context for the re-activation of attachment behaviour, which can enable the little creature to stir.

At the severe end of the spectrum, what can be needed to enable the little creature to have a different sort of existence is not an updating of internal working models as such but the construction for the first time of a benign rep-resentational model of caregiving and careseeking. This is based on the experience with the therapist as a secondary caregiver. This process entails what Stern (1997) refers to as the 'wordless and static' type of narrative of trauma to be reconstructed based on a different type of experience.

A helpful conceptualisation of the kind of experience which can make a dif-ference is provided by Heard and Lake (1997). The authors extend Bowlby's work by proposing two major instinctive modes of relating. There is a sup-portive companionable mode and a contrasting pattern of dominating and submissive forms. Supportive companionable (SC) relating takes a protective, explanatory and exploratory form. It is a pattern of caregiving integrated with interest sharing. Dominating and submissive (D/S) relating is primarily a defensive pattern that provides for self-care and self-management when SC relating is unavailable and caregivers cannot be trusted.

In my view, the kind of experience which can make a difference to the little creature involves finding a way of breaching the defensive exclusion of attach-ment needs within the system and promoting supportive companionable (SC) relating between its fragmented parts.

I think, therefore, it is not sufficient to replace the disconnection of the dis-crepant IMERs in a dissociated person with a connection. A connection between associating selves can still be problematic unless the style of relating between them is based on some kind of bond and a sense of shared interest seen in SC relating.

STAGES OF THERAPEUTIC WORK

Stage 1: assessing the system

Key therapeutic task: recognition of the existence of the little creature

A clue to most hidden selves can be severe, persistent symptoms which may have little or no obvious explanation and are resistant to treatment. They may be manifested in attacks on the self in various forms. The individual often belongs to the group described as 'heart sink' patients. Alternatively, at other points on the spectrum, individuals can experience themselves as cut off from feelings, or suffering from self-condemnatory self-dismissive attitudes or simply without a coherent narrative of their past.

Therapeutic methods of assessment such as the SCID-D (Steinberg 1993) can convey recognition and understanding of existence of the little creature and other parts of the system

Therapeutic issues

THE ESTABLISHMENT OF A SECURE BASE

In addition to considerations of safety and stability (see for example Herman 1992 and van der Kolk et al. 1996), a key objective is the provision of a secure therapeutic base which can facilitate the exploration of individual real life experiences (Bowlby 1988; Heard and Lake 1997; Holmes 1993).

In the context of dissociative conditions, a therapeutic alliance may be needed with several different parts, based on an understanding of their individual IMERs: 'Each individual personality needs that outside contact, some way of connecting with the outside world that is different from the abuse she experienced' (Bryant et al. 1992).

To avoid the mistake of forming too strong an alliance with the little creature and of getting trapped in the system, Ross (1997) recommends taking on the role as consultant to the system. In attachment-based therapy, the alliance offers different parts of the self a relationship with the therapist as a caregiver. This can be internalised as the basis of an SC model for self-care and management and bring the fragments into a more secure attachment relationship with one another.

SUPPORTIVE COMPANIONABLE RELATING

The therapist's stance is a key influence. It is important that it conveys verbally and non-verbally a non-pathologising attitude of respect for the survivor's experience and coping mechanisms (Briere 1992). Most crucially, it needs to convey a willingness to relate in a supportive companionable way (Heard and Lake 1997).

Kluft (1993) in outlining some key principles of therapeutic work with dissociative conditions work comments that: 'The therapist can anticipate that passivity, affective blandness, and technical neutrality will be experienced as uncaring and rejecting behaviour and that therapy is better served by taking a warm and active stance.' He details a number of reasons why this stance is so important in work with trauma victims, such as the need to manage traumatic transferences and difficult counter-transferences.

I propose that a key purpose is to create a context for the re-activation of attachment behaviour which will enable the little creature to stir and establish the affectional bonds which are needed to create a new representational model of self as a trusted adult

Stage 2: accessing the system

Key therapeutic task: creating a context for the development of internal relating

Therapeutic issues

BREACHING THE DEFENSIVE EXCLUSION OF ATTACHMENT NEEDS

I feel that it is paradoxical to use the word 'breaching' with D/S connotations. A dilemma, reflected in the poem, is the need to relate to the fear of being related to. In the poem, the type of relating needed is identified as something non-anxiety-provoking provided by someone who is perceived by the little creature as prepared to sit by her side, and who is sufficiently trustworthy and sufficiently attuned to the fears and anxieties concerning proximity to be allowed to do so.

Accessing the system begins at the assessment stage. The identification of the dissociated parts can be very exposing for the system since it gets behind the defensive exclusion of information, needs and feelings.

Recognition of underlying emotional states which may constitute hidden selves may not be shared by the system as a whole at this stage. The goal-directed behaviour of the system is still to avoid proximity. Since the client may well have internalised Liotti's (1992) 'frightened and frightening parent' any interaction with the little creature tends to be characterised at best by anxiety, avoidance or ambivalence. Signals from the little creature can go unheard, be ignored or responded to angrily or anxiously. Exploratory behaviour might be discouraged and feared as dangerous. The little creature's sense of agency can only be exercised covertly, often via dangerous or alarming symptoms. This situation can risk leaving the therapist in receipt of mixed messages and feeling somewhat discouraged.

ATTUNEMENT

Stern (1985) asks the question: How can you get 'inside of' other people's subjective experience and let them know you have arrived there, without using words?

Stern was referring to infants of between 9- and 15-months-old but we are exploring the inter-subjective exchange which needs to take place long after that chronological age has come and gone and the experience at that stage of development has been missed. Attempting to provide SC relating to a system based on D/S principles is very difficult. The system can't change until it can trust another person. Attunement has a key role in establishing trust and is a key aspect of the therapeutic task of reconnecting with the severed self.

TYPES OF ATTUNEMENT

My experience is that little creatures make rapid assessments of one's usefulness as therapist based on the quality of affect attunement and 'goal-corrected empathic attunement' (McLuskey et al. 1999). Goal-corrected empathic attunement is defined as an 'intuitive grasp of the underlying emotional state of the other that draws on empathic knowledge and is an acknowledgement of that state'.

In addition to goal-corrected empathic attunement, which is a verbal activity, I would add the non-verbal dimension of affect attunement to the assessment of dissociative states. This entails entering via 'empathic knowledge', the domain of 'the earliest forms of the self, the self that was communicating and making sense of how it and others fitted together and understood each other long before language was available, and at a time of extreme physical dependence' (McLuskey et al. 1999).

When working with a dissociative system, attunement has a particularly important role in permitting the re-activation of attachment needs. As Stern (1985) points out, attunement behaviours 'recast the event and shift the focus of attention to what is behind the behaviour, to the quality of feeling that is being shared'.

This can be a slow and taxing process for the therapist who may be working with the equivalent of a pre-verbal infant. As in the poem, it involves much 'sitting patiently by'. It can mean entering the equivalent of a world of a crying baby without signalling too much danger to the system's defences and without loss of boundaries. It can often induce empathic strain (Wilson and Lindy 1994) in the therapist.

ATTUNING TO MULTIPLE SELVES, MULTIPLE FEELING STATES AND MULTIPLE ATTACHMENT STYLES

Because of the need to attune to multiple selves, multiple feeling states and multiple attachment styles there is a danger of misattunement. I am not referring here to 'purposeful misattunement' (Stern 1985) which can regulate and extend behaviour but to the stopping of therapeutic exploration by parts of the system who do not feel attuned to, do not want to be attuned to, or fear what might result from the process of attunement.

One explanation dimension might be the existence of abuser alters (Blizard 1997b) who function as internalised abusive caregivers and can be threatened or frightened by empathic statements.

Another issue is what Goodwin (1998) refers to as 'getting to the language of the protest cry'. Protest means the exercise of agency and might be seen as dangerous to the artificially constructed IMER, which maintains an attachment to the abuser. Affect attunement to a fragmented system therefore needs to be like forming a set of roving alliances. These alliances need to be at levels which can be tolerated. They may need to be different in response to the different attachment issues affecting different parts of the system.

In my experience the most hidden part – the little creature of the poem – is the most in need of being attuned to, the hardest to reach but paradoxically the most responsive. He or she responds to signals that his or her existence is known. The most avoidant parts appear to be the most in need of teaching about attunement. They need to observe it happening, and to learn that it need not result in complete disorganisation and that it is possible to learn from misattunements and mistakes.

Stage 3: chaos and disorganisation

Key therapeutic task: the beginnings of co-existence and the creation of a shareable inter- and intra-personal world

A key therapeutic task at this stage is the creation of shareable inter- and intra-personal worlds: a belief that parts can co-exist without destruction. Initial steps towards this can lead to a stage of increased disorganisation so that pacing is important.

The point is being reached where the therapist is able to 'patiently sit by her side' and demonstrate that care is available to enable previously separated parts to have contact with one another.

Because survival has been equated with internal separation, proximity can set off panic and fears of disintegration, i.e. 'fearing the trembling must turn to such severe shaking the vibration would dissolve her entirely, scattering her being irrevocably wide'.

'Painful disassuaging information' (Heard and Lake 1997), formerly segregated in different IMERs is becoming less closed off. For example, for one person receiving caregiving was experienced initially as triggering feelings of devastation. This was different from the better functioning she had expected.

Therapeutic issues

A very safe context in which experience and associated affect can be shared is best promoted by the method described below.

KEEPING IN SC MODE AND MAINTAINING AN EXPLORATORY ALLIANCE

A crucial goal is to promote healthy inter- and intra-personal relating based on inter-dependence rather than dominance and submission. Therapy needs to remain a co-operative rather than a prescriptive endeavour. This calls for enormous trust in the little creature who is the emerging Guntripian withdrawn self and the key partner in the co-operative endeavour.

Alice Miller (1986) in describing her own therapeutic process says that she had to put her trust in a 'nearly autistic being who had survived the isolation of decades'. She says she had to allow this hesitant, inarticulate self to take her by the hand and lead her into territory 'I had been avoiding all my life because it frightened me – the place I had attempted to forget so many years ago, the same place where I had abandoned the child I once was'.

It is interesting to note that Miller refers to what can be understood as the mentalising ability of this so-called autistic being: 'She had a remarkable sensitivity, which enabled her to detect even the tiniest hint of design, manipulation or dishonesty. In this regard she was adamant and unwavering' (Miller 1986).

The therapeutic alliance needs to provide sufficient support to other parts of the system whose mentalising capacities may be more restricted and who are being asked to accept not only the emergence of this self but also its capacity to offer new leadership.

Moving from chaos to the language of the hidden self tends to be characterised by the developments described in the next stage of therapeutic work.

Stage 4: ambivalent relating

Key therapeutic task: the development of an incipient careseeking and caregiving system

The development of an incipient careseeking/caregiving system involves moving from avoidance to a belief that inter-subjectivity can be equated with survival. This can be very anxiety provoking. One person described it as a 'crisis of attachment'. Any past internal relating is likely to have been highly ambivalent at best. This is a phase in which internal beliefs, such as being unworthy of care, which were formed in an identification with the perpetrator, are challenged. The little creature may perceive both caregiving and careseeking as dangerous. He or she may fear being vulnerable to further abuse or exploitation and 'flinches, expecting pain again'.

Some fears of receiving care may relate to Bowlby's (1988) view that the discovery of the true self entails helping the person own their own yearnings for love and care as well as acknowledging their anger towards those who failed to provide it. This can be complicated in situations where parts of the system might be seen as actively persecutory and responsible for self-neglect and/or self-harm. The individual may have to face actual physical damage or other life restrictions imposed by past methods of coping. Some may have harmed their actual children and, in some cases, have to face that it may be too late to resume their care.

Engaging the 'internalised abusive caretaker' (Blizard 1997b) who responds to increased proximity by defensive reactions can come into sharp therapeutic focus.

In my experience, this stage can be one of very anxious attachment to the therapist. Access to the therapist's presence as a secondary caregiving model can be vital to avoid. As one person put it, it is like being in a sinking ship without a lifeline. It can tax the boundaries of therapy and its management can be demanding for both therapist and client alike.

DEALING WITH FEARS OF AGENCY/DEVELOPING AUTONOMY

It is important to remember that the little creature is the active bit of the self which had to retreat in order to maintain attachment to the abuser. His or her emergence can appear dangerous because it threatens those attachments and other relationships built on submission. He or she has the capacity to protest and to be agentic. He or she has retained' maturational ideals' (Heard and Lake 1997), i.e. potentially realisable developmental ideals. The therapist needs to support the growth of the latter and to promote the idea that autonomous development can be compatible with safe attachment.

RECONNECTING WITH THE BODY

Some individuals may have problems identifying with a physical self. Some parts may have no physical identity at all. Others may only have an identity based on a physically anguished self, such as an anorexic body. In this example, weight gain can make the person feel that the body does not belong to them. Connection with the body in a more united self means that existing physical problems may be felt with more impact. For example, one person recognised for the first time that she and her body were one and the same and she could no longer pretend to be unaffected by what the body had suffered.

WORKING IN THE ZONE OF PROXIMAL DEVELOPMENT

The 'zone of proximal development' (Vygotsky 1978, quoted in Heard and Lake 1997) is the space between an individual's actual and potential development. It is important to keep reinforcing developmental capacities without precipitating fears of abandonment (development being seen as incompatible with maintaining attachment) or pushing the person beyond the limits of current competence.

Stage 5: the beginnings of secure internal relating

Key therapeutic task: the development of internal attachment bonds and an inner supportive environment

Therapeutic issues

CONTINUING ROLE OF THERAPY AS A SECURE BASE

The external therapeutic relationship remains a template for the kind of SC relating needed as an internal model. At the same time, this stage facilitates the role of the therapist as a consultant to the system.

FACILITATING GRIEF AND MOURNING

The amount of grief which can be involved is potentially overwhelming and needs to be carefully managed. The following may be among the many things to be mourned for: guilt about self-inflicted damage; responsibility for any damage to others; replacing an idealised image with a realistic appraisal of the extent of traumatic damage; coming to terms with limitations; the collapse of defensive non-maturational ideals.

THE DEVELOPMENT OF NEW COPING MECHANISMS

All past roles need to be honoured for their part in survival and reframed as helpful before new coping strategies can be developed. The ability to internalise the relationship with the therapist as a caregiver is key to the individual's ability to provide for self-care and management (Heard and Lake 1997).

Stage 6: secure internal relating

Key therapeutic task: the transfer of external attachment bonds to a secure internal base

Therapeutic issues

INTERNAL RESTRUCTURING

At this stage, the possibility of peaceful co-existence and/or integration with the little creature is becoming a working reality. One person developed the metaphor of a co-operative to explain the internal shifts which were taking place.

CHANGE IN GOAL-DIRECTED BEHAVIOUR

The goal of the little creature is now to end his or her isolation and to work, in proximity to the rest of the system, on forming a united rather than a fragmented identity. This represents a move to agency by parts which had formerly seen submission or avoidance as their only options.

CHANGE IN METACOGNITION

A new and shared state of mind enables an increasing amount of information to be available to consciousness. The system as a whole can allow the little creature's metacognitive abilities to monitor progress and to keep self and the therapist informed about what is going on and what is needed. One person saw her task as taking charge of her life in a different way with the best interests of all parts at heart.

RECONSTRUCTION OF THE NARRATIVE

Alice Miller (1995) summarises the signs of a shift in narrative as follows:

> the patient does not make light of manifestations of herself anymore, does not so often laugh or jeer at them, even if she still unconsciously passes them over or ignores them, even in the subtle way her parents dealt with the child before she had words to express her needs.

RENEGOTIATING THE THERAPEUTIC RELATIONSHIP

At this point the therapist might have to learn new ways of co-operating too! The system no longer needs interventions focused on overcoming avoidance. Therapy can be a forum for the fledgling united self to practise new ways of relating before trying them out elsewhere.

CONCLUSION: THE SURVIVAL OF THE ATTACHMENT DYNAMIC

An attachment-based approach to dissociative conditions demonstrates the survival of the attachment dynamic (Heard and Lake 1986) throughout life. Following even the severest trauma, an interested, supportive companionable stance can help individuals to meet the challenge of transforming and remodelling traumatic internal memories of experiences in relationships. The little creature's responsiveness to supportive companionable experience confirms Alice Miller's (1995) opinion that:

> People whose only experience has been the wall of silence cling to the wall, seeing in it the solution to their fears. But if they have once glimpsed an opening in it, they will not endure its illusory protection.

REFERENCES

Barach, P. (1991) 'Multiple Personality Disorder as an Attachment Disorder', *Dissociation*, 4, 117–123.

Blizard, R.A. (1997a) 'The Origins of Dissociative Identity Disorder from an Object Relations and Attachment Theory Perspective', *Dissociation*, X, 4, 223–229.

Blizard, R.A. (1997b) 'Therapeutic Alliances with Abuser Alters in Dissociative Identity Disorder: The Paradox of Attachment to the Abuser', *Dissociation*, X, 4, 246–254.

Blizard, R.A. and Bluhm, A.M. (1994) 'Attachment to the Abuser: Integrating Object Relations and Trauma Theories in Treatment of Abuse Survivors', *Psychotherapy*, 31, 373–382.

Bowlby, J. (1980) 'An Information Processing Approach to Defence', in *Attachment and Loss, Vol. 3: Loss*, Hogarth Press and Institute of Psycho-Analysis, London.

Bowlby, J. (1988) *A Secure Base*, Routledge, London.

Briere, J. (1992) *Child Abuse Trauma: Theory and Treatment of the Lasting Effects*, Sage, London.

Bryant, D., Kessler, J. and Shirar, L. (1992) *The Family Inside: Working with the Multiple*, Norton, London.

Coleman, J. (1994) 'Satanic Cult Practices', in Sinason, V. (ed.), *Treating Survivors of Satanist Abuse*, Routledge, London.

Fonagy, P. et al. (1995) 'Attachment, the Reflective Self, and Borderline States: The Predictive Specificity of the Adult Attachment Interview and Pathological Emotional Development', in Goldberg, S., Muir, R. and Kerr, J. (eds), *Attachment Theory: Social, Developmental and Clinical Perspectives*, The Analytic Press, London.

Fonagy, P. (1998) 'Attachment, the Development of the Self, and its Pathology in Dissociative Disorders', *Bulletin of The Menninger Clinic*, 62, 147–169.

Fonagy, P. (1999) 'The Male Perpetrator: The Role of Trauma and Failures of Mentalisation in Aggression Against Women – An Attachment Theory Perspective', paper presented at the 6th Annual John Bowlby Lecture, Centre for Attachment-based Psychoanalytic Psychotherapy, London.

Goodwin, J. (1998) Presentation at 4th ISSD(UK) Conference, Chester.

Guntrip, H. (1968) *Schizoid Phenomena, Object Relations and the Self*, Hogarth, London.

Hartman, C.R. and Burgess, A.W. (1993) 'Information Processing of Trauma', *Child Abuse and Neglect*, 17, 1, 47–58.

Heard, D. and Lake, H. (1986) 'The Attachment Dynamic in Adult Life', *British Journal of Psychiatry*, 149, 430–439.

Heard, D. and Lake, H. (1997) *The Challenge of Attachment for Caregiving*, Routledge, London.

Herman, J.L. (1992) *Trauma and Recovery*, Basic Books, London.

Holmes, J. (1993) *John Bowlby and Attachment Theory*, Routledge, London.

Howell, E.F. (1997) 'Desperately Seeking Attachment: A Psychoanalytic Reframing of the Harsh Superego', *Dissociation*, X, 4, 230–239.

Kluft, R.P. (1993) 'The Treatment of Dissociative Disorder Patients: An Overview of Discoveries, Successes, Failures', *Dissociation*, VI, 2/3, 87–101.

Liotti, G. (1992) 'Disorganised/Disorientated Attachment in the Etiology of the Dissociative Disorders', *Dissociation*, 5, 196–204.

McLuskey, U., Hooper, C.A. and Bingley Miller, L. (1999) 'Goal-corrected Empathic Attunement: Developing and Rating the Concept within an Attachment Perspective', *Psychotherapy Theory, Research, Training and Practice: Journal of the Division of Psychotherapy*, APA, 36, 80–90.

Main, M. (1991) 'Metacognitive Knowledge, Metacognitive Monitoring and Singular (Coherent) vs. Multiple (Incoherent) Models of Attachment: Findings and Directions for Future Research', in Harris et al. (eds), *Attachment across the Lifecycle*, Routledge, London.

Messler Davies, J. (1997) 'Dissociation, Repression and Reality Testing in the Countertransference', in Gartner, R.B. (ed.) *Memories of Sexual Betrayal: Truth, Fantasy, Repression and Dissociation*, Aronson, New York.

Miller, A. (1986) *Pictures of a Childhood*, Farrar, Strauss and Giroux, New York.

Miller, A. (1995) *The Drama of being a Child*, Virago, London.

Nightingale, C. (1988) *Journey of a Survivor*, Constance Nightingale, Bristol.

Nijenhuis, E. (1998) 'Dissociation Masterclass', ISSD(UK) Conference, Chester.

Perry, B.D. (1998) 'Homeostasis, Stress, Trauma, and Adaptation: A Neurodevelopmental View of Trauma', *Bulletin of Child and Adolescent Clinics of North America*, 7, 1, 33–51.

Richardson, S. and Bacon, H. (eds) (1991) *Child Sexual Abuse: Whose Problem? Reflections from Cleveland*, Venture Press, Birmingham.

Ross, C. (1997) *Dissociative Identity Disorder*, Wiley, London.

Steinberg, M. (1993) *Interviewers Guide to the Structured Clinical Interview for DSM-IV Dissociative Disorders (SCID-D)*, American Psychiatric Press, Washington, DC.

Stern, D. (1985) *The Interpersonal World of the Infant*, Basic Books, New York.

Stern, D.B. (1997) 'Discussion: Dissociation and Constructivism' in Gartner, R.B. (ed.) *Memories of Sexual Betrayal: Truth, Fantasy, Repression and Dissociation*, Aronson, New York.

van der Kolk, B.A., McFarlane, A.C. and Weisaeth, L. (eds) (1996) *Traumatic Stress: The Effects of Overwhelming Experience on Mind, Body and Society*, Guilford, London.

Winnicott, D.W. (1965) *The Maturational Processes and the Facilitating Environment*, Hogarth, London.

Wilson, J.P. and Lindy, J.D. (eds) (1994) *Countertransference in the Treatment of PTSD*, Guilford, London.

Zulueta, F. de (1993) *From Pain to Violence: The Traumatic Roots of Destructiveness*, Whurr, London.

Chapter 10

Profound desolation

The working alliance with dissociative patients in an NHS setting

Peter Whewell

> My soul looked down from a vague height, with Death,
> As remembering how I rose or why,
> And saw a sad land, weak with sweats of dearth,
> Grey, cratered like the moon with hollow woe
> And pitted with great rocks and scales of plagues
> Wilfred Owen 1918

Some eight years ago one of the teams working at the Regional Department of Psychotherapy in Newcastle began to specialise in assessing and treating Borderline Personality Disorder (BPD) patients. This specialisation attracted an increasing referral of such patients from around the Northern region, leading to the situation where the team moved entirely to treating BPD patients, and renamed itself the 'Borderline team'. Among the referrals are severely disturbed patients, who would not have been traditionally assessed as being suitable for analytical psychotherapy, and within this group are a small number of Dissociative Identity Disorder (DID) patients, who also carry a diagnosis of BPD. Very little has been written about DID patients in Britain, and so the team was faced with a challenge both theoretically and in terms of organising a treatment setting.

Both Borderline and Dissociative Identity Disorder patients are characterised by a disturbance in the sense of self. As Sandler and Joffe (1969) have pointed out, in psychoanalytic literature the concept of self can be seen to have two facets; first, a subjective sense of one's conscious experience, second, a structural organisation which is out of subjective experience. The importance of childhood trauma in the creation of unconscious structured splits in the self was carefully elucidated by Ronald Fairbairn. In his 1943 paper 'The Repression and the Return of Bad Objects', Fairbairn describes his work examining children who had been the victims of sexual assaults and postulates that as a result the experience is accompanied by the internalisation and repression of a bad object representing the abuser. He says (p. 63):

the position is that the victim of a sexual assault resists the revival of the traumatic memory primarily because this memory represents a record of a relationship with a bad object . . . it is intolerable in the main not because it gratified repressed impulse, but for the same reasons that a child often flies panic-stricken from a stranger who enters the house. It is intolerable because a bad object is always intolerable and a relationship with a bad object can never be contemplated with equanimity.

Fairbairn here is commenting upon the importance of fear in the perception of a bad external object that is then structurally internalised. Later in the same paper he discusses shame also as a predisposing factor in the experience of a bad object. The perception of bad object experience in childhood is a repeated finding in the histories of our Borderline patients, with childhood sexual, physical and psychological abuse being very common. The histories of the patients with an additional DID diagnosis differ only in that the experience of trauma is especially severe among these patients. All have suffered severe, chronic and sadistic child abuse as young children from a number of adult perpetrators who themselves were organised together in their abuse of children. The degree of terror and shame involved seems to distinguish between the BPD patients and those carrying dual DID and Borderline diagnoses such that our particular sample of patients represent a pathogenic trauma continuum, with the DID patients at an extreme end.

In his 1944 paper 'Endopsychic Structure Considered in Terms of Object Relationships', Fairbairn goes further in stating the bad object is split into two, as it is internalised, into what he calls rejecting and exciting objects. He emphasises that both these objects are unsatisfying. In response to the internalisation of the two bad objects, the central ego splits in conjunction with each bad object, giving two self-states – a rejecting/rejected self (the anti-libidinal ego) and an exciting/excited self (the libidinal ego). Both of these self-states become structuralised and repressed.

While both Borderline and DID patients have structuralised splits in unconscious self representations, they differ in their subjective experience of being able to call to mind preceding self-states. Thus Borderline patients may operate in one self-state while a preceding self-state is kept temporarily out of mind, but can be recalled when memory is triggered. However, DID patients maintain a degree of amnesia between self-states, so that previous self-states cannot be remembered; instead a powerful trigger will precipitate the DID patient back into another self-state rather than trigger a memory of a previous self-state. Neither Borderline nor DID patients are capable of object permanence and they are therefore unable to retain evocative memory of one self-state during another.

Fairbairn continued to struggle with the nature of internalisation of good experiences. In his original 1944 paper he felt that good experiences, because they were satisfying, were not internalised in terms of psychic structure.

However, in his 1951 addendum to the same paper he seems to accept that some satisfactory internalisation of a bad object can occur, secondary to the object being stripped of its rejecting and exciting aspects. He goes on to say (p. 135):

> It will be noticed that, in accordance with my revised conception, the central ego's 'accepted object' being shorn of its over-exciting and over rejecting elements, assumes the form of a desexualised and idealised object which the central ego can safely love after divesting itself of the elements which give rise to the libidinal ego and the internal saboteur [the anti-libidinal ego]. It is significant, accordingly, that this is just the sort of object into which the hysterical patient seeks to convert the analyst – and the sort of object into which the child seeks to convert his parents, usually with a considerable measure of success.

Fairbairn sees the internalisation of the good aspects of the bad object as strengthening the ego. The perception of the therapist as an idealised object is usually the basis for the therapeutic alliance with a Borderline patient. However, it seems that our DID patients have great difficulty in internalising anything good – it is as if there is nothing left of the object once stripped of its exciting/rejecting aspects. This may be because the terror and shame associated with the bad object experiences were of sufficient force to overwhelm the possibility of anything good remaining.

The DID child's experience of relationships prior to the overwhelming sexual trauma may be an important factor here. All our Borderline DID patients had a history of a poor or abandoning relationship with their mothers before the sexual trauma occurred. Whereas Borderline patients can find solace with their idealised therapists, and this solace can be (but not consistently) recalled, DID patients are unable to recall the therapist as an internal solacing object between sessions. They seem to be inconsolable and to live in an intensely desolate world, denuded of all goodness and positive meaning. Their choice seems to be to live in that world of desolation or emotionally disengage and view the desolation from a detached position.

The usual treatment setting for our Borderline patients is once-weekly out-patient psychoanalytic psychotherapy with a standard 50-minute session. The complexity of the DID patients in terms of multiplicity of symptoms, the depth of distress and behavioural disturbance, the transference generated and the countertransference pressures involved for the therapist all argued for the need for more frequent sessions than our standard weekly format. However, to provide this sort of service has been beyond the treatment resources of the Borderline team. Consequently we have employed our standard technique with these DID patients, and one of the results has been a struggle to maintain a working alliance with them.

Putnam (1992) has described the extreme difficulty DID patients have in trusting their therapists and warns (p. 106):

No therapist will ever seriously err by overestimating the distrust that victims of abuse have in others. One should not depend on trust as the foundation for a therapeutic alliance. Nor should one expect these patients to concede that one is doing what one has to do for their own good.

Our DID patients have suffered extreme experiences of neglect and intrusive abuse at the hands of maternal and paternal caregivers, with the latter being involved in an organised way in sexual abuse. Working within the NHS we are, as therapists, part of a system that has its own logic and values that can be experienced by the DID patient as not consistent with their own needs, and can be felt to be cold, detached and abusive. First, there may be a fleeting and tantalising (from the point of view of both patient and therapist) ability to find the therapist helpful while the patient is in contact with him or her, but there is always the fear for the DID patient of the therapist changing into a malign object, of realising they have been tricked again. Second, there is the problem not only of object constancy but of object permanence, whereby the therapist ceases to exist as an object between sessions. Third, there is the problem of the therapist being introjected by one personality, and that link being then enviously attacked by another personality in a way which is hidden from the view of the therapist.

The aim of our treatment of Borderline patients has been to facilitate the integration of their split selves and objects, and this aim remains the same with the DID subgroup. A neutral and reliable environment creates conditions in which the whole patient can present difficult aspects of herself in terms of the emergence of other personalities. These personalities are subject to containment in the countertransference, clarification and interpretation as any presenting aspect of a Borderline patient would be. We have learned that if the therapist is worried about a vulnerable or upset alter leaving the session, the alter is gently asked to switch to a more stable alter shortly before the end of the session. Before the end of the session a summary of the content of the interaction with a preceding alter is given to the stable alter (usually the host) so no secrets are kept between therapist and individual alters. The aim is therefore to establish, if possible, a working alliance with each alter, and to analyse each alter when it appears. However, no pressure is placed on the patient to be, or switch into, any specific alter. Whatever the patient presents is the focus for the therapeutic work.

CLINICAL MATERIAL

Margaret sits in the waiting room radiating psychic pain. A small, blonde woman in her late twenties, she rocks back and forward in an apparent attempt at self-calming, looking desperately disconsolate. As the youngest of three children she felt she was unwanted by her mother, who behaved violently and cruelly towards her. Margaret records the following memory:

> My mother dragged Margaret by the hair and threatened her with a knife and locked her in the shed. My father seemed to go along with what mother was doing. He repeatedly told Margaret he cared for her but he seemed to side with mother when they were not alone. Margaret couldn't stand the pain *he* was inflicting. She knew what to expect from mum, she never expected anything different – but dad – it hurt, far far more what he kept doing and somehow Joanne took over. Nothing hurt Joanne, she never let him near her, she could deal with his weakness and lies. She felt nothing, she was able to treat people with contempt.

This memory was recorded in a letter to me written by an obscure alter personality, Jean, who seems to represent a psychic helper. The letter was explaining that in not supporting her struggle for more community support in a more vociferous way than I had been doing, I was behaving just like her father. The letter said that Joanne would never present herself directly to me.

Before the age of this memory Margaret had been sent away to stay for summers with her maternal uncle, a successful employee of a large public organisation. The visits to her uncle began at the age of 4 and went on until she was aged 8. Margaret was subject to repeated penetrative, perverse abuse at first at the hands of her uncle alone. He would act in a seductive way, telling her how nice her hair was, buying her sweets before and after the abuse. Gradually the abuse extended to include two men who worked with her uncle, and involved Margaret being forced to undergo sexual acts with dogs, which were photographed. The abuse was terrifying and among other current sequelae it has left Margaret with an intense phobia of dogs.

Intense shame is another long-term effect of this abuse. At the time of the abuse, Margaret seems to have split into two child selves: Jill, a terrified hurt abused body self; and Petal, a split-off child self who was able to enjoy eating the ice creams her uncle gave her. The alters hate Petal, blaming her collusion and seductiveness for the uncle's abuse of her.

Margaret had been in psychiatric care for over a decade before her referral for psychotherapy, initially with a diagnosis of a chronic depressive illness. After a number of years Margaret was able to trust her female psychiatrist sufficiently to let her know about her alter personalities, but shortly after this the psychiatrist left, referring Margaret to our department concurrently. When Margaret was initially seen she did not mention her multiplicity (nor did the referral letter) as she was not sure whether this would be seen as merely signalling her badness – 'copping out and not facing up to life' – or would be disbelieved. It was only when she was established in therapy that she was able to gradually reveal her alter personalities.

Margaret is the host personality. She does have some knowledge of the existence and nature of other personalities but experiences repeated losses of time and retrospective blanknesses on a daily basis when she assumes she has switched into other personalities. Margaret usually presents in therapy sessions.

Her personality resembles that of an avoidant, narcissistic personality, with a strong masochistic element, and is suffused with shame. There have been presentations at sessions of two other personalities – Meg and Janet. These personalities have arrived as Meg or Janet and have left in the same mode; switching has not occurred during a session. Each personality has arrived unannounced, and I have been expected to pick up on the different presentation and be empathic to that personality in much the same way that Margaret expects empathy. Janet is a self-confident angry alter who characteristically is contemptuous of attempts to help Margaret. Meg is a highly compliant self, close to Winnicott's concept of a false self (1960), who does what others require of her at all times. This Meg self seems to predominate at home and in the outside world.

Between sessions I have had letters from all the personalities described except for Petal, the seductive child self and Margaret has wondered if Petal has 'been killed', possibly by Jane. Jill, the abused child self, has written infrequently, in a very childish handwriting, a typical communication being:

I hurt my tummy hurts
My head hurts. Teddy got hurt too
I scared. I bad. Help Teddy
Make him better. Help.

Here the damage to good objects extends to her transitional object, leaving her without solace.

The main personality presenting to therapy sessions is Margaret. Margaret feels and behaves in an avoidant, narcissistic manner, centred upon a suffering bad self and who is destined to endlessly repeat cycles of rejection and punishment. She says: 'I know the pain, the fear, the price, the horrendous helplessness of it all. There's no help, nowhere to turn to, nowhere to hide.'

Margaret is racked by fear and shame, and cannot turn to another for comfort. She is beset by flashbacks, both visual and olfactory, of her childhood abuse which generate self-loathing. She talks about 'The unspeakable truth, things so bad there are no words.' Margaret has for many years hurt herself in secretive ways. She has often cut herself and she rubs her skin with a pumice stone. However, the relief of tension is only temporary and has to be repeated. She often thinks of suicide; this offers a degree of solace and the prospect of triumph over her persecutors.

At the beginning of therapy just over two years ago, Margaret appeared locked in a cycle of self-hatred, self-blame and punishment. All her material linked to herself being to blame, and at times she moved into transient psychotic episodes in which she was convinced the police were going to arrest her for being such a bad person. Because of the severity of self-harm, a contract was agreed whereby Margaret agreed to limit her self-harm in return for the provision of a reliable therapy. By and large she has managed to stick to this contract which has now, like the fate of Winnicott's transitional object, fallen into limbo.

Margaret began to feel more confident that I would not contaminate the sessions with my own agenda and this seemed to lead to increasing attacks on therapy, with the focus being her uncertainty whether I could be a trustworthy and reliable person. She repeatedly talks about my inability to understand what it is like to be her, given the depth of her fear and shame.

I seem real in sessions, but as soon as the session ends she is left 'with guilt and a big hole'. She is very sensitive to waiting and if I am late in taking her in for a session she experiences a depressing emptiness. In the wait, even for a short time, I am equated with an absent object and all hope turns into hopelessness. There is a fear I will turn into a bad object, but also an expectation of this. She notes that I am a paid member of an organisation (the NHS) and she expects that if she criticises me she will be punished or ignored; that in arranging CPA reviews I will gang up with fellow professionals and we will act out of our own motivation against her; that people in power will lie to her and trick her. She is more able to trust the room than trust me, but is attentive to even small changes in the room, such as a vase having been moved, because they portend instability.

Margaret has only brought one dream to our sessions, a recurrent dream where 'An unknown faceless woman lies dead. Maggots crawl out of her eye sockets.' The dead woman seems to represent both Margaret's dead, congealed, internal world as well as the therapy between us. Nothing lively can exist, nothing good can be seen as our capacity for insight is invaded and destroyed by persecutory introjects. A rendering of a hopeless state of being living yet dead was represented in the following poem:

A Child's Grave

A child, buried deep within a tiny grave
That's overgrown and hidden from the world
It happened years ago, her death
She had to die, she could not bear her suffering anymore
No one can remember, now, quite who she was
The headstone of a cherub holds a book
That bears her name and dates that mark her birth
And death are noted, too.
She really was a person, really lived for just a few short years,
But that was long ago, no one mourns this little one.
All have forgotten now the pain in which she died
I wonder if they know, or even cared, about her fate
I stand and stare but I am not surprised
To see my name upon the stone
It is myself that's buried there

For I am just a memory she left behind
The whisper of her name upon the breeze
Her ghost, tortured still, goes on but finds
No rest or peace.

The poem poignantly captures the fragmentation of Margaret's child self at an early age, and the lack of any empathic other that might have mitigated or healed this split. There is the legacy of unreality and suffering which extends into the present. In giving me the poem there is the implicit hope that I may understand something of her story and experience her hopelessness.

From a countertransference point of view the problem of maintaining a working alliance is to metabolise feelings mobilised by contact with Margaret's suffering selves and to maintain hope in the face of a deadly hopelessness without becoming emotionally detached from, or emotionally overwhelmed by, highly persecutory material.

Kerry is a tall, thin red-haired woman in her mid-thirties who looks older than her years. At interview Kerry presents with an unnerving passivity, staring expectantly in the hope of a response she can comply with. As a small child Kerry was abandoned by her mother, and was placed in foster care from the age of 2 to 5. There are no bad memories of this time. However, at 5 she was transferred to a children's home she experienced as cruel and depriving. The children, including Kerry, were subject to systematic sexual abuse from their house parents, and her main attachments were to other children. Kerry kept up contact with her foster mother, and eventually at the age of 7 was adopted by this woman. At about this time Kerry met her father, apparently by accident, when out playing. He continued to meet her secretly and then introduced her to a paedophile ring with which she continued to be involved until her early adult life. The ring seems to have been highly organised around perverse sexual abuse and violence and to have used a variety of coercive techniques to induce compliance in its victims, including the induction of extreme terror and the deliberate production of alter personalities by hypnosis while the victim was in a state of terror. Kerry apparently escaped from the ring by marrying and moving from London to the north-east, though her marriage subsequently broke down. However, it continues to be unclear whether Kerry, in the form of an alter, Declan, is still in touch with the ring.

Kerry is the host personality, and shows the characteristics of a severe dependent personality disorder. By her passivity she forces activity in the other person, then fits in with the expectations of the other person. Behind this compliant façade there is a vacuous emptiness. Although Kerry usually begins sessions she is liable to switch into alter personalities during sessions, the triggers for the switches being a high level of anxiety or a specific cue such as a visual memory. Alter personalities which have appeared have been Declan, who appears to be cruel, hateful and potentially abusive in identification with her childhood abusers; Dana, who is chronically suicidal and despairing; Kelly, a traumatised, sensitive young girl; and Kieley, a seductive and eroticised young girl. There have been hints that further alters, hypnotically programmed by her abusers, exist.

Kerry was referred to the department via her general practitioner following private therapy. She had previously avoided psychiatric systems as she had been told by her abusers that her story would not be believed, and that she would be treated as mad and given ECT. It was during the private therapy that Kerry's multiplicity emerged; this in turn led to her therapist becoming enmeshed and over-involved and eventually abandoning her abruptly. Therapy with me began 2 years ago, and was initially characterised by sessions of great anxiety as she began to tell her story. Two of the first sessions were followed by Kerry leaving in a fugue state, and so to protect her from wandering she arranged to be accompanied to and from sessions by a friend. The process of putting together a coherent story of her life has been assisted by writing a diary which she posts so that I can read it before the session and return it to her.

The diary quickly became a source of inter-alter conflict, with Declan threatening, and at times succeeding, in destroying the diary. In sessions Declan initially appeared cold, detached and arrogant, but as therapy has progressed he has become more thoughtful and less intolerant of the other alters. It seems likely that this is secondary to the experience of being tolerated by me over a period of time. It soon became apparent that Kerry was extremely sensitive to separation, and that if sessions were missed, or when there were planned breaks, there would be dangerous acting out involving amnesia and alter switches. As an example Kerry returned from a short break in therapy with severe bruising on her arms, saying she had lost my appointment card. She said she could not remember exactly what had happened to her, but she vaguely recalled being abducted into a van by two men, who may have been part of the paedophile ring, and made to take drugs. They had found her appointment card and questioned her about therapy. She wondered if I might be in danger because I knew too much about her story. This was conveyed in an affectless, flat tone of voice, the effect in the countertransference being to make me feel, on behalf of herself and myself, an element of the terror that she herself must have experienced as a child. The concurrent problem in the countertransference is keeping an open mind and being able to think about internal and external realities. The sequence can be interpreted as dream; in the break in therapy she is unable to hang on to me as a good object and her inner world is overpowered by an internal narcissistic gang who question her dependence and attack it by destroying her appointment card. At the same time she is bruised and battered and an external enactment of this state of affairs is a possibility and the issue of Kerry's safety has to be taken up with her.

As therapy progressed, the suicidal alter, Dana, became more prominent. In part this was due to Kerry becoming more aware of the destructive Declan aspect of herself, with the emergence of shame and feelings of badness at a conscious level. This led to a sequence of overdoses, one of which was nearly fatal, that revealed the extent of Kerry's internal anarchy, and the difficulties of creating a therapeutic alliance. Kerry herself claimed no knowledge of each overdose attempt, and though she was aware of tablets in the house she was unable or unwilling to take responsibility for ensuring her own safety by removing them. Kerry seemed both intractably passive and unable to exert any control over the activity of her alters. The situation was complicated by the damaged little girl alter, Kelly, being in touch with Dana, but being unable to communicate directly with Kerry, but was eased by Dana appearing in sessions and by my allowing her to talk about her suicidal wishes, and by Dana then beginning to think about the effect she was having on Kerry and Kelly, and in the transference upon myself via her suicidal acts. At first it seemed that Dana saw me as Kerry's therapist, and not her therapist, but over time a working alliance with Dana is being established.

CONCLUSIONS

It is possible to discern similarities in the self-structure of Margaret and Kerry that can be matched against Fairbairn's tripartite structuralisation and also against Winnicott's description of the false self. Both patients have a compliant false self which has no resonance or depth and which serves a defensive structure of the central ego. In the case of Kerry this false self is Kerry, and is her usual presentation in therapy; in the case of Margaret the false self, Meg, is dominant at home while Margaret seems to represent a more real suffering central ego self that is her usual therapy presentation. The real, suffering self in Kerry's case is her alter Dana, and she has been less easily contactable in therapy – perhaps indicating a greater degree of ego splitting due to more powerful repetitive trauma. Both patients have split off angry and destructive alters (Janet and Declan) who seem to represent internal saboteurs in Fairbairn's scheme. Damaged and abused selves fixed in childhood represent Fairbairn's libidinal ego (Jill and Kelly) but it is clear that in Fairbairn's terms the libidinal ego is further split with seductive child selves (Petal and Kieley) being dissociated from the traumatised child selves. In the case of Margaret her seductive child self (Petal) has not been available, whilst Kerry's seductive child self (Kieley) has occasionally appeared in sessions.

The problems of establishing a working alliance with Margaret and Kerry has in both cases been concerned with making contact in a hopeful way with a regressed, despairing and suicidal true self. In the case of Kerry this process has been complicated by the presence of a vacuous, dependent false self (Kerry herself). The suicidal and despairing cathexis of the central, regressed false selves in both cases seems to be very powerful, and can be seen as the inevitable consequence of extreme and prolonged childhood sexual abuse on an already deprived ego, the traumatic splits being driven by shame in Margaret's case and terror in Kerry's case. The power of suicide as triumph over an overwhelmingly persecutory situation is described by Wilfred Bion in his autobiographical writing about his experience of prolonged exposure to shellfire on Wyschaete Ridge in 1917 (1997: 94):

> It did not take long for interest in life to die out. Soon I found myself almost hopeless. I used to lie on my back and stare at the low roof. Sometimes I stood for hours at a small piece of mud that hung from the roof by a grass and quivered to the explosion of the shells . . . This may seem hardly possible to you. But the fact remains that life had now reached such a pitch that horrible mutilations or death could not conceivably be worse. I found myself looking forward to getting killed, as then, at least, one would be rid of this intolerable misery . . . I was merely an insignificant scrap of humanity that was being intolerably persecuted by unknown powers and I was going to score off these powers by dying . . . With this new idea before me, I felt better. I didn't feel afraid anymore.

The integration of the personalities into which both of these two patients are split involves the remembering of the traumatic experience split off into each of the personalities, together with the intensification of the overall persecutory experience that the splitting defended against in the first place. For the patient and therapist to hold a working alliance there has to be hope that something good can be internalised in order to prevent retraumatisation of the patient. If this cannot be established then suicide is the logical outcome. There is implicit hope for life in the fact of the patients continuing to attend for appointments and their continued survival, but in addition the therapist has to hang on to hope for the patient via metabolism of the shame and terror shared with the patient and the belief in the goodness of the therapist's own analytic internalisations.

REFERENCES

Bion, F. (1997) *W.R. Bion. War Memories 1917–19*. London, Karnac Books.
Fairbairn, W. (1943) 'The Repression and Return of Bad Objects'. In *Psychoanalytic Studies of the Personality* (1952). London, Tavistock.
Fairbairn, W. (1944) 'Endopsychic Structure Considered in Terms of Object Relationships'. In *Psychoanalytic Studies of the Personality* (1952). London, Tavistock.
Owen, W. (1918) *The Poems of Wilfred Owen* (1985). London, Chatto & Windus.
Putnam, F. (1992) 'Are Alter Personalities Fragments or Figments?', *Psychoanalytic Inquiry* 12, 95–112.
Sandler, J. and Joffe, W. (1969) 'Towards a Basic Psychoanalytical Model', *International Journal of Psychoanalysis* 50, 79–90.
Winnicott, D. (1960) 'Ego Distortion in Terms of Time and True Self'. In *The Maturational Processes and the Facilitating Environment* (1965). London, Hogarth Press.

Dark dimensions of multiple personality

Phil Mollon

Over the past decade I have attempted to work in psychotherapy with a small number of patients with multiple personalities. Since writing a book on the subject (Mollon 1996) I have been contacted by various colleagues from around the country who have also found themselves struggling to understand and help such patients, often finding that conventional psychodynamic and psychiatric paradigms prove inadequate. The more experience I have gained, the more complex and ambiguous these structures of mind seem to be – and the more hazardous the work to both patient and therapist.

DISSOCIATION AND CONFABULATION

Some years ago, a patient, Rebecca, came to her usual psychotherapy session, curled up in her chair and appeared very frightened. She seemed to be trying to fight off someone who was hurting her. My attempts to communicate and enquire with words evoked only a gasping whisper of 'hide!' and 'get hurt'. After a few minutes she got up from the chair and hid on the floor behind it. She did not utter any more words that session. Despite this odd presentation, which appeared very removed from the present reality, she was able to leave when I indicated it was the end of the session. I had been seeing this patient for about a year. She had not previously behaved in this strange manner during her therapy.

Following this session, Rebecca telephoned later in the day to apologise for not coming that morning. She 'explained' that although she had come to the hospital she had not felt able to attend her session because she had been feeling so upset about certain events during the week. I tried to tell her that she had in fact come to her session. She seemed to presume that I was misunderstanding her and repeated her explanation. At her next session she again apologised for not having come the previous week. When I tried to present her with the reality of her attendance, she appeared puzzled and confused, and said I must be lying but she could not understand why I would want to tell her this lie. After some minutes of unproductive discussion, there was a sharp change of demeanour. She looked straight at me and assertively said: 'Tell her the name of the one who came last week'. I asked what this name was. She replied 'Tiny'. I asked who was speaking to me at the moment. She replied 'Zoro'. Abruptly the demeanour changed again, to the puzzled, depressed and withdrawn manner. I said 'I think the one who came last week may have been called Tiny'. Looking shocked and bewildered, she asked how I knew that name. She protested that it was a name known only to her within her own mind. I explained that 'Zoro' had told me. She became even more agitated, exclaiming that Zoro was a box in her mind, a box that she would put things in – 'How can a box come out and talk to you? It doesn't make any sense!'

Over the ensuing months there were many other extremely dissociative phenomena shown by this patient. For example, my secretary might tell me that 'Zoro' had phoned, asking me to call. When I then phoned, the call might be answered by another part of the patient, who would deny any knowledge of either Zoro or myself. Space does not permit description of the range of complex dissociative behaviours and experiences displayed, with often dense amnesia between the different dissociative states. Needless to say, in some states of mind she would present accounts of very severe and unusual childhood abuse, some of which she would represent in drawings, which unfortunately she would always carefully tear up and remove at the end of the session. Rebecca stopped attending her therapy after informing me that she had been told by an abusive network that my safety, as well as hers, was under threat if she continued.

One crucial point about this patient is that in what one might think of as her main personality state, the one in which she first presented for therapy, she did not know that she had a multiple personality. In this state she was unaware of her various dissociative behaviours. Moreover, judging from her responses on the telephone on occasion, in at least one of Rebecca's personality states she was unaware that she had therapy. Thus her relationship to reality and her awareness of reality was severely compromised. Alongside this is the observation that some of her accounts of traumatic experiences in both her childhood and her current adult life, while not appearing completely beyond the bounds of possibility, did seem most unusual in a way which invited scepticism. As so often in the case of accounts of unusual abuse, it is difficult to know which would be the more naïve: to think the events described could not happen; or to think the events described could indeed happen.

In the years since I saw Rebecca I have sometimes reflected upon some worrying possibilities. Supposing I had persisted in trying to talk about her dissociation to a part of her that was unaware that she had a multiple personality. Might that part of her then have concluded that I had some preoccupation with a particular diagnosis that I was trying to impose on her – that I was indeed attempting to elicit a multiple personality. Could she then have accused me of malpractice? Moreover, she had sometimes referred to another doctor having raped her. Could she have accused me of raping her?

While her perception of reality appeared profoundly defective, her confidence in her perceptions seemed secure.

Around the same time I saw another patient, Stephanie, who told me that she had several personalities. Unlike Rebecca, her multiple personality was presented freely and overtly from the beginning. Shifts from one personality state to another were sudden and sharply defined, usually indicated by a jerk of her head. Often the new personality would indicate its identity by name. In addition to describing and presenting various adult personalities, which carried out different tasks of adult life – e.g. one who went to work, one who was sociable, one who could be flirtatious and a depressed one who was regarded as the main personality – she also described child parts and, more surprisingly, some non-human entities. These latter parts included an angel and a demon, both of which would on occasion appear to take executive control of Stephanie and would speak to me. The 'angel' would appear profoundly wise and compassionate, exuding peace, while the 'demon' would appear extremely malevolent, threatening to kill Stephanie and pursue me forever if I did not cease the therapeutic work. These two parts were utterly opposed to each other, seeming to represent a cosmic war taking place within Stephanie's psyche. Sometimes Stephanie would report being plagued by continuous 'whisperings', cruel taunts, blasphemies against her religion, and seductive invitations to suicide.

Initially I naïvely thought it might be possible to help Stephanie work towards fusion of her dissociated personalities – and indeed for a time this work seemed to proceed. However, over the ensuing years I found that Stephanie had a capacity to generate an apparently limitless number of new personalities. Situations of stress would find her again in the grip of hysteria, with a new personality having emerged somewhere in the system. Always it was possible to find psychodynamic sense in these developments, but Stephanie did not appear able to surrender her resort to dissociation as her fundamental response to both exogenous and endogenous stress.

Having grappled over some years with a small number of very dissociative patients, I have been struck by the implicit optimism of many American texts on this subject. Almost without exception, they suggest that such patients can be cured!

Concepts of multiple personality or Dissociative Identity Disorder have been in vogue only for the last 10 years or so. However, patients presenting such clinical states are not a new phenomenon. The Kleinian analyst, Rosenfeld (1987) describes the case of Caroline who was clearly severely dissociative, although he did not have available the current understanding of dissociation. Rosenfeld's experience was not encouraging.

Rosenfeld described Caroline as a doctor in general practice, with a part-time psychiatric appointment. She appeared slightly manic and diagnosed herself as having a schizoid personality, but seemed happily married with a small child. Rosenfeld related how he became concerned and puzzled over an incident that occurred after about a year and a half of analysis. Caroline disclosed that she had been dismissed from her job in the psychiatric clinic, apparently without any reason being given. She also reported that some nurses had been observing her when she visited the lavatory, as if suspecting her of drug addiction; she felt this was ridiculous because she had never used drugs, although she had treated some drug addicts at her clinic.

After her dismissal from her psychiatric post, Caroline went on to specialise in treating drug addicts at an NHS clinic. One day she mentioned to Rosenfeld that the police had questioned her about possible criminal drug prescribing, following a newspaper article. She appeared extremely upset about this, protested that she was completely innocent, and speculated that an envious colleague was trying to defame her. Following this, Caroline was arrested and was refused bail so that she could not attend her sessions. Some time later, Rosenfeld was visited by Caroline's solicitor who told him that unfortunately the allegations appeared to be true, and that Caroline had been selling prescriptions for large sums of money. The solicitor asked Rosenfeld to tell the court that he was treating her for schizophrenia. At the same time, Caroline was writing to Rosenfeld from prison, still protesting her innocence and asking him to tell both the court and her solicitor that she was both sane and innocent. Subsequently, Caroline was examined by a professor of psychiatry at a London teaching hospital, who found no evidence of any severe mental illness. Then, while in prison, Caroline tried to hire someone to murder her assistant. It was not until she was found guilty of attempted murder, as well as the other charges, that Caroline's mental state became more overtly disturbed, as she began to show signs of schizophrenia.

Rosenfeld described the outcome of Caroline's psychoanalytic treatment as 'a severe shock'. He remarked: 'What seems so incredible even now is the extent of the split between the destructive criminal part of the patient and the part with which she related to me' (p. 136). He was clearly in no doubt that, in the part of her mind which related to him as her analyst, she was completely unaware of her own criminal activities and believed herself to be innocent of the charges against her. Therefore there must have existed a dense amnesia between the criminal part and the caring doctor part of her mind. When Caroline was confronted with evidence of her own criminal activity, she resorted to confabulation to explain this to herself and to Rosenfeld – e.g. her belief that an envious colleague was trying to defame her.

One point about this and the other examples is that they illustrate how a person's relationship with reality can be profoundly impaired as a result of dissociation. Delusional explanations can be constructed to fill in the 'gaps' in awareness.

A further striking instance of dissociative impairment of the relationship to reality is provided by Ross (1994). He describes a patient, Pam, who one day reported to her therapist that her mother had died. Pam then appeared to proceed through a normal pattern of mourning, except that she also described odd behaviour from her father; she claimed that he had formed a relationship with another woman almost immediately after her mother's death, and to add further insult, this woman was now, with gross insensitivity, sending her postcards signed 'Mom'. Eventually one of Pam's alter personalities admitted that 'he' had generated the delusion that the mother had died, in a misguided belief that this would provide a solution to some problems that Pam was experiencing with her mother.

Here is yet another example. A patient speaks of her parents as having abused her extensively over many years. She appears distraught and despairing as she describes this. Suddenly there is a change of demeanor and body language. She 'introduces' herself by a different name. The new personality declares that she has different parents from the one who was speaking previously; her parents are, by contrast, extremely caring but live in a different country.

What is going on here? We are invited to believe in a charade, a piece of make-believe of obvious absurdity. And yet such a travesty of logic and reality sense is presented as if completely acceptable and indeed unremarkable. These are patients who appear to have found a way of living in a world of pretence whilst at the same time maintaining a degree of relationship to reality. How do they differ from those suffering from schizophrenia, or other forms of psychosis?

PSYCHOTIC ASPECTS OF MULTIPLICITY

Although patients with multiple personalities generate quite a different emotional quality from those who are regarded as schizophrenic, I find it actually rather difficult to specify formally how they differ. Indeed the more I have reflected upon this point, the more striking I find the similarities between the two kinds of patients.

Steinberg (1993) lists a number of similarities between schizophrenia and Dissociative Identity Disorder (DID): both conditions show dissociative symptoms, identity confusion, auditory hallucinations, Schneiderian symptoms (e.g. experiences of being influenced, thought insertion, etc.), impaired reality testing, comorbid mood disorders (sometimes), and impairments in general functioning. On the other hand, she argues there are clear differences: for example, schizophrenic symptoms occur in the context of bizarre delusions (unlike those in DID), the auditory hallucinations of DID are limited to the voices of alter personalities and are located internally (unlike those of schizophrenia), and the impairment in functioning in DID is temporary (unlike that in schizophrenia). However, I am not persuaded that these distinctions are actually so clear and consistent. Although most hallucinatory voices in DID are located internally, I have found on occasion that patients will report experiences of externally located voices. Moreover, there is no easy way of distinguishing between the voices of alter personalities and any other internal voices. Regarding other hallucinatory phenomena, one could construe the striking amnesias in DID as instances of 'negative hallucination'; for example, the patient (Rebecca) who asked me to phone her and then, when I did, denied any knowledge of ever having met me. As described above, DID states of mind abound in confabulations, which can be considered forms of delusion. The whole experience of DID, the belief that one consists of a number of different personalities, could itself be seen as a fundamental delusion about identity. A more controversial point relates to the narratives of childhood presented by DID patients; some would argue that accounts of ritual abuse contain elements of delusion as well as areas of historical truth (Kluft 1997). Altogether it is not possible to distinguish clearly and reliably between schizophrenic and DID patients in terms of descriptions of symptoms. Might DID and schizophrenia be essentially the same condition?

If the symptoms of schizophrenia and DID are so difficult to distinguish, why do clinicians not more readily conclude that DID patients are indeed schizophrenic. The answer lies, I suggest, in the rather different affective quality of DID patients as reflected in the response of the clinician. DID patients, in some states of mind, are warmer and more socially appropriate than schizophrenic patients. They can be extremely appealing, especially when presenting as vulnerable children. It is remarkable how quickly the clinician can come to feel that work with multiple 'people' in the one body is quite normal – at least while in the consulting room. Perhaps this provides the clue – the seductive presentation of DID patients obscures how essentially odd the whole picture is.

A further observation is that sometimes there may be at least one part or personality within a person with DID which demonstrates more overtly schizophrenic symptoms – e.g. reporting externally located hallucinations, hypochondriacal delusions, incoherent thought, blunting of affect, extreme withdrawal, etc. Alongside this can be considered the point that schizophrenic patients make use of dissociation. Like DID patients, those who are schizophrenic will withdraw from an external world felt to be unbearable and will construct an alternative 'pretend' or delusional world in which to dwell. Within this alternative internal world, the patient may feel dominated by dissociated voices, experienced as both belonging within the self but also separate. Like DID patients, the schizophrenic can appear relatively well at one point, but then under stress can become more overtly disturbed. Moreover, British psychoanalysts are used to conceptualising the existence of dissociated psychotic and sane parts of the mind living side by side, alternately assuming greater control (e.g. M. Sinason 1993; Bion 1957). This point of view could well be applied to the situation which occasionally arises, in which one may begin therapy with a patient who appears troubled but essentially sane, only to find some months, or even years later, that the patient shows psychotic manifestations, or reveals a hidden multiple personality.

What schizophrenia and MPD/DID clearly have in common is that both involve a retreat to a private world of fantasy or pretence, as a defence against a reality which is felt to be unbearably painful. The impression given by MPD/DID patients is that the retreat from reality to fantasy is driven by repeated trauma and abuse, while in the case of schizophrenia, there often appears to be more of a biological vulnerability which renders interpersonal life particularly difficult and painful.

In the case of both schizophrenia and MPD/DID, the private inner world is designed to be private. Internal voices and secret organisations do not take kindly to being discovered. As with disclosures of secrets of the mafia, there may be dangers both to the one who tells and the one who hears. Rage and relentless hostility may be unleashed towards the therapist when the hidden system is discovered or revealed. The system is, after all, organised on the basis of opposition to reality and to relatedness to external others. An internal world of fantasy others, concretised representations of aspects of self, are substituted for external relations. Thus in essence, the MPD system is both psychotic (in its avoidance of reality) and narcissistic (in its avoidance of relations with external others). Although parts of the system are allowed to relate to others, the idea that the system as a whole might relate to, or be known by, others is perceived as abhorrent and utterly dangerous.

Narcissism is often seen as inherently destructive (Rosenfeld 1971). Certainly, there can be moments in work with MPD/DID where one encounters the fury of narcissism discovered. The therapist and the therapy are viewed with implacable hostility, indeed hatred. Some religiously minded patients may use the image of the devil or satan to represent this hatred of reality and the scorn for vulnerability and relationships. The bizarre narratives of satanist ritual abuse, which so often emerge with such patients, indicate that either the patient herself, or those who abused her, believed that it is possible to create and dwell in an alternative world of pretence, fantasies of omnipotence, and reversal of values, scorning truth and love and spewing out confabulation and cruelty. Either the abusers or the patient are, in their hearts, psychotic and dedicated narcissists.

THE CONTENT AND PROCESS OF MPD

Multiple personality appears to represent a development of the basic reaction of dissociation in response to trauma. Dissociation, in the sense of detachment, numbing, feelings of depersonalisation and derealisation, amnesia etc. are recognised as common features of trauma responses and of post-traumatic stress disorder. Studies of Vietnam war veterans contributed greatly to an understanding of this constellation (van der Kolk et al. 1996). Some traumatised people, including those who were repeatedly abused in childhood, will describe experiences of feeling they were outside their body looking on at what was being done. This seems to represent a further stage of dissociation. Much rarer is the development of the full Dissociative Identity Disorder in which multiple personalities are created – dissociated behavioural states, each with specific identities, modes of cognition, characteristic moods and attitudes.

These 'alter' personalities can assume almost any identity since they seem to be constructed on the 'logic' of dream or trance, in which anything is possible. Thus alters may be male or female, adult or children, human or non-human. Quasi-spiritual entities are not uncommon. Usually, but not always, there is one personality that the system as a whole regards as the main identity which is presented to others. Often different personalities are created for particular roles – e.g. going to work, being sociable, being sexual, etc. Traumatised children are also commonly found. These may be guarded by special protector personalities, who may be hostile to the therapist if the children are perceived as being in danger. The degree of awareness of the overall system varies among the personalities, some having very limited awareness and others having considerable overview.

The extent to which the different personalities come out and take executive control varies between patients. With some, the switching between overt behavioural states is very clear – often signalled by a marked shift of body posture, or a sudden jerk of the head. The resulting change of mood, attitude and general demeanour may be striking. Moreover, the personality which has taken the driving seat, so to speak, may actually identify him/herself by name. With other patients, the multiple system may be much more covert or latent, its presence revealed only gradually, or the other personalities may be reported as internal influences which rarely take overt control but are experienced in the form of internal voices. Sometimes there may be switches of personality but these are so subtle that they are not easily apparent to the therapist. In such cases the patient may express surprise or irritation that the therapist has not realised there has been a change of personality.

In severe cases there may be dense amnesia in one personality state for what has taken place in another personality state. Thus the patient may describe waking up in bed with a stranger, or finding herself in a hospital or a police station, or discovering evidence of having been out during the night and returning with soiled clothes, but with no recollection of these events. Such a patient may have very limited conscious recollection of what has transpired during a psychotherapy session if there have been changes of state. After a particular alter has finished speaking and has 'retired', the 'main' personality may report no awareness of what has been said, or might describe a sense of hearing a conversation as if from a great distance.

What happens to alter personalities when they are not in executive control? Patients usually describe these as either being active in the background, listening or commenting, or else in a state resembling sleep. Sometimes alters appear to disappear for long periods of time, perhaps months. On returning they may describe having been in a state of deep dissociation. They may be disoriented, expecting the surroundings and the time of year to be as it was when they were last conscious. For example, a patient's teenage alter emerged, convinced that the year was 1965 and was very frightened that her parents would come to punish her for speaking. In an effort to convince her of the truth that her parents had died many years previously, she was shown a newspaper with the date indicating 1995. This greatly puzzled her. Looking out of the window she was astonished by the modern cars quite different in style and colour from the ones she knew. On being shown a modern clock with a battery she had to acknowledge that the world was indeed not quite as she expected.

Where the multiple system is capable of revealing its origins, the situation often described is one in which there was repeated abuse by a caregiver or other person who had regular access to the child and from whom there was no means of external escape. Other adults would either actively collude with the abuse or would turn a blind eye. Crucially, there would be no one who could act as a soothing and protective presence. The abuser would convince the child that there was no escape and that worse punishment would follow if the child attempted to tell. The child's resort to dissociative defences may have been mirrored upon dissociation inherent in the environment. For example, the perpetrator may abuse the child in one context while appearing loving and respectable in other contexts; the abuse that takes place in one situation is not referred to in another situation. The child may learn, in situation A, not only not to talk about the abuse that takes place in situation B, but also not even to think about it. Once dissociation has been discovered as an effective escape from pain, it may be resorted to ever more readily as a means of dealing with life's problems. The resulting dissociative structure may become very complex.

Can MPD be an iatrogenic creation, resulting from a combination of a suggestible and compliant patient and a crusading therapist who believes in this particular condition? Certainly some have argued this (e.g. Aldridge-Morris 1989; Ross 1997; Spanos 1996). Some such patients can be very suggestible, responsive both to externally and internally (self) derived suggestions, and also compliant, sensing what the therapist might expect or be interested to find, and generating an appropriate role play. The question is whether all cases of MPD/DID are generated in this way. The fact that patients do present for treatment with a fully developed multiple personality already apparent, and sometimes with no prior knowledge of the literature or television programmes about the condition, indicates that MPD can be present without any possibility of coaching by a therapist.

A corollary of the argument about therapeutic iatrogenesis is the claim, made by some MPD patients, that groups of dedicated abusers may deliberately create dissociation and multiple personality in their child victims. Certainly any kind of severe childhood regime, involving prolonged discomfort and fear, is likely to enhance tendencies to dissociate – and this may be valued in some cultural contexts. There have also been suggestions of interest in possible military uses of MPD (Marks 1979). Naturally it is extremely difficult to know what truth there might be in such allegations.

Although MPD/DID is usually assumed to have a basis in childhood trauma, Mair (1999) cautions that this may not always be the case. The grounds for assuming a basis in childhood trauma are, first, such patients usually report childhood abuse, and, second, dissociation is understood as one of the responses to trauma. However, some people who have not been traumatised may be naturally prone to dissociation and absorption in fantasy and score highly on measures of hypnotisability (Gudjonsson 1992). It is certainly the case that we should not assume that the fact of someone having a multiple personality necessarily means they have suffered childhood abuse. There may be other, as yet not clearly understood causes of MPD/DID.

What is clear is that MPD/DID is based in the use of pretence for psychodynamic purposes. Pretence is, in its nature, malleable. In one sense, a patient with a multiple personality is a patient pretending to have a multiple personality.

MEMORY AND DID

Multiple personality disorder is often dragged into the debates about recovered and false memory. For example, it might be alleged that a person recovered memories from a state of dissociation. Such a claim reflects a misunderstanding of dissociation and a confusion with repression (Mollon 1998).

If a piece of mental content (e.g. a feeling, a memory, a fantasy, a perception) is in a state of repression, it is not directly available to consciousness. Its existence may be inferred from its displaced and disguised expression. For example, a patient who is angry with the therapist may speak of anger with someone else – a kind of unconscious hinting. Gradually the patient may become more consciously aware of the previously repressed material.

By contrast, the feelings, memories and other mental contents of dissociated parts of the mind may be quite accessible to consciousness in that state of mind. Those contents may not be available, however, when the patient is in a different state of mind, or when another personality is in executive control. It is not that the objectionable mental content is kept in 'the unconscious' (a horizontal splitting, implying a hierarchical gradation of consciousness), but rather that consciousness is distributed among the dissociated parts of the mind.

Thus in state of mind A the patient may speak of a narrative of events of which he or she appears completely unaware when in state of mind B. When asked what she thought about the accounts of abuse which she had presented, in a childlike state of mind, during a previous session, a patient replied that she had no idea whether the memories were true or not because they were not her memories. In this way, what is claimed in one state of mind may be disowned in another state of mind. There may be a repudiation not only of the content of what has been said, but also of the fact of ever having said it.

Obviously, the existence of a mind which is severely dissociated raises questions about who is forgetting and who is remembering. In a dissociative structure, there is no unitary self which can remember or forget. Rather than a self making use of repression to avoid disturbing memories, there has been a resort to an alteration in the self as a central and coherent organisation of experience. MPD/DID involves not just an alteration in content but, crucially, a change in the very structure of consciousness and the self.

CHARACTERISTICS OF THE DISSOCIATIVE MIND – THE DISTRIBUTED CONSCIOUSNESS

The Freudian topographic model of the mind portrays a hierarchy of consciousness, with horizontal semi-permeable barriers regulating the passage of information from the unconscious to the conscious mind. In the later structural model, the emphasis was shifted from the topographical layering of consciousness to a concern with the ego functions of mediating between the instincts (id), the internalised caregivers (superego) and the external world. Nevertheless, the idea of a layering of consciousness, horizontal splitting (repression), remained intrinsic to Freud's vision of the mind. Melanie Klein's accounts of multiple splitting and projection began to weaken the assumption of a hierarchical consciousness, as did Fairbairn's (1952) description of a multiplicity of internal objects. Fairbairn actually published his Masters thesis on Multiple Personality Disorder.

The model of the dissociative mind renders a purely hierarchical view of consciousness hopelessly simplistic. Instead of consciousness and unconsciousness, what is found is a distributed consciousness. One patient put this very clearly. She told me that her different personalities remembered different aspects of what had gone on in her childhood; they did not know what each other knew and none of them knew all of what had gone on; the knowledge existed within her mind but was distributed among the different parts.

Dissociation as a defence may be compared with Bion's (1959) rather similar concept of 'attacks on linking', an extreme variant of the Kleinian schizoid position, in which splitting is the primary mode of relieving anxiety and mental pain. Dissociation is indeed an attack on linking, a mutilation of consciousness, engaged in as an act of desperation in order to reduce overwhelming emotional or physical agony. Thus linkage may be severed between one area of awareness and another, between memory and affect, between words and affect, and between experience and identity. Areas of experience may be denied access to words, with the result that experience is known but cannot be thought about – a variant of Bollas' (1987) 'unthought known'.

The varying experiences of self and other may be compartmentalised and therefore unintegrated – so that there may be multiple representations of self and other.

Those whose minds are not organised on the basis of multiplicity tend to experience the self as having relative coherence and cohesion, a sense of 'I' which persists through varying and conflicting experiences and which has continuity across time. By contrast, the experience in multiplicity may be of having no central self, but instead consisting of a group of disparate personalities, each of which at any particular point may regard him/herself as the self. The more extreme the dissociation, the more each fragmented part of the self is likely to assume an egocentric position. Each part may feel haunted or inhabited by the intimidating voices of the 'others'.

As well as coherence, cohesion and continuity in time, the self-experience of those who are not multiple, is of having depth. Some aspects of the self are clearly visible to others – above ground, so to speak. Other aspects are more hidden, both from consciousness and from others. In psychoanalysis, and other forms of emotional exploration, these hidden depths may gradually be discovered. Part of our sense of having roots or foundations, may lie in the early experience of safety (Sandler 1960), the feeling of being supported, held securely and 'backed up' – Grotstein's (1981) 'background selfobject of primary identification'. The person whose early life has been pervaded by terror, pain and betrayal (Freyd 1996) may lack this background of safety and experience of soothing. Instead of feeling able to surrender securely, for example during sleep, the person may experience a dread of falling into a nightmare. What should be a bedrock of safety becomes infiltrated with the uncanny, a distorting mirror that offers not soothing but mockery.

Despite the radical alteration of the structure of self-experience in MPD/DID, it should not be assumed that this is like a smashed or shattered state of mind, as found sometimes in more simple instances of PTSD. The multiple system of personality is highly organised, each part carrying out particular functions and having relationships to one another, as in any complex organisation. Functions may involve particular tasks in the person's current life, or may be to do with containing particular experiences or affects. As with any complex organisation of people, there will be group dynamics, including jostling for position and control, and the use of projection. The latter is apparent, for example, when one personality is the repository of all the most intense feelings of depression; quite understandably, such a part may feel ragefully suicidal at having to carry all this unbearable affect dumped by the others. Commonly, those parts which contain the most agonising affect or experiences of trauma may feel considerable resentment towards other dissociated parts who are free of these.

Although the dissociated personalities may appear to act relatively independently, especially if there is dense amnesia between them, there appears always to be a meta level of the system where it functions as a whole. For example, studies of implicit learning show that what is learned in one personality state may have an influence on learning in another personality state, even though this is not a conscious transfer (reviewed in Mollon 1998). Similarly, statements can be addressed to the system as a whole and there will be an appropriate response; for example, in the case of Rebecca, described above, she was able to get up and leave when told it was time for the session to stop, even though she had spent the session seemingly in a terrified child state of mind, completely disoriented from present reality. I find that a common dilemma is that if one addresses the patient as if he or she were multiple, this can be felt to impose a distortion, but if they are addressed as if having a unitary personality, this also is felt not to recognise their subjective reality. The patient is both multiple and a coherent unity. One patient represented this by the image of a molecule – a constellation of distinct parts, which nevertheless comprise a coherent whole.

SOME PRINCIPLES OF TREATMENT

The presence of a dissociative disorder is of such clinical and therapeutic significance that careful assessment is always advisable when considering taking on a patient for psychotherapy. It is not uncommon to hear of instances where a psychotherapist takes on a patient who seems only moderately troubled, only to discover months or even years later that a severe dissociative structure has become manifest – at a point when the psychotherapeutic voyage is well under way and it is too late to turn back. It is a sensible precaution therefore to screen routinely for indications of dissociative tendencies, perhaps through enquiries about amnesia, depersonalisation, derealisation, identity confusion and identity alteration; these are the five areas covered by Steinberg's Structured Clinical Interview for the assessment of DSM Dissociative Disorders (SCID-D). Another helpful tool is the use of screening questionnaires, such as the Dissociative Experiences Scale (Bernstein and Putnam 1986), or the Dissociation Questionnaire (Vanderlinden et al. 1993).

If there are indications of a Dissociative Identity Disorder, the next question is whether psychotherapeutic treatment is indicated or contraindicated. Psychotherapy always has the potential to worsen a patient's mental state, especially if the psychic equilibrium is fragile. This is likely to be the case if there has been severe and repeated abuse trauma in childhood, or if there is a latent psychosis, or if there is a multiple personality system. It is appropriate for both patient and therapist to be extremely cautious. Psychotherapy with a multiple personality system will destabilise that system through the very fact of its existence being disclosed – such systems are intended to be secret.

Disclosures and requests for help by one part of the system, without the agreement of other parts, are likely to generate internal civil war. This may be particularly intense if there is an idea that the therapist would favour fusion of personalities or abolition of certain troublesome personalities. This would be equivalent to an external agency taking sides in a conflict within a country.

One point that cannot be emphasised too highly is that for many patients a multiple personality system has been established as a means of surviving. To threaten this system may be experienced as a threat of death. In this way the therapist may be perceived as utterly dangerous, either through malevolence or ignorance. Nevertheless, the fact that the patient is presenting for treatment at all means that in some respects the system created for defence is breaking down, and this creates the motive for therapy.

My own stance is to tell the patient explicitly that the model I work with is one which aims to facilitate the development of internal communication and democracy. I explicitly use this political metaphor, emphasising that it is not my role to impose a solution, or to take sides. Therefore, the fundamental task for the personality system is to decide whether there is an internal consensus to proceed with therapy and what the goals might be. What may then happen is that the patient reports a kind of internal meeting having taken place, perhaps imagining the various personalities gathered around a table or debating chamber, and an agreement having been thrashed out. There may be further questions about aims and ground rules and conditions.

If agreed, therapy should proceed cautiously and slowly. The patient's safety and stability should remain a paramount concern. At times there may need to be careful discussion of practical tasks in the patient's life. Embarking on therapy may unleash a psychic stampede as the various personalities rush and compete to communicate with the therapist. The patient may neglect essential life tasks, including attention to job and family. At the same time, other parts may express intense alarm and hostility about what they perceive as the insane enterprise that has been embarked upon. There may be serious self-harm. In such crises it is necessary to remind the patient that the re-establishment of stability is the crucial task and that therapy is not viable if it continues to provoke such an overt worsening of his/her mental and behavioural state.

There will certainly be crises. One of these is likely to be what I call the 'crisis of trust'. This occurs as child parts of the patient begin to press to come forward in hope of being helped by the therapist. Paradoxically, the more that trust is felt by some personalities, the greater the anxiety, since trust is felt to be extremely dangerous. In response, those parts that have had the responsibility for maintaining or protecting the system and, in particular, the guarding of the 'children', may undertake drastic action to sabotage the therapy. In one example of this, a system protector generated an internal hallucinatory fantasy in which the patient followed the therapist to his house and stabbed him. This provoked alarm and chaos among the personalities, and serious self-harm in the form of cutting. The protector responsible for generating this image subsequently apologised to the rest of the system and to the therapist, acknowledging that the results had been more dangerous than 'he' had intended. Subsequently it was possible to negotiate with this part. The point was made to the protector that 'he' had demonstrated his capacity to wreck the therapy; the therapist was impotent to help unless this part agreed; it was not safe to allow the therapy to continue without the agreement of this part; the therapist would agree to take serious note of concerns expressed by this part at any stage; the therapist and this protector both wanted the best for the patient even if their perspectives were different. In this way, the initially hostile protector was transformed into an ally – grudging and scornful, but nevertheless an ally.

The mode of therapy I favour with such patients tends to be conversational and systemic, while always informed by psychoanalytic principles. Consistently with the non-hierarchical nature of consciousness in dissociative patients, I find that I make relatively little use of interpretation. Listening and facilitating communication and enquiry are more important much of the time. Simple explanations are sometimes relevant, however; for example: 'The sense of confusion and tension among you at present may be because you are all experiencing such different emotions about your stepfather's death.'

Inevitably, multiple selves mean there will be multiple transferences. Whatever the demeanour and attitude of the personality state in executive control at any particular moment, there will be others listening in the background, and these may have quite different attitudes towards the therapist. Another phenomenon that may arise is that of multiple therapists. For a person whose mind is organised on a dissociative basis, there may appear no contradiction in the idea of seeing different therapists concurrently.

The need for caution with regard to narratives of childhood events is clear. Deliberately seeking memories of trauma is not advisable because (a) this may encourage confabulation, and (b) the patient may be plunged into a state of retraumatisation. Memory is obviously prone to many distortions and, like a dream, is a psychodynamic product. Without independent corroboration, there may be no means of knowing what is literally true and what is confabulation in a memory narrative. Accounts of ritual or other bizarre abuse, I have always found perplexing. However, regardless of the question of its literal truth, my impression is that if a patient presents material of this kind the work is likely to be extremely difficult and hazardous.

The principles of work with MPD/DID may be summed up as follows: (1) assess carefully; (2) proceed cautiously; (3) facilitate internal democracy and communication; (4) emphasise that the therapy cannot continue if it appears to be producing a consistent worsening in the patient's state of mind; (5) firmly state that it is not for the therapist to find or impose a solution for the patient's internal conflicts; (6) keep expectations realistic and modest; (7) accept dissociation but do not encourage it; and (8) maintain extreme caution.

One further point I would advise is that a third party, a doctor such as the GP or a psychiatrist, is always kept in the picture. Without this, the therapy has the potential to be experienced as secretive and therefore abusive.

HAZARDS TO THE PSYCHOTHERAPIST

In previous writings (e.g. Mollon 1996, 1998) I have emphasised the hazards to the patient of embarking on therapy. Here I will state some ways in which therapists may be in danger from patients with multiple personalities.

It is commonly alleged that MPD/DID is an iatrogenic creation, a product of suggestion by an overenthusiastic therapist who is excessively invested in a particular theory. Actually, the truth, in part, may be a reversal of this. Such patients are often highly skilful actors who effectively hypnotise the therapist as well as 'themselves' – and who manage to convince the therapist of their subjective reality.

The MPD system as a whole is a kind of psychosis, albeit one created out of despair, terror or other unmanageable affect. Once created, it may itself become a monster, a malevolent organisation run on terror. Its purpose seems to be to maintain some basic engagement with the surrounding world, while concealing most of the dissociative self in a secret fortress. Obviously such an organisation is not going to co-operate in its own destruction. Instead it will try to incorporate the therapist into its own world. Indeed it will seek not only to maintain itself, but also, like any organisation, will tend to expand, consuming reality and substituting fantasy.

Patients presenting with these problems can often appear very appealing, evoking strongly protective or maternal responses in the therapist, and fantasies of rescue. Accounts of therapeutic work with MPD/DID abound with examples of the therapist trying hard to accommodate the patient, stretching boundaries, endeavouring to present a more 'human' rather than professional stance, and generally behaving in therapeutically unusual ways. These can then leave the therapist vulnerable to accusations of deviant practice.

In some instances a patient may present at certain times in ways which display dissociation and invite a diagnosis of MPD/DID, but subsequently deny this and claim it to be a therapist's creation. This may then be followed by a vicious turning against the therapist, including making complaints to employers or professional organisations and, in the USA, pursuing litigation (Macdonald 1999). The patient has created a delusion, drawn the therapist into it, and then condemned the therapist.

As Chu (1998) comments, in his excellent book:

> It is sadly ironic that these patients accuse others of having believed the very behaviours that they so diligently tried to portray, and that the accusations prolong the attention on them that they pathologically crave.
>
> (p. 200)

Such manoeuvres, while deeply traumatising for the therapist, are really no surprise in view of the likely basis of MPD/DID in childhood betrayal. Of course the early experiences of betrayal will be enacted and probably reversed.

This is both obvious and shocking. The experience of betrayal gives rise to the wish for revenge. Someone has to pay – and it may well be the therapist. The patient may switch from a vulnerable child state to one of manic triumph, in which the bad or vulnerable self is projected into the therapist. This may be evoked particularly by the threat during therapy of approaching an area of unbearable annihilatory pain. At such points the therapist is perceived as a lethal threat which must be destroyed.

The hatred of the therapist may rest partly upon the tendency towards a psychotic transference. Instead of an 'as if' transference perception, the therapist is experienced quite concretely as abusive or malevolent. It should be remembered that the worst abuse the patient may have suffered in childhood is likely at some point to inform the transference image of the therapist.

A psychotherapist considering work with an MPD/DID patient should think carefully about what he or she is taking on. The endeavour, begun with such good will, may consume years of work and create immense stress and turmoil for both therapist and patient. Indeed, if therapeutic work with an MPD patient goes awry, it may consume an entire career.

REFERENCES

Aldridge-Morris, R. (1989) *Multiple Personality. An Exercise in Deception*. Hove: Erlbaum.

Bernstein, E.M. and Putnam, F.W. (1986) 'Development, reliability and validity of a dissociation scale'. *Journal of Nervous and Mental Disease* 174: 727–735.

Bion, W.R. (1957) 'Differentiation of the psychotic from the non-psychotic personality'. *International Journal of Psycho-Analysis* 38. Also in *Second Thoughts* (1967) London: Maresfield.

Bion, W.R. (1959) 'Attacks on linking'. *International Journal of Psycho-Analysis* 40: 308–315. Also in *Second Thoughts* (1967) London: Maresfield.

Bollas, C. (1987) *The Shadow of the Object. Psychoanalysis of the Unthought Known*. London: Free Association.

Chu, J.A. (1998) *Rebuilding Shattered Lives. The Responsible Treatment of Complex Post-traumatic and Dissociative Disorders*. New York: Wiley.

Fairbairn, R. (1952) *Psychoanalytic Studies of the Personality*. London: Routledge.

Freyd, J.J. (1996) *Betrayal Trauma. The Logic of Forgetting Child Abuse*. Cambridge, MA: Harvard University Press.

Grotstein, J.S. (1981) *Splitting and Projective Identification*. New York: Aronson.

Gudjonsson, G.H. (1992) *The Psychology of Interrogations, Confessions and Testimony*. Chichester: Wiley.

Kluft, R.P. (1997) 'Overview of the treatment of patients alleging that they have suffered ritualised or sadistic sexual abuse'. In G.A. Fraser (ed.) *The Dilemma of Ritual Abuse*. Washington, DC: American Psychiatric Press.

Macdonald, G.C. (1999) *The Making of an Illness. My Experience with Multiple Personality Disorder*. Toronto: Laurentian Press.

Mair, K. (1999) 'Multiple personality and child abuse'. *The Psychologist* 12(2): 76–80.

Marks, J. (1979) *The Search for the Manchurian Candidate. The CIA and Mind Control.* New York: Norton.

Mollon, P. (1996) *Multiple Selves, Multiple Voices. Working with Trauma, Violation and Dissociation.* Chichester: Wiley.

Mollon, P. (1998) *Remembering Trauma. A Psychotherapist's Guide to Memory and Illusion.* Chichester: Wiley.

Rosenfeld, H. (1971) 'A clinical approach to the psychoanalytic theory of the life and death instincts: an investigation into the aggressive aspects of narcissism'. *International Journal of Psycho-Analysis* 52: 169–178.

Rosenfeld, H. (1987) *Impasse and Interpretation.* London: Routledge.

Ross, C. (1994) *The Osiris Complex. Case Studies in Multiple Personality Disorder.* Toronto: University of Toronto Press.

Ross, C. (1997) *Dissociative Identity Disorder.* New York: Wiley.

Sandler, J. (1960) 'The background of safety'. *International Journal of Psycho-Analysis* 41: 191–198.

Sinason, M. (1993) 'Who is the mad voice inside?' *Psychoanalytic Psychotherapy* 7: 207–221.

Spanos, N.P. (1996) *Multiple Identities and False Memories. A Sociocognitive Perspective.* Washington, DC: American Psychological Association.

Steinberg, M. (1993) *Interviewer's Guide to the Structured Clinical Interview for the DSM-IV Dissociative Disorders (SCID-D).* Washington, DC: American Psychiatric Press.

van der Kolk, B.A., McFarlane, A.C., and Weisaeth, L. (1996) *Traumatic Stress. The Effects of Overwhelming Experience on Mind, Body and Society.* New York: Guilford Press.

Vanderlinden, J., Van Dyke, R., Vandereycken, W., Vertommen, H. and Verkes, R.J. (1993) 'The dissociation questionnaire: development and characteristics of a new self-report questionnaire'. *Clinical Psychology and Psychotherapy* 1: 21–27.

Part IV

Practical diagnostic and administrative issues

Labels

a

I've been silenced all through my life
The labels I carry I never hide
I got them through triggers
Planted in my mind

b

Labels are awful
Labels are sad
People use them
Thinking you're bad
But they just don't know
The pain that's inside
And the labels are the mask
Behind which you hide

Beverley

Look Nurse, Look Nurse, what can you see?
An attention seeking, manipulative trouble-maker
Who dresses like a tart and acts like a flirt
Look Nurse, Look Nurse, that's not this person
I mean to be
That's not the person locked up in this prison
Called me!

Toisin

Chapter 12

Dissociative disorders
Recognition within psychiatry and RAINS

Joan Coleman

As medical students in the 1950s, we learned during the course on psychiatry, that there was a rare condition known as Hysterical Multiple Personality, which occurred almost exclusively in young women. My student psychiatric text book (Henderson and Gillespie 1950), stated that:

> 'Double' and 'Multiple' personality are the terms applied when the same individual at different times appears to be in possession of entirely different mental content, disposition and character, and when one of the different phases shows complete ignorance of the other, an ignorance which may be reciprocal. Each 'sub-personality' . . . is said to be 'dissociated' from the total personality.

There was no stated causal theory such as childhood trauma, but the definition was not unreasonable for that time.

In 1973–5 while retraining in psychiatry, my mind became more or less closed to the idea of multiple personality, which was again mentioned very briefly and only in the context of hysteria. The main textbook used then was *Clinical Psychiatry* (Slater and Roth 1969), which, although warning of the dangers of misdiagnosing all tics and stammers as hysterical, none the less is sceptical and derogatory about 'double and multiple personalities' which are once more linked exclusively to the female sex. 'It seems that these multiple personalities are always artificial productions, the product of the medical attention (and also the literary interest) that they arouse'. There is still no suggestion of any relationship to childhood trauma.

The Companion to Psychiatric Studies (Alistair Forrest 1973), was considered then to be *the* comprehensive psychiatric textbook for those seeking a higher qualification. The 1973 edition contains only one reference to 'dissociation' and none to multiple personality, even under 'hysteria'. So, like most other psychiatrists I put the concept to the back of my mind as of little interest or importance. Significantly, none of these textbooks mentioned child sexual abuse (CSA) either, despite describing patients with eating disorders, given to self-injury, incapable of sustaining relationships, sometimes very promiscuous but often frigid. These disorders were attributed to attention seeking or to unconscious unresolved infantile conflicts and were included among the personality disorders or the neuroses.

Many such patients came through the 'revolving door' of the hospital I worked in, and they were usually diagnosed as borderline personality disorder. Some were said to be hysterics. Rarely did they disclose abuse in the early years, but if they were brave enough to do so, they were told that that was all in the past and were advised to put it firmly behind them and concentrate on their present behaviour. Most continued intermittently to harm themselves. Some gave up trying to get help and killed themselves.

How was it that we were all so blind?

I was as blinkered as the rest until the mid-1980s when, by chance, I found myself working with a patient who had various 'psychosomatic' disorders and was also subject to trance-like states. She attributed her frequent overdoses to her inability to cope with these. After my having investigated her for temporal lobe epilepsy, with a negative result, and puzzled over her for two or three years, she eventually began to talk. It finally emerged that she had been brought up within a satanic cult which was currently operating, and that these trance-like episodes were dissociative phenomena.

Since then I have worked clinically with a number of other survivors of Satanist ritual abuse, most of whom clearly showed multiple personality. In addition, I have, through RAINS (Ritual Abuse Information Network and Support) spoken to at least 300 therapists, all of whom have clients who have suffered alleged ritual abuse. These therapists have described high levels of dissociation among their clients, many of whom are showing evidence of what we now know as Dissociative Identity Disorder (DID). Most have already been through the psychiatric services and have received little help from them. I have also encountered, more directly, a large number of survivors claiming to have been ritually abused and it is very clear that dissociation of some degree is the norm. Many were brought up in families that had practised Satanism through several generations, and the usual procedure, according to them, was for abuse to start in infancy. I now find myself surprised when generational ritual abuse survivors do not show any sign of DID. It seems to be a survival strategy that is almost inevitable, if any relationship with their parents or carers is to be sustained.

Multiple personality usually develops in the presence of severe and repeated trauma, beginning at a very early age, when the personality is developing. Ritual abuse fulfils these criteria; much of it is generational and starts almost at birth; in addition, it involves profoundly sadistic sexual and physical abuse which includes torture, also psychological abuse which includes enforced perpetration. This psychological abuse is devastating as it forces upon the child impossible choices with no available positive option; whatever choice is made it will result in extreme guilt or further punishment. It is hardly surprising that many survivors of ritual abuse develop DID in order to preserve their own sanity.

Sadly, psychiatric training still includes far too little on the very serious psychiatric sequelae of childhood trauma, especially CSA. There is inadequate recognition within mental health services of the prevalence and importance of Dissociative Disorders, sufferers of which are frequently misdiagnosed as Borderline Personality Disorder (BPD), or, in the cases of DID, schizophrenia.

This is to some extent understandable as some of the features of DID appear superficially to mimic those of schizophrenia and/or Borderline Personality Disorder. These are as follows:

1   Losing time. Periods lasting minutes, hours or days for which the person is subsequently amnesic. These are explained by another alter (personality) being present (in charge of the body). These times could conceivably be mistaken for the amnesia that many schizophrenics display for acute psychotic episodes.

2   Sudden dramatic changes in mood. People with DID can appear to be in the depths of despair or uncontrollable panic one minute and suddenly switch to a calm, rational and even cheerful state when another alter takes over. These changes could erroneously be regarded as incongruity of affect as seen in many hebephrenics, or as the mood swing often apparent in patients with personality disorder.

3   Bizarre behaviour. Some alters may be loyal to the perpetrators and show considerable hostility to the therapist or anybody whom they feel is undermining the group's activities. Sometimes they are programmed to carry out aggressive acts such as fire-setting, or threats of harm to others. People who display such behaviour are usually regarded as psychopaths, but combined with other symptoms may appear psychotic.

4   Hallucinations.

   a   Visual, olfactory, gustatory, haptic, painful, etc. All or any of these may occur when experiencing memory flashbacks or when reliving with vivid intensity experiences from which their conscious memory has been dissociated. They are often described as body memories and they are impressive to witness. Those involving pain are convincingly real. These body memories frequently precede narrative memory. In therapy it gradually becomes apparent that there is an association with a specific past event, unlike most of the hallucinations of schizophrenics.

   b   Auditory. Patients with DID usually admit to hearing voices. They describe these as being inside the head, whereas those in schizophrenia are more commonly heard as if coming from outside. In DID these are often the voices of alter personalities, but sometimes they may be the voices of perpetrators repeating past commands or tormenting them with threats. This is probably a result of post-hypnotic suggestion and programming, especially in SRA victims: sometimes they are the voices of perpetrators who have been introjected as alters. In these cases it is worth establishing whose voice they are hearing and also the content of the hallucination.

5   Paranoid features. Those who have been hurt by Satanist abusers may have a tough time when trying to leave the group and may live for months or years in perpetual fear of being found. In this state they can read sinister motives into all manner of events, at least some of which may be innocent. At other times there may be sound foundation for their fear. Paranoid fears under these conditions should not be interpreted as psychosis, even though this may score highly in psychometric tests. Of course, childhood trauma and DID do not protect anyone from developing paranoid schizophrenia and occasionally people are seen with both conditions. This can confuse the issue immensely but sorting out this situation is beyond the scope of this chapter.

6   Self-injury: cutting and overdosing. This is more likely to be attributed to personality disorder than schizophrenia. Many who are diagnosed as BPD have in fact been either physically or sexually abused in childhood and have low self-esteem, strong feelings of guilt and shame extending sometimes to self-hatred. Through frequent hospital admissions many have learned maladaptive behaviour patterns. But these features are also often seen in DID patients who may have alters who have been programmed to injure themselves. They frequently dissociate prior to cutting, then return, bewildered, to find themselves holding a razor blade and bleeding. There are many reasons why abused people injure themselves and it is worthwhile exploring these. It is rarely due to the motive normally attributed to them; that of self-pity and attention seeking.

There is, thus, virtually no provision for treatment within the NHS. It would appear that the diagnosis of Post-traumatic Stress Disorder (see de Zulueta, Chapter 3) is more commonly accepted and treated, but usually without acknowledgement of the degree of accompanying dissociation.

However, intelligent new psychiatry books like the *UCH Textbook on Psychiatry* (1990) do devote more time to DID and recommend *Sybil* as a book describing psychoanalytic treatment of DID (see also Brett Kahr, Chapter 16). There have in addition, during the last few years, been more clinical accounts.

However, there is still an urgent need for psychiatric training to include considerably more information regarding CSA and SRA together with their subsequent effects, with special emphasis on dissociative disorders. Only then is there likely to be adequate provision for appropriate psychotherapeutic treatment within mental health services.

REFERENCES

Forrest, A. (ed.) (1973) *Companion to Psychiatric Studies*, Churchill Livingstone, London.

Henderson, D. and Gillespie, R.D. (1950) *A Textbook of Psychiatry*, OUP, Oxford.

Slater, E. and Roth, M. (1969) *Clinical Psychiatry*, Bailliere, Tindall & Cassell, London.

Wolff, H., Bateman, A. and Sturgeon, D. (eds) (1990) *UCH Textbook of Psychiatry*, Duckworth, London.

Chapter 13a

How does a telephone help?

Patricia Pitchon

Working in a clinic with patients suffering from Dissociative Identity Disorder involves answering calls from people who have experienced severe trauma and generally have a background of prolonged abuse. Key issues that arise from this aspect of the work include the difference between helpful listening and therapeutic intervention, the ability to listen to stories of torture and terror and their traumatic aftermath, ways of relating to those who may communicate in more than one personality state, and the development of trust.

Goals include establishing a relationship with the person in any and all personality states, contributing to a developing awareness of the existence of those states helping with the processing of unbearable memories.

In answering such calls we neither investigate possible crimes – however disturbing the evidence – nor engage in therapy. But we can support these individuals and be an adjunct to their therapy by developing a relationship with the caller which never violates their autonomy. The caller takes the initiative in communicating, and a space is provided where some traumatic aspects can be communicated and shared reflection becomes possible.

Accounts emerge with grim and unfailing regularity from people who are isolated, often do not know of any others who share their plight, and whose loneliness is often extreme. I think 'torture' is a more accurate, and more descriptive term, than 'abuse'.

The suffering of such people is as much moral as physical, mental and emotional. It often seems that those involved in ritual abuse, either consciously or instinctively, in a deliberate and organised fashion, have gone to great lengths to compromise these survivors. They apparently wish to destroy the ability of such survivors to forgive themselves for what they were initially coerced into, and to discredit them as witnesses. This type of suffering is even more difficult to bear than the memories of tortures they themselves have undergone.

Our current legal and medical procedures do not adequately assist such vulnerable people. These attitudes compound the difficulties of the various counsellors, therapists, GPs, psychiatrists, child protection officers and members of the legal profession who may have succeeded in understanding what has happened to a given individual even if they are no closer to being able to provide quick solutions, much less develop appropriate legal redress for those who seek it among this particular group of severely damaged people.

This is why sympathetic listening, and the ability to stay with the caller in any of the personality states which may present themselves, can become a valuable service. What is communicated is often powerful and revealing, so that our understanding grows accordingly.

Take this succinct explanation for the creation of alternative personality states. I was speaking to 'Susan' and after some minutes a childlike voice said 'Hello? This is "Billy"'. I asked, 'How old are you?' The answer was, 'I'm ten'. I spoke as I would to any 10-year-old child, and 'Billy' related some distress-ing memories of animal sacrifice. The same episode had been related in a more mature way by Susan as herself. 'Billy' also told me about one or two other young ones, their names, and how they hurt themselves when they could not stand the memories, including a recent episode of self-harm where 'Susan' had to go to hospital. 'I came out in the ambulance', said Billy. I said, 'You must have been very frightened'. He agreed. I asked, 'Were you in pain?' He said, 'No, but there was blood everywhere and I was scared'. During another call, 'Susan' described how she suddenly found herself with her arms slashed, bleeding profusely, and managed to call an ambulance, not knowing how this had happened to her. Later during the call, 'Billy' re-emerged to explain that 'we' (the various child-like personality states, with a sense of identity involv-ing specific gender, age, name and separate memories) 'came out so Susan would not feel the pain'.

One caller informed me that she had been through four therapists but had never been able to describe the ritual abuse – aspects of which she had just related to me – to any of them. I asked whether it was easier to tell me because we could not see each other and she said yes. This highlights how difficult it is to reveal the grimmest details of this type of abuse, and at the same time how telephone work can serve as a link to therapy.

The clinic receives several thousand phone calls each year. Many of these come from concerned carers, relatives and professionals, as well as abused and dissociative people. This highlights the severe lack of provision for this group of people, and the need to provide services to help and support them.

Issues around administrating in a clinic for patients with Dissociative Identity Disorder

Claire Usiskin

Most patients have a troubled psychiatric history, with various past diagnoses. This leads to files being large and complex.

As different personalities produce different kinds of communications, filing structures have to be flexible. Some will send five emails a day, some will send poems or drawings, others will communicate by phone and these conversations will need to be written down and filed. Patients may also wish photos or school records to be kept for safety, away from cult-identified relatives.

The files are literally multiple, as most patients generate a lot of material, and may be known under different names. It is important to be organised as, for example, one patient may have an alter with the same name as the host personality of another patient and mix-ups are possible.

Psychologically it feels necessary to have good recall of patients' different personalities and their histories. Perhaps this is a reaction to the fact that the patients are dissociative – it engenders a wish for one person at least to be able to contain all the information known about them at the same time.

Memory is also important in keeping track of the various other agencies which may be involved in a patient's life, as often an extensive amount of liaison is necessary.

When answering the telephone the administrator needs to understand that child alters or very distressed patients may call. It is important to ask who is speaking and to understand that some people may not wish to give their names or any details. As an administrator rather than a helpline operator I have felt frustrated, guilty and worried at not being able to help a distressed caller if the helpline worker is not there and the caller does not know me.

Some of the visual material produced or sent in by patients can be very shocking and disturbing. It is essential to file and label this clearly so that it is not found unexpectedly by anyone.

A related matter is the disclosure of details of severe abuse which may be present in a patient's file. This disturbing material is not easy to forget (and as mentioned above, sometimes it feels important *not* to forget it), and supervision with someone who understands the issues is therefore essential. While clinicians are trained to protect themselves from the impact of this kind of material, an administrator is trained to remember detail, which can leave them vulnerable to the effects of dealing with it. Secondary traumatisation is a real risk when doing this type of work.

Even from an administrator's point of view it is sometimes difficult to maintain clinical and professional boundaries around patients with DID. They may call in desperation out of office hours, or at risk of suicide, wanting and needing an immediate response even if the therapist is not available. This creates a dilemma – the anxiety of the patient is transmitted directly to the administrator, and it can be difficult to contain, resulting in a wish to break clinical boundaries and interrupt the therapist's session with another client.

Having been a researcher and administrator on projects working with both child sexual abuse victims and young sexual abusers, I can say that there is a noticeable difference in the emotions experienced when working with dissociative ritual abuse survivors. The terror experienced by these patients is very real and powerful to witness, even many years after their abuse has ended. One is compelled to accept the truth of what to most people would seem like horrific fiction. This is not an easy thing to do and sometimes this knowledge can feel unwelcome and disillusioning. However the bravery of the patients in disclosing these facts must serve as an example.

Finally I would say that this is a very inspiring group of patients to work with, in terms of their strength, tenacity, resourcefulness and creativity. It is a privilege to witness their hard work and to be able to help them in however small a way.

Legal issues around Dissociative Identity Disorder

Short notes

Valerie Sinason

The courts in England are not experienced in dealing with Dissociative Identity Disorder. However, the growing awareness of the need to provide access to justice for vulnerable victims means that it is extremely important that further education takes place. Many DID individuals have been taking legal advice in terms of the ways in which their cases could be aided. Key questions that have not yet been tested in court include the responsibilities of the 'main' person for possible offences committed by other states when there is genuinely no co-consciousness. Police also have to deal with difficult circumstances where one 'state' tells where an offence has taken place but they are loyal to the alleged abuser and give a wrong detail. When the 'main' state appears to give their account of the alleged abuse the police might not have the time to deal with this and the possibly useful witness is discredited for being too unreliable and vulnerable. Memory tests conducted by experienced psychologists in this field can help to show if there is real unreliability or whether each 'state' can give consistent evidence.

Of increasing concern to all who come into contact with these children and adults is the current position where crimes against someone suffering with DID can go unpunished. Rape is sadly all too often one person's word against another's and only a tiny percentage of cases even get to court. Where the alleged victim has a learning disability or a dissociative disorder the odds are even smaller.

However, the increasing role of advocates in the mental health system and the rise in lawyers concerned for such individuals provides hope for the future. Here below is a brief list of points that lawyers have made in terms of legal issues to consider in the case of offences, but the legal issues cover far greater areas than this. What is the right of a single 'state' to the home of their choice or the medical treatment of their choice when another 'state' disputes that choice? Clinicians will be required to think about the systemic needs of the whole person.

Legal points:

1   *Trespass to the person* is subject to a 6-year limitation period which runs from the date of the abuse or, if later, the date at which the claimant attained

majority. Dissociation can mean an individual is only capable of taking action when the time limit has already expired.

2   *Claim for negligence* can allow judges the discretion to extend time following 533(3) of the 1980 Limitation Act which takes into account reasons for delay and disability.

3   *Expert assessments* Despite the new scientific evidence from brain research on the reality of DID, few British psychiatrists are up to date in their ability to diagnose or evaluate this condition.

4   *DID in Court* There appears to be no legal precedent in this country as to how multiplicity would be dealt with. This makes it harder for the 'innocent' state to confess to the police what another state has done.

5   *The Home Office 1998 Report* on the treatment of vulnerable or intimidated witnesses emphasises the extra support needed for such individuals where mental or physical disability, disorder or impairment exists. Unfortunately, a change of identity is not possible for someone who is severely dissociative.

6   Those wishing to disclose details of murders they were implicated in under duress are held back by fear of imprisonment. They see themselves in a similar position to Pattie Hearst, just freed by outgoing President Clinton, who eventually took part in the bank raids the group who kidnapped her involved her in. Although the issue of brainwashing was thoroughly, discussed, lengthy imprisonment still followed.

Part V

Other frames of reference

I thank you for believing

I thank you for believing
And for not turning me away
I know it must be awful
To hear the things I say

I know I've still a long way to go
But at least I know it won't be alone
Things will get better as the triggers disappear
And the realisation will take away my fear

Never think you've wasted your time
Knowing how it's done has opened my eyes
Never once have you said, 'It's all in my mind'
Through telling me it's not you've helped save my life

Beverley

Chapter 14

The di-vidual person

On identity and identifications

R.D. Hinshelwood

> The dialectic between Janet and Freud continues a century later.
> Ira Brenner 1994

The idea of a number of persons occupying one body is manifestly absurd. And yet psychiatry has got very excited about this in the last couple of decades. Some psychiatrists repudiate the idea altogether, while others insist on the phenomenon in the most literal terms.

What should we make of this debate and the 'unscientific' excitement it has generated?

Dissociation, repression, splitting, fragmentation, annihilation . . . The plethora of terms that deny the basic functioning unity of the person do suggest it is an elusive thing, and yet one which cannot be ignored. The individual, one has to say, is not inevitably indivisible, but potentially divided – hence a 'di-vidual'.

INTRODUCTION

Multiple Personality Disorder (MPD), or Dissociative Identity Disorder (DID) are names for a condition which is variously thought to result from trauma, organic change or iatrogenic pressure. Serious claims of a very far-reaching kind are made. A whole series of different phenomena are aggregated together: altered states of consciousness, autohypnosis, depersonalisation, abrupt switching of identification, iatrogenic influences (also forensic), post-traumatic stress disorder. All these can be taken as more or less synonymous with the core idea of 'seemingly autonomous alters' (Brenner 1994).[1]

The plethora of confusing descriptions, the dismaying overlapping of distinct terms such as dissociation, repression and splitting, the quality of a gripping drama, the disconcerting affront caused by some patients, and the popular assumption of the credulity of psychiatrists has led naturally and frequently to the conclusion that there is no reality at the bottom of all the excitement.

Certainly, the confusions, sloppily used terminology and professional disagreement suggest that there is probably not any one thing at the bottom of it all. However, something creates this fascination, builds professional careers, and dedicates many patients to lives of illness. I want to address some of the terminological and conceptual issues in this currently raging debate.

So many people have come back to this phenomenon in their own ways. What exactly is it? Do all those terms mean the same thing in different people's languages, or are there important differences? Are there ways in which an individual is divisible? And, if so, do we need a catalogue to find our way?

In order to try to bring some order to this array of phenomena with competing aetiological factors, Wilson (1993) categorised four possibilities:

1   *Multiple personality is a normal enough condition.* It differs only in degree from the extreme states encountered clinically; and Wilson quoted Freud – 'perhaps the secret of the cases of what is described as "multiple personality" is that the different identifications seize hold of consciousness in turn' (Freud 1923: 30–31).[2]

2   *Multiple personality is a false entity promoted by malingerers with the aid of gullible medical practitioners.*[3] For many patients, and some legal offenders, the diagnosis will relieve them of various obligations, responsibilities and potential punishment. Hypnotic influences would play a considerable role in this explanation.

3   *Multiple personality is a mental disorder* sui generis. Two or more distinct personalities exist in the same body. Amnesia exists, at a conscious level, between these separate personalities, and thus each is taken as an autonomous person with paradoxical results in the area of autonomy and responsibility (for example Braude 1995).

4   *Multiple personality is a symptom in a range of primary pathologies.* The plethora of conditions is great and it leaves the essential nature of the condition undecided.

A fifth tendency appears to be growing, in which multiple personality is *a common root cause of an increasing array of diagnoses*. Mollon (1996), for instance, makes one such inclusive claim that 'dissociation is about detachment from an unbearable situation' (p. 4). He includes everything from the 'hidden' observer in hypnosis (Hilgard 1977) and the observing ego of Fenichel (1938) to the major amnesias and multiple autonomous personalities, and some hallucinatory states close to schizophrenia. Gathering such a wide spread of phenomena under one sweep is making a very large claim to explain a very large panorama of psychopathology.

This unifying view has then stimulated attempts, usually on theoretical grounds, to implicate a common underlying factor causing this widespread phenomenon. Some (Kluft 1984) postulate an elegant specificity: interest in Multiple Personality Disorders (MPD) has coincided with the revelations of the incidence of childhood abuse, therefore one of these (abuse) is attributed as the cause of the other (MPD).

There is among many people a reactive hesitation to accept this hegemonic aspiration of MPD/dissociation. In addition, the fact that these ideas have historically been, gone, and come back again, points us directly towards a significant socio-historical factor in explanation of them.[4] Hacking (1999) has explored the social meanings of this disorder thus minimising all elements of actual psychopathology.[5] In the present account, the psychopathology of this particular condition will be briefly traced.

TWO HISTORICAL PHASES OF MULTIPLE PERSONALITY DISORDERS

Interest in dissociated parts of the person has reached a peak in two separate historical periods. The first was in the last two decades of the nineteenth century. A considerable therapeutic pessimism within psychiatry at that time prompted a reaction, particularly in France, where psychology and psychotherapy experiments with hypnosis were carried out (Charcot 1889; Bernheim 1884). Altered states of consciousness, known as hysteria, became a dominant field of interest at the turn of the century. The condition could be conceptualised within current psychological theories (based on dissociation), and it prompted specific forms of therapy (Bernheim 1884; Dejerine and Glaucker 1913) but above all it could challenge the prevailing pessimism and assert a new *fin-de-siècle* optimism. In addition, Charcot's pictures of swooning young women under the control of male doctors exemplified the quality of excitement these new interests could arouse.

Interestingly, that fascinated interest became linked, in Britain, to the investigation of spiritualism and the attempt to contact those in 'the other world' (Myers 1904; Oppenheim 1985). This quasi-religious significance progressively gave way to scientific attempts at understanding. However, Janet (1899) in France and Morton Prince (1906) in the US formalised their psychiatric status; Prince with his study of Sally Beauchamp, a medium who had several personalities,[6] was particularly influential in the US.

More recently, interest resurfaced in a second phase. In the last couple of decades of the twentieth century, a renewed popularity emerged. Like 100 years ago, it started as a recessive strand to contemporary psychiatry. But once again it had to escape from the shadows of the dominant physical explanations of psychosis – the new neuroscience.

This historical periodicity needs understanding, and this can be done only with some thought about the dominant sets of attitudes and conceptualisations of the person as they evolve in the modern period. I shall argue that what we see is a particular historical shadow cast upon our own times. Posing as a medical issue, it is one married to contemporary concerns about personal identity. Nor are these concerns limited, in our own day, to medicine alone. There is considerable philosophical uncertainty, too, over the nature of the individual and its supposed singularity (Nagel 1971; Parfitt 1984; Glover 1988; Hinshelwood 1995). I shall try to disentangle some of the factors which contribute to our contemporary notion that a divided individual is pathological.

A HISTORY OF INDIVIDUALITY

The debates of the last hundred years are not the beginning of this interest in multiple personalities (see also Ellenberger 1970; Whyte 1979; Taylor 1989; Rose 1990). A trend occurs throughout history in which the divided individual is actually accepted as commonplace. For example, Wilson (1995) has briefly cited instances, as follows. Plato famously described the human being as one half of a person seeking to come together with the other half in a coupled unity. Shakespeare comments, in *Twelfth Night*, 'How didst thou make division of thyself?' And Elizabethan drama was occupied with the device of disguised and mistaken identity – often cross-dressing.

Stevenson in his *Dr Jekyll and Mr Hyde* celebrated the phenomenon in a very concrete way: 'I hazard a guess that man will be ultimately known for a mere polity of multifarious incongruous and independent denizens' (quoted in Wilson 1995: 73). Today, we continue to be fascinated by the ventriloquist and his dummy. So, the idea of an individual having diverse identity has not always been abnormal.

At a certain point, however, that notion of divided selves became submerged as a non-dominant trend in the view of persons. That contrast with the ideal view of the individual, was described explicitly 100 years ago by Myers, a prominent researcher, at the time of the first phase of interest in multiple personalities:

> The earlier enquiries which men have made about consciousness have been of a merely ethical or legal character – simply aimed at deciding whether at a given moment a man was *responsible* for his acts, either to a human or a divine tribunal. Common sense has seemed to encourage this method of definite demarcation; we judge practically either that a man is conscious or that he is not; in the experience of life intermediate states are of little importance.
>
> As soon, however, as the problem is regarded as a psychological one, to be decided by observation and experiment, these hard and fast lines grow fainter and fainter. We come to regard consciousness as an attribute which may possibly be present in all kinds of varying degrees . . . We must approach the whole subject of split or duplicated personalities with no prepossession against the possibility of any given arrangement or division of the total mass of consciousness which exists within us.
>
> (Myers 1904, vol. 1, pp. 37–38)

Myers is stating the contrast between the ideal notion of the individual as avowed culturally and the state of affairs which is revealed by empirical investigation. At this time, the end of the nineteenth century, the social dislocations of the industrial revolution had atomised society and dislocated individuals, while the Enlightenment notion of the discrete, undivided individual was pressed upon people.

The moment when the individual became endowed with a discrete and indivisible identity and consciousness came about earlier, and formed a slow trend. Taylor (1989) tracked the rise of the notion of the individual, with its component characteristic 'inwardness'.

The term 'individual' itself began to be in common use in the seventeenth century during the period of agricultural reform and the sudden eruption of wealth as a commodity that can be accumulated like any other. The notion of the individual man, contrasting with (or standing out within) his society, is inextricably linked as an idea with these specific cultural changes[7] – those which founded the system we know as capitalism. In the seventeenth century it was understood that accumulated wealth (capital) of a joint stock company could reproduce itself, resulting in the recognition of companies as legal entities and correlating with individuals as personal/moral entities; both were radical novelties in this cauldron of new ideas in the period of the Enlightenment. So, the nature of being individual became a special issue of modernity. Thus the origins of this modern idea were in a moment in the seventeenth century which brought a confluence of renaissance art, Enlightenment philosophy and science, the new use of rationality, the revolutions in agriculture, manufacturing and the political process, entrepreneurial capitalism (the revision of the relations of ownership), and reformation of the church.

At the same time, the new medical science, psychiatry, categorised those phenomena which did not fit the new notions of the person as pathological entities. In fact, psychiatry owes its origins, as a modern science, to just this development of the notion of the individual.

So, the supremacy of the notion of the singular, autonomous individual relegated the more diverse notion of the individual to a state of abnormality. According to Wilson (1995), the earliest reports of multiple personalities occur during this period; and therefore represent a consequence of the new ideas. This consequence, the normalising of individuality, entailed hunting down abnormalities.[8]

In the eighteenth and nineteenth centuries the phenomenon was progressively medicalised and seen as the effects of abnormal natural substances and functions. It became thus a socially required (and engineered) diagnosis. In Foucaultian terms the rise of the 'individual' created new problems in the relation of the person to the state – itself in a radical transition. Those problems were solved, in part, by the state's hegemony over the individual's mind and body, through the process of medicalisation.

The emphasis on the new notion of the individual also created a natural philosophy of the person and of the mind, in effect, a psychology. This is typified by Locke (1690) and Hume (1739). In turn, their views on normal psychology spawned more explicit medical notions about abnormal individuality, or the psychopathology of the personality.

Locke (1690) gave philosophical expression to these new ideas when he described the mind as composed of the binding together of perceptions into concepts and memories. Such binding together was called 'association'. Associationist psychology has it that the mind is a set of connections between experiences. This binding into coherence results in a sophisticated personality. The mind and the person, composed of connections – or associations – was reflected in psychology and eventually, in the early nineteenth century, in neuroanatomy. Knowledge of the nervous system developed, notably with the discovery of the reflex arc which seemed a physical representation of 'association' – in this case, the association of sensation with behaviour. This supported the idea of links, Locke's associations, as the basis of mind. The recognition later in the nineteenth century of nerve cells and their complex connectivity with each other, gave a further biological support to the associationist idea of bundles of sensations, bound together (Young 1970).

HISTORY OF NINETEENTH-CENTURY NEUROPSYCHIATRY

During the nineteenth century psychiatry became a medical profession. The origins of the medicalisation of deviancy in the eighteenth century had prompted a more humane trend in the care of the insane (Porter 1987; Scull 1981) and an early Victorian optimism. However, in the course of the century, the asylums filled up and both patients and staff were helpless to prevent that flood of derelict persons with its familiar ensuing degradation. By the end of the century, there was a profound therapeutic pessimism about mental disorders. The disease condition was regarded as an inevitable and progressive disintegrative state of the brain.

In the course of that transition two different theories of pathology succeeded each other. In the more optimistic first half of the century, a functional theory of mental illness was dominant (phrenology), but as pessimism overran the discipline an associationist theory of pathology was evolved.

In the earlier functional theory the various faculties of mind could become atrophied, or hypertrophied. Phrenology was then an attempt to link these philosophical, or proto-psychological, notions to physical signs. The bumps on the head were taken to indicate underlying faculties of the brain which were functioning normally, and the dips in between indicated areas of diminished functioning where the brain had shrunk locally. With a map of the skull that plotted the underlying functions of the brain, the degenerating functions could be identified as the dips between the bumps. Specific treatment regimes (so-called 'moral treatment') aimed to stimulate those declining functions.

As potential treatments were gradually recognised as ineffective, there was little that could be done for people admitted to the asylums. Generally those suffering mental illnesses were inevitably believed to be in an unstoppable decline. The asylums filled up. Pessimism grew. Interest moved from the inmates of the asylums to their brains when they were dead.

This move was enhanced by the increasing knowledge of neurophysiology and anatomy. Hughlings Jackson (1931) influenced this approach with his theory of higher and lower mental functions. That theory said the lower functions were bound together by higher functions of the mind, which in turn were held together by yet higher ones. With this theory he was bringing together the functionalist neuropsychiatry of his time with an associationist binding-together psychology. The civilising higher levels bound the lower level functions into a whole personality. Jackson's ideas developed at a time when the idea of disintegration of mental functions as the basis of disorders of mind was becoming dominant. Illness was seen as a progressive organic deterioration of the binding function of higher centres (the civilised ones) – a dissociation in the brain.

This notion of the hierarchically arranged levels of brain functioning allowed a theory of psychopathology that could explain the decivilising degeneration of asylum inmates as the lower functions escaping from the control of higher integration. It also fitted evolutionary notions at this time, as the debates about evolution reached their peak.[9]

Thus as phrenology declined so an associationist theory came to be propounded. Derived ultimately from Locke in the seventeenth century, it acquired strong anatomical and physiological dimensions, and was turned specifically to explain psychopathology, not the normal mind.

In the late nineteenth century the notion that insanity was to do with the coming apart of the person, led Charcot (1887), a neurologist in Paris, to explore the phenomenon of hypnosis, hitherto highly suspect.[10] He argued that the idea that mentally ill people progressively deteriorate towards a less civilised condition, could be modelled in the hypnotic trance state in which the subject gives up his higher functions to the hypnotist. In fact, Charcot thought that hypnosis was possible only because of this propensity to disintegration, or 'dissociation' as it was then coming to be called by French psychiatrists (Janet 1899). Those people who were hypnotisable, he suggested, were just those susceptible to organic deterioration, and he believed their hypnotisability was prodromal.

Disorders of the mind then seemed naturally to be the unhinging of those bundles with the release of lower level sensations and perceptions. While Charcot (1887) explored the use of hypnosis to investigate mental illness, others (Bernheim 1884; Dejerine and Glaucker 1913) experimented with hypnosis as a therapeutic method. They aimed to inhibit the dissociation of specific thoughts, through making small links in the cognitive functioning of the person. The aim was, at least, to delay the degenerative processes.

Mental illness, conceived as the coming apart of the mind, was applied to hysterical patients at the end of the nineteenth century. They held a key place in the theoretical conceptions of the time. The professional journals then carried more articles on hysteria than on any other condition.[11] Dissociation became, under the influence of Hughlings Jackson and the French psychiatrists, the dominant explanatory concept in psychopathology at the end of the century.[12]

The diagnosis of hysteria incorporated many and very varied conditions, including florid hallucinosis as well as functional 'conversion' symptoms. Its decline in importance occurred as a new diagnosis came to dominate psychiatry – this was dementia praecox, defined in 1883 by Kraepelin (in Kraepelin 1919); and renamed 'schizophrenia' by Bleuler (1911). This condition then took up an increasing acreage of the diagnostic territory, including paranoias, various paraphrenias such as catatonia and hebephrenia, as well as forms of dementia and idiocy.[13] Hysteria as a topic of interest in psychiatry shrank rapidly throughout the twentieth century, only sustained one might say by the nostalgic respect for Freud's earliest interest.

FREUD'S ADVERSARIAL VIEW OF DISSOCIATION

Like other psychologists at the end of the nineteenth century, Freud was steeped in the ideas of association and dissociation. He started his work by studying the French psychiatrists and the possible scope of hypnosis. Under the influence of his Viennese colleague, Josef Breuer, Freud developed a different view of hysteria, and of the dissociative process. While using hypnosis, Breuer discovered that quite contrary to the idea of something lost in a degenerative process (an association), the mind of the hysteric has *accumulated* something, something which needs release. Freud confirmed this and developed the view that hysterics suffer from memories. He thought that certain memories act as focal points of associations which become in some way energised so that discharge of that energy is blocked. Energised tension progressively builds up until its overflow in some inappropriate form becomes inevitable. This is manifest in a short-circuiting process which results in strange ideas, behaviours and symptoms.

Discharge under hypnosis, or 'catharsis' as Breuer and Freud called it (Breuer and Freud 1893; Freud and Breuer 1895) released the blocked energy under controlled conditions. Freud went ahead on his own to develop these ideas while dropping the hypnotic method. The notion of an idea forming the kernel of a lot of associations was akin to Jung's term 'complex', which became generally accepted once Freud and Jung had joined forces (around 1906)[14]. Psychoanalysis, as it then evolved, had adopted the idea of association, and evolved a method based on revealing the various normal and abnormal associations that make up a person's mind.

Thus the psychoanalytic theory of psychopathology emphasised abnormal associations, which opposed the French idea of *dis*sociation (loss of association). Freud's 'dissociation' meant that ideas (and their associating links, complexes) were removed from ordinary consciousness, and located separately in a different category, or zone – the unconscious. It did not necessarily mean the total loss of a binding association.

Janet's formulation was of an idea stripped of all associations which remained adrift in the mind ('idée fixe', or 'a screw loose' in common parlance) available to link indiscriminately and arbitrarily with other thoughts. Instead, for Freud, 'dissociation' became the basic idea of the separation of the conscious from the unconscious. So Freud's appropriation of the term 'dissociation' was a serious modification of the French one and to which in the end he rightly gave a different name – 'repression'.[15]

Freud's system was coherent theoretically, and it led directly to a treatment method. Freud could proclaim that the therapeutic pessimism of nineteenth-century psychiatry was over. He did so vehemently, although it involved a cost, which was to accept a considerable amount of theory regarding the sexual life of children, at a time when children were viewed as innocents. Freud inveighed against the French forms of psychotherapy based on hypnosis and suggestion. A battle was joined for a period of two decades before the First World War. Freud's claim of an effective and theoretically understood method of treatment gained ground rapidly with the military authorities who sought to reduce the wastage of manpower at any price. The altered somnambulistic states of many 'shell-shock' victims could, it seemed, be tackled by psychoanalytic interpretation more hopefully than with the methods of the dissociationists which were still linked, rightly or wrongly, with organic degeneration theories and with evolution. Freud's strategic escape from the pessimism of psychiatry ensured, in Europe at least, a surging advance and pre-eminence of psychoanalysis in psychiatry. In effect, there was no other overarching psychiatric theorisation until after the Second World War.[16]

Despite setbacks within psychiatry, psychoanalysis steadily gained ground, at admittedly an uneven pace, to become an orthodoxy among the psychotherapies. However the suggestive therapies did not simply disappear. Prior to the First World War the French methods had remained particularly strong in France, and also in the United States. In Britain they were of more interest to the researchers into spiritualism,[17] rather than in psychiatry, where a fundamental reserve and suspicion remained towards hypnosis and its old link with fallacious unqualified quacks.

While psychoanalysis developed a hegemony during the 1920s and 1930s in Europe, the practice of hypnosis and the suggestive therapies continued in America. Key to the interest in America is probably the work of Morton

Prince (1906) (as well as Smith Ely Jelliffe who translated a number of continental psychiatrists and psychotherapists, and William Alanson White, an American psychiatrist who founded an early psychoanalytic society in New York).[18] The later hypnotherapy work of Milton Erickson (Erickson and Kubie 1941) also stands out as well as psychological treatments derived from learning theory (notably behaviour therapy). They ensured that a continuing therapeutic undercurrent turned away from psychoanalysis to those methods that are aimed at correcting the person's mind, as opposed to encouraging its greater expression.

Freud's work was thus predicated on a model of the mind in which separation of parts did not mean they existed unrelated to each other. The conscious and unconscious react with each other. This interactive model of the mind reached its most sophisticated form in two of Freud's later theoretical innovations. First was his theory of depression as the internalisation of external, or 'alien', persons into the inside of the personality where they remained in a similar relationship to the subject (Freud 1917). And, second was his structural theory in which the ego, the id and the super-ego form an interacting stable structure to the personality (Freud 1923). Instead of severed links between parts of the person, he instituted a quite different model in which the person is a number of *interacting* parts, held together in a structure of coherent, 'internal' relationships. With this idea of an integrated structure of identifiable parts, Freud was taking and modifying Hughlings Jackson's hierarchical model of parts interacting under control.

THE PSYCHOANALYTIC RETURN TO DISSOCIATION

By the 1930s psychoanalysis had moved from the analysis of symptoms to become an analysis of character. The focus was increasingly on the integrating function of the ego (the school of ego-psychology). Naturally the weaknesses of the ego in this respect were pushed to the fore in the practice with disturbed people. Within British psychoanalysis, this seems to have become an interest in the early states of the ego, when it might be experienced as in parts. For instance, Melitta Schmideberg described some children's experience of parts of the self, experienced primitively as parts of the body that feel to be quite separate persons:

> there is a still deeper anxiety, that of independent hostile parts of the body. The infant first projects its love and hate feelings on to various parts of its body. The parts which give pleasure (e.g. the erotogenic zones, mainly the genitals) become good ones and are narcissistically loved. The parts which cause displeasure (pain or frustration) are hated and feared. Hence the tendency to hurt hurting parts . . . The anxiety of hostile parts

of the body fighting each other and the fear of disruption can best be observed in schizophrenia, but also in such everyday phenomena as in the anxiety of clothing . . . In nail-biting, e.g. parts of the body fight each other. In thumb-sucking this aggression is overcompensated by excessive love of these parts. But in thumb-sucking too aggression may manifest itself.

(Schmideberg 1935: 458–459)

The body, Schmideberg claimed, is the arena on which a whole *dramatis personae* play out fantastic but compelling dramas.

Fairbairn (1944) classically chided Freud for his move towards depression, and, faithlessly as it were, leaving behind the dissociating hysteric upon which psychoanalysis was founded.[19] Fairbairn is less perspicacious on why Freud made this move. However, Fairbairn is right in connecting the dissociative phenomena of hysterics with schizoid phenomena, and in calling for a move 'back to hysteria' (Fairbairn 1944: 74). Although these two phenomena – hysteria and schizophrenia – were diagnostically separated by Kraepelin and Bleuler, they have common qualities residing in the division of the personality into apparently separate parts:

my own investigations of patients with hysterical symptoms leave me in no doubt whatever that the dissociation phenomena of 'hysteria' involve a split of the ego fundamentally identical with that which confers upon the term 'schizoid' its etymological significance.

(Fairbairn 1944: 74)

In effect Fairbairn's conclusions dismantle the essential division between these two categories – hysteric and schizoid/schizophrenic patients.

These writers, Schmideberg and Fairbairn, describe parts of the mind between which there remains a functioning relationship, albeit a violent conflictual one. However, Glover (1943) made a similar plea for the return of the core term 'dissociation' despite the assertion that 'the history of the term dissociation is a chequered one' (p. 12). However he described dispersed ego-nuclei, between which there was *no* interaction.

Winnicott (1945) at this time discerned the earliest state of the ego as one of unintegration, which leads to a primary struggle for integration (before processes of splitting can then take place).[20] Glover and Winnicott are describing parts of the mind between which there are *no* functioning relations.

Notably, these authors come from the British tradition of psychoanalysis, while ego-psychology in Vienna and the US considered 'splitting of the ego' as much less important, and did not seek it in the primitive processes of infancy. As an example, Federn (1938) considered the adult ego, describing multiple personalities in terms of separate cathexes:

> If we base the ego on a unitary cathexis the splitting of the ego in hysteria loses much of its enigmatic character. We begin to understand that in extreme cases of double personality the representatives of the object are accessible to both ego units by undirected access, though they are not in consciousness at the same time and the unities of ego cathexis themselves are connected in the bodily ego only.
>
> (Federn 1938: 192–193)

Also Fenichel (1938) used the idea of splitting of the ego as an achievement of maturity that created a separation between the 'experiencing ego' and the 'observing ego', though the subsequent parts remain in relation to each other. Federn and Fenichel described interacting parts of the person which, though at variance with each other, do relate together unconsciously. The parts Fenichel discerned even relate consciously.

Freud gave authority at the end of his life to the concept of 'splitting of the ego' (Freud 1940a, b):

> as a result of the continuous irruptions of the id, [the ego's] organization is impaired, it is no longer capable of any proper synthesis, it is torn by mutually opposed urges, by unsettled conflicts and by unsolved doubts.
>
> (Freud 1940a: 180–181)

His descriptions clearly are of a situation in which the parts of the mind do *not* communicate with each other. Freud remarks on how delayed his appreciation of this ego process has been (Freud 1940b). However, he does not indicate how his reluctance must have been due to his battles over many years around the turn of the century against Janet, dissociation and the French suggestive therapies.

On the basis of much of this work, Klein (1946) began a comprehensive theory of splitting of the ego, which, like Freud's late consideration, is not a function of immaturity (in contrast to Glover and Winnicott); it is an active defence. In addition, unlike Fairbairn, Klein followed Freud's late view in which there is no relation between the subsequent parts.[21] She stressed the effect on identity, as these splitting processes radically adopted or divested themselves of certain identifications with other objects (see Hinshelwood 1997a).

The phenomenon of splitting of the ego, in which the resulting parts are *not* in interaction, either primarily or as a secondary defensive occurrence, is the equivalent of the term 'dissociation'. Nevertheless, 'splitting' is often, and confusingly, used synonymously for 'repression' (Hinshelwood 1999b). The term 'multiple personality' was not much in use in psychoanalysis, in mid-century. The return of interest in the 1980s, therefore, drew from a number of different sources. The tradition of Morton Prince had survived strongly in the US and was supplemented by the development of other psychotherapies from hypnotism and the continuing descendants of the French suggestive therapies. These joined with psychoanalytic traditions, including those arising from both Freud's dominant ideas based on repression, and also those resting upon his late idea of 'splitting of the ego'. In the US, the phenomenon of splitting of the ego has been pressed upon psychoanalysts by these non-psychoanalytic cases (see for instance Brook 1992; Berman 1981), rather than by the psycho-analytic phenomena. The current use of, and later development in, these terms from many origins have created a fruitful potential for confusion. That potential has been fulfilled.

IDENTITY AND IDENTIFICATION

Persons are influenced in 'who they think they are' and in what they think their identity is, by external pressures, but also by pressures within themselves. There are two broad dimensions to the plethora of conditions that are currently included in the multiple personality disorders:

- First, the issue of whether the ego originates in an unintegrated state; or if disintegration/dissociation occurs later (possibly as a defence).
- Second, the issue whether unintegrated states imply an ongoing, albeit unconscious, interaction between the resulting parts of the person, or whether we have to consider a structure of completely non-communicating parts.

The first of these issues touches on how personal identity itself comes about. This remains unresolved – either by psychologists or philosophers, both of whom have actively worked on this central aspect of individuality. Does the original ego have a sense of identity, that is a coherent sense of being and possessing its own characteristics and relationships? Or is this developed only slowly in the early stages of life, emerging perhaps from much discontinuity which has to come together in the course of development? Current work in this area suggests that the person of the infant is surprisingly coherent (Stern 1985), but its originary state remains elusive (Tustin 1990; Alvarez 1992).

More important perhaps for the present topic is the second issue above. There is a quite normal process familiar in social psychology when a person behaves – and actually feels – differently from time to time – changes which are determined by changed social contexts and also, we know, by changed internal psychodynamics. I refer not to separate identities; instead we might call them *changes of identification*. When I am at work lecturing, I can feel myself a different person from when at home with my children doing a jigsaw puzzle. This choice of different identifications, bounded by transitions in time, should be distinct from those autonomous sub-divisions of the person.

We need to distinguish these two – identity and identification. I suggest that the key difference is that separate identifications can exist in a person who is functioning in a largely integrated manner. This would correspond to the more historical descriptions of Shakespeare, Stevenson, etc.

But it contrasts with separate parts of the person that do not communicate with each other, and one can truly say that the identity contains a fault line that fully separates non-interacting identities.

However, from outside observation, it is difficult to tell whether we see a true case of distinct identities, or a dynamic flux between identifications that are under some mutual alternation with each other. Really, only a deeper probing – for which psychoanalysis and psychoanalytic psychotherapy are the only tools – is necessary.

CONCLUSIONS

The simple assertion that a 'divided individual' is pathological cannot be sustained simplistically. The two phases of interest, in the late decades of both the nineteenth and the twentieth centuries, indicate a definite socio-historical factor; and my survey can contribute to sorting out some of the issues that are currently run together.

The Multiple Personality Disorders, or Dissociative Identity Disorders, occupy a complex multi-dimensional space comprising social, historical, psychological and biological factors, across which persons may be spread very widely. If these dimensions are ignored or collapsed into each other, then the topic is delivered into greater and greater imprecision and will ultimately fall from use. If these varied dimensions are taken into account, then some discrimination may be possible between the conditions, which range from quite usual to highly abnormal, from disadvantageous to fascinating.

The relatively inadequate means of observing these deeply interior states has created a new cauldron of bubbling terms, ideas, claims and counter-claims. The following summarise the factors and processes operating to create these states, which I have encountered in my descriptions in this chapter.

1   Quite possibly, the primary state of mind in infancy, in which the person is divided, may survive as a failure of the normal integrative process, due perhaps to innate developmental abnormalities.
2   Division of the person may occur, with altered consciousness in later stages of development as a defensive mechanism – often after actual trauma.
3   Certain processes result in truly non-communicating 'sub'-personalities or 'alters'. And these divided states of mind may be stable or changing.
4   Certain of these processes would allow unconscious relations to continue between the separate parts of the individual. Though I have denoted this as a normal enough result of various identifications, some highly conflictual

identifications can result in states of mind that present for treatment. Conflict, though, is a relatedness.

5   Certain sub-cultures may prioritise (and thus encourage) certain states of mind or altered consciousness – notably deprived and low status cultural groups.
6   Similarly, medical, forensic and other social pressures may inadvertently encourage presentation of apparently disintegrated states of mind which conform to any of the above patterns.
7   Finally, actual organic disorders may well add to all these other factors.

I conclude that there is no simple condition of multiple personality. Each must be explored to a depth beyond consciousness.

This complex diagnostic field is further complicated by other factors. I shall mention only two: sexuality and the politics of psychotherapy.

I have mentioned the quality of excitement that attaches to discussion of these conditions. It may in itself pose a problem to the responsible professional observer, since excited fascination can operate detrimentally against calm reflection. The often excited quality of debate and dispute around this issue, and the holding of impassioned positions generally give rise to suspicions about the protagonists. However, psychodynamically, strongly felt affect can enlighten a significant aspect of the issue itself – provided it is also something which can be reflected upon. We can sometimes discern, and use, the characteristic affective reactions to certain diagnoses (Hinshelwood 1999a). For instance, it is typical of other personality disorders in psychiatry (borderline or narcissistic) that they attract an angry rejection by staff as unworthy; or patients with schizophrenia attract a distancing and depersonalising response from staff. Multiple personalities, in common with the adjacent issue of recovered memories of abuse, provoke an excited and disputatious response from those attending these patients.

Such excitement would imply there are undercurrents of unconscious messages between patients and professionals imbued with unacknowledged sexuality. Freud was influenced by such surreptitiously eroticised relations when first studying his hysterical patients. This led to his discovery of children's hidden erotic and sexual lives. It also led to Breuer's taking flight from the emerging psychoanalysis altogether. And it is also responsible for the highly energised disputes that take place among professionals and the public today. That excitement itself needs to be reflected upon. The starting point, it seems to me, for such reflection is that our own reactions should draw us towards excitement as a key element of the condition. We might therefore seek the origins of some of these conditions in sexuality and its traumas.

A second aggravating factor is the plight of psychotherapy within psychiatry in many western countries. Because of current political pressures within scientific, pharmacological psychiatry, psychotherapy feels beleaguered. As a result, a widely reported and highly fascinating condition with a clear psychological form offers an important opportunity to claim the importance of psychotherapy. The psychological nature, diagnosis and treatment of multiple personalities point to the specific need for psychotherapists. Thus the promotion of the diagnosis of multiple personality implicitly includes a political promotion of psychotherapy within psychiatry. Such political pressures involve highly personal aspects of the professional himself – his status, his financial security, his reputation and so on – and therefore constitute influences potentially interfering with the clarity of clinical thinking.

The idea of being a multiple, a 'di-vidual', is a disorder conceived in the modern world, a disorderliness deriving from the inadequate conception of the 'individual' to which modernity clings. It would seem that a daunting and perhaps unwelcome conclusion to my historical argument is that truly to understand the nature of MPD/DID will include dissolving a whole cultural set of baggage that is deeply invested in the notion of the undivided individual. The 'di-vidual' however was a non-issue until modernity.

NOTES

1 It is to be noted in the recent literature how scrupulously the term 'hysteria' is avoided.
2 F.W.H. Myers wrote in surprisingly similar terms from his researches into spiritualism about 'the tendency of the individuality to split itself up into various co-ordinate and alternating trains of personality, each of which may seem for a time to be dominant and obsessing, while yet the habitual sense of the ordinary self may persist through all these invasions' (Myers 1904, vol. 2, p. 423).
3 I leave aside the instances of conscious misrepresentation (e.g. Rieber 1999), and refer to unconscious collusion between both parties.
4 Ioan Lewis (1971) has linked the phenomena of trance states in ecstatic religions with groups of low socio-economic status and deprivation.
5 Susan Sontag (1989) attempted a similar cultural explanation for a preceding generation of 'fashionable' illnesses.
6 The high point of this tradition occurred when Hollywood conferred the seal of popular approval by filming Thigpen and Cleckley's (1957) *Three Faces of Eve*.
7 Perhaps Rembrandt's extraordinary series of 75 (at least) self-portraits exemplifies this reflective gaze upon one's own identity and self, typical of the new seventeenth century *Weltanschauung*.
8 At first, and for a brief period, these were seen in religious terms. At the end of the seventeenth century, there was a sudden interest across the Christian world in witchcraft, the possession of one person's body by invaders, or demons or the Devil himself. Segments of some more advanced countries (England, Germany and the North American colonies) became preoccupied with witches (Roper 1989). The brutality and irrationality of witch-hunting led probably to its own swift decline in a period of advanced rationalism. Interestingly those charged with witchcraft were of the deprived and oppressed – mostly women, also poor and very poor. This connects with Lewis's correlation of altered consciousness with social marginality (see Note 4 above).
9 A hierarchy of controlling brain functions can be seen as the projection back into the world of nature of those social arrangements which bourgeois society wished

to regard as natural. Just as Darwin could naturalise the free-market economy as the principle of the survival of the fittest species.

10 Hypnosis, originally peddled by quack healers in the early nineteenth century, was so suspect that it was one important factor leading to the professionalisation of medicine and establishing statutory regulations for valid medical training, in order to exclude such quacks.

11 See Hinshelwood (1991). Hysteria and the conditions later grouped together as dementia praecox, and as schizophrenia, were not separated then. Those diagnoses had not been delineated nor the words coined.

12 Hysteria was also the phenomenon of spiritualist mediums, who claimed religious significance. Psychiatrists (Janet 1899; Prince 1906) were interested in these mediums for their seeming wilful division of their personalities. They postulated the existence of separate states of consciousness, and tried to assay the conditions under which one consciousness could come into the ascendancy rather than another. Interestingly, independent researchers such as Myers (1904) (and the Society for Psychical Research which he was involved in establishing) explored the possibility that these psychiatric conditions might be a scientific route through to the spirit world and could therefore form the foundations of a scientific approach to religion.

13 Increasingly, perhaps as the stress on individuality grew culturally, a similarly increasing stress occurred on the abnormality of the sense of being – a core problem of the schizophrenic.

14 See Satinover (1986) for Jung's early comments on multiple personality.

15 Perhaps, Freud was not always aware of exactly the distinction he had made between repression and dissociation, although Freud did realise that his views were in conflict with the French and there was an energetic 'war' between the two men before the First World War (Hinshelwood 1991). He also became a member of the SPR and contributed a paper on the unconscious in 1910.

16 So, after the military armistice, Freud was in a position to offer his own armistice to other psychotherapies in his 1919 visionary paper on the future of psychoanalysis by discussing the advisability of an 'alloy' of psychoanalysis with suggestive methods.

17 However, prior to 1914 some newly created clinics did attempt to use all forms of psychotherapies (Boyle 1905; Boll 1962).

18 This was one reason for Freud's frequent dismissal of psychoanalysis in America during his lifetime (Gay 1988). It was also the mission of the exiled German-speaking psychoanalysts in the 1930s, to establish pure psychoanalysis in America.

19 Anna O, Breuer's founding case of psychoanalysis, suffered from having two states of consciousness (Breuer and Freud 1893). This of course is a clinical description formulated in the terminology current at the time, but it is the kind of description Fairbairn intends to return to – parallel autonomous aspects of the self.

20 Winnicott's views changed to a much more integrative picture later on (Winnicott 1960) when he thought of the infant as existing in a state of primary omnipotent union with the whole of its experienced world (saying, famously, 'there is no such thing as a baby').

21 The question of whether the ego can conduct a defence of splitting in which there is no link between the parts was disputed by Sartre, and formed the core of his view of psychoanalysis as 'bad faith' (see my discussion of this in Chapter 4 of *Therapy or Coercion* – Hinshelwood 1997b).

REFERENCES

Alvarez, Anne (1992) *Live Company*. London: Routledge.

Berman, Emanuel (1981) 'Multiple personality: psychoanalytic perspectives'. *International Journal of Psycho-Analysis* 62: 283–300.

Bernheim, H.-M. (1884) *De la suggestion et des applications à la thérapeutique*. Paris: Doid. (Reprinted in *Suggestive Therapies* (1900). London: Pentland.)

Bleuler, Eugen (1911) *Affectivity, Suggestibility, Paranoia*. Utica: State Hospitals Press, 1912.

Boll, Theophilus (1962) 'May Sinclair and the Medico-Psychological Clinic in London'. *Proceedings of the American Philosophical Society* 106: 310–326.

Boyle, Helen (1905) 'Some points in the early treatment of nervous and mental cases'. *Journal of Mental Science* 51: 676–681.

Braude, Stephen (1995) *First Person Plural: Multiple Personality and the Philosophy of Mind*. Lanham: Rowman and Littlefield.

Brenner, Ira (1994) 'The dissociative character: a reconsideration of "multiple personality"'. *Journal of the American Psychoanalytic Association* 42: 819–846.

Breuer, Josef and Freud, Sigmund (1893) 'On the psychical mechanism of hysterical phenomena: preliminary communication'. In *The Standard Edition of the Complete Psychological Works of Sigmund Freud 2*. London: Hogarth.

Brook, J.A. (1992) 'Freud and splitting'. *International Review of Psycho-Analysis* 19: 335–350.

Charcot, J.-M. (1887) *Leçons sur les maladies du système nerveux*. Paris. (Reprinted in *Lectures on Diseases of the Nervous System* (1889). London: The Sydenham Society.)

Dejerine, J.-J. and Glaucker, E. (1913) *The Psychoneuroses and their Treatment by Psychotherapy*. Philadelphia: Lippincott.

Ellenberger, Henri (1970) *The Discovery of the Unconscious*. New York: Basic Books.

Erickson, Milton and Kubie, Lawrence (1941) 'The successful treatment of a case of acute hysterical depression by a return under hypnosis to a critical phase of childhood'. *Psychoanalytic Quarterly* 10: 583–609.

Federn, Paul (1938) 'The undirected function in the central nervous system – a question put to physiology by psychology'. *International Journal of Psycho-Analysis* 19: 173–198.

Fenichel, Otto (1938) 'Ego-disturbances and their treatment'. *International Journal of Psycho-Analysis* 19: 416–438.

Fairbairn, R.D. (1944) 'Endopsychic structure considered in terms of object-relations'. *International Journal of Psycho-Analysis* 21: 30–37.

Freud, Sigmund (1917) 'Mourning and melancholia'. In *The Standard Edition of the Complete Psychological Works of Sigmund Freud 16*. London: Hogarth.

Freud, Sigmund (1923) 'The Ego and the Id'. In *The Standard Edition of the Complete Psychological Works of Sigmund Freud 19*. London: Hogarth.

Freud, Sigmund (1940a) 'An outline of psychoanalysis'. In *The Standard Edition of the Complete Psychological Works of Sigmund Freud 23*: 144–207. London: Hogarth.

Freud, Sigmund (1940b) 'The splitting of the ego in the process of defence'. In *The Standard Edition of the Complete Psychological Works of Sigmund Freud 23*: 275–278. London: Hogarth.

Freud, Sigmund and Breuer, Josef (1895) 'Studies on hysteria'. In *The Standard Edition of the Complete Psychological Works of Sigmund Freud 2*. London: Hogarth.

Gay, Peter (1988) *Freud: A Life for our Time*. London: Dent.

Glover, Edward (1943) 'The concept of dissociation'. *International Journal of Psycho-Analysis* 24: 7–13.

Glover, Jonathan (1988) *I: The Philosophy and Psychology of Personal Identity*. London: Allen Lane, The Penguin Press.

Hacking, Ian (1999) *Mad Travellers: Reflections on the Reality of Transient Mental Illness*. London: Free Association Books.

Hilgard, E. (1977) *Divided Consciousness: Multiple Controls in Human Thought and Action*. New York: Wiley.

Hinshelwood, R.D. (1991) 'Psychodynamic psychiatry before World War 1'. In German Berrios and Hugh Freeman (eds), *150 Years of British Psychiatry*, pp. 197–205. London: Gaskell/Royal College of Psychiatrists.

Hinshelwood, R.D. (1995) 'The social relocation of personal identity'. *Philosophy, Psychology, Psychiatry* 2: 185–204.

Hinshelwood, R.D. (1997a) 'Primitive mental processes: psycho-analysis and the ethics of integration'. *Philosophy, Psychology, Psychiatry* 4: 121–143.

Hinshelwood, R.D. (1997b) *Therapy or Coercion: Does Psychoanalysis Differ from Brainwashing*. London: Karnac.

Hinshelwood, R.D. (1999a) 'The difficult patient: the role of "scientific" psychiatry in understanding patients with chronic schizophrenia or severe personality disorder'. *British Journal of Psychiatry* 174: 187–190.

Hinshelwood, R.D. (1999b) 'Controversy is the growing point: repression and splitting'. Lecture to the British Psychoanalytical Society, October 1999.

Hume, John (1739) *A Treatise of Human Nature*. Oxford: Oxford University Press (1978).

Jackson, J. Hughlings (1931) *Selected Writings of John Hughlings Jackson*. London: Hodder and Stoughton.

Janet, Pierre (1899) *Traité de therapeutique appliqué*. Paris: J. Rueff.

Klein, Melanie (1946) 'Notes on some schizoid mechanisms'. In *The Writings of Melanie Klein* 3. London: Hogarth.

Kluft, R.P. (1984) 'Treatment of multiple personality: a study of 33 cases'. *Psychiatric Clinics of North America* 7: 9–29.

Kraepelin, E. (1919) *Dementia Praecox*. Edinburgh: Livingstone.

Lewis, Ioan (1971) *Ecstatic Religions*. London: Penguin.

Locke, John (1690) *An Essay Concerning Human Understanding*. London: Penguin (1997).

Mollon, Phil (1996) *Multiple Selves, Multiple Voices: Working with Trauma, Violation and Dissociation*. Chichester: Wiley.

Myers, F.H.R. (1904) *Human Personality and its Survival of Bodily Death*. London: Longmans.

Nagel, Thomas (1971) 'Brain bisection and the unity of consciousness'. *Synthese* 2: 396–413. (Reprinted (1979) in Thomas Nagel *Mortal Questions*. Cambridge: Cambridge University Press.)

Oppenheim, J. (1985) *The Other World: Spiritualism and Psychical Research in England 1885–1914*. Cambridge: Cambridge University Press.

Parfitt, Derek (1984) *Reasons and Persons*. Oxford: Oxford University Press.

Porter, Roy (1987) *A Social History of Madness*. London: Weidenfeld and Nicolson.

Prince, Morton (1906) *The Dissociation of a Personality*. New York: Longmans.

Rieber, Robert (1999) 'Hypnosis, false memory and multiple personality: a trinity of affinity'. *History of Psychiatry* 10: 3–11.

Roper, Lyndall (1989) *The Holy Household: Women and Morals in Reformation Augsburg*. Oxford: Oxford University Press.

Rose, Nikolas (1990) *Governing the Soul: The Shaping of the Private Self*. London: Routledge.

Satinover, J. (1986) 'Jung's lost contribution to the dilemma of narcissism'. *Journal of the American Psychoanalytical Association* 34: 401–438.

Schmideberg, Melitta (1935) 'Bad habits in childhood: their importance in development'. *International Journal of Psycho-Analysis* 16: 455–461.

Scull, Andrew (1981) *Madhouse, Mad-doctors and Madmen: The Social History of Psychiatry in the Victorian Era*. Philadelphia: University of Pennsylvania Press.

Sontag, Susan (1989) *AIDS and its Metaphors*. London: Allen Lane.

Stern, Daniel (1985) *The Interpersonal Life of Infants*. New York: Basic Books.

Taylor, Charles (1989) *Sources of the Self: The Making of the Modern Identity*. Cambridge: Cambridge University Press.

Thigpen, Corbett and Cleckley, Hervey (1957) *The Three Faces of Eve*. New York: McGraw-Hill.

Tustin, Frances (1990) *The Protective Shell in Children and Adults*. London: Karnac Books.

Whyte, Lancelot (1979) *The Unconscious before Freud*. London: Julian Friedman.

Wilson, Stephen (1993) 'Multiple personality'. In Stephen Wilson (1995) *The Cradle of Violence: Essays on Psychiatry, Psychoanalysis and Literature*. London: Jessica Kingsley.

Wilson, Stephen (1995) *The Cradle of Violence: Essays on Psychiatry, Psychoanalysis and Literature*. London: Jessica Kingsley.

Winnicott, Donald (1945) 'Primitive emotional development'. *International Journal of Psycho-Analysis* 26: 137–145.

Winnicott, Donald (1960) 'The theory of the parent–infant relationship'. *International Journal of Psycho-Analysis* 41: 585–595.

Young, Robert (1970) *Mind, Brain and Adaptation*. Oxford: Oxford University Press.

Chapter 15

Dissociation and spirit possession in non-western countries
Notes towards a common research agenda

Leslie Swartz

Roughly a century after the pioneering work of Janet and Freud, there has been a return to an interest in dissociation. This interest has been tied not only to an apparent increase in dissociation in the consulting room but also to central concerns of postmodernity – questions of fragmentation, disputed identity, interpersonal violence and trauma. Dissociative Identity Disorder, apart from being the stuff of television talk shows, internet romances and popular literature, has become the fractured mirror within which we see ourselves refracted at the start of the twenty-first century.

Ours is a world of increasing multiplicity of images and toying with reality through the pop video and the computer-altered photograph, a world of refugees and wars, of nations and identities making and unmaking themselves. It is a world of banal genocides and careers built on the representation of horror in forms both shocking and palatable enough to suit the sensibilities of consumers of information. The primary consumers represent that shrinking but globalising proportion of the world who have access to the technology and the funds comfortably to act as witnesses to, rather than participants in, these horrors. As we watch the plight of those in Kosovo and Rwanda, in Angola and Afghanistan, part of what we cannot help but do is to be grateful for our own predictable lives, and our own sense of a future which can be planned or insured for. The more the world fragments, the more the images of fragmentation define the comforting contours of our own sense of continuity.

Mental health professionals have always played a role not only in caring for individuals but also in acting as agents of defining the best ways to live in our society. The professed neutrality of some such professionals in allowing clientele (and the public at large) 'choices' about how to live and how to relate to others, in creating more space for individual freedom and responsibility, is of course not a neutral stance at all but one deeply influenced by a liberal western value of individualism. Any psychotherapist working at the boundaries of this value – with clients for whom the search for individual fulfilment is culturally strange – will be familiar with the dilemmas of taking on a role which though in one sense is about giving choices, in another is about cultural brokerage and even cultural imperialism of a type, however benign. In this

context, the therapeutic ideal of individual integrity, of personal responsibility with relatively small reference to the constraints placed on that personal
responsibility by social role ascriptions, becomes difficult to strive for without
question. In my own work, especially in the volatile political context of a
changing South Africa, I have often been confronted with clients and with crit-
ics of psychotherapy who have argued that the psychotherapeutic support for
individual development is at odds with both communal African values and
with the politics of the struggle for national liberation. Though these arguments can and should be countered in various ways, I do find some relief in
seeing the modern ideal of the autonomous integrated whole being subverted
in the context of postmodernism. Suddenly, the lack of autonomy, the fragmented lives of people marginal to the psychotherapeutic mainstream, become
not particular problems of the marginal or of the politically oppressed but concerns of everyone.

Postmodernism is partly about identity politics – about the multiple and
mutually incompatible identities we may hold at different times and contexts,
and also about the external imposition of identities and role ascriptions on
individuals and groups of people. It is also about what Hacking (1994) has
termed 'memoro-politics', about the ways in which our images of the past are
policed and constructed through the lens of current power relationships
(Nuttall and Coetzee 1998; Sinason 1999). One of the ways in which our past
is constructed is through images of people currently alive whom we see as representing that past – images of the 'primitive'. There are different ways in
which primitivity can be represented, and Lucas and Barrett (1995) have identified the key bifurcation between the arcadian image of the peaceful,
prelapsarian noble savage, and the barbaric image of the violence of the
untamed savage. When I was training as a clinical psychologist some twenty
years ago in South Africa, I was taught that catatonia, though currently rare in
the developed world, could still be seen in South African blacks, and trainees
were taken to see the latest admission to the hospital of a catatonic schizophrenic. We were not given any overt explanation of why this relic could still
be seen in South Africa, but the implication was that more sophisticated cultures had more sophisticated ways of expressing themselves. Similarly, there
was (and in many quarters continues to be) a belief that depression was rare
among black and other 'unsophisticated' people – a view entirely unsubstan-
tiated by any respectable epidemiological evidence. In fact, all the indications
are, for obvious reasons, that depression is more common among people who
are oppressed or have to struggle to survive (Swartz, 1998).

The idea that through our work in South Africa we were somehow more
closely linked to the past than were those in Europe and North America was
further reinforced for me by an admission to our ward of a 'coloured' woman
who would find herself lying on the pavement with her legs apart and her
knickers in her hand. After similarly finding herself 'coming to' in the corridor of the hospital ward one day, again with her knickers in her hand, she

claimed that she had been raped. I can no longer recall how or whether we helped this woman, but what I do recollect was the excitement that we were seeing a true Freudian hysterical or dissociative state before our eyes. I was told by trainers that though modern Europe may seem far away from Freud's world, we had a nineteenth century bit of Vienna in our black townships. This fascination with the primitive and the archaic in our context probably made some contribution to the great interest in Jung in South Africa, and to the fact that the first fully recognised analytic training in this country has been a Jungian training.

In the international literature on culture and mental health there is, as Lucas and Barrett (1995) show, a prominent strain of work which produces, for modern consumption, images of the primitive against which we can implicitly gauge our own modernity. This strain is certainly not without its rigorous empirical foundations – for example, Leff (1988) has carefully shown how hysteria, though once common in the west was relatively rare in Europe by the 1980s but still prominent in nonwestern[1] countries; similarly the diagnosis of neurasthenia has all but disappeared in the West but is common in China (Kleinman 1988). Leff (1981) has posited a developmental theory of the differentiation of the language of emotions, with people in western cultures having a more differentiated linguistic repertoire for distinguishing, for example, between anxiety and depression. The storm of protest which greeted Leff's (1981) earlier proposition of this view (Kleinman and Good 1985), as well as his reformulation of it (Leff 1988; Swartz 1998) may not be entirely fair to Leff's intentions, but it does speak of the sensitivity within the transcultural psychiatry field about allegations of political conservatism and evolutionist views in which the modern western individual was seen as the pinnacle of human intellectual and emotional development.

Spirit possession is very much a feature of interest in transcultural psychiatry internationally, and once again there is an implicit contrast made between the primitive world of those who believe in spirit possession and the rational world of those who do not. In South Africa, for example, there is an increasing literature on both negative and positive possession, and I shall give a brief description of a form of each.

Amafufunyana has been described as a form of spirit possession caused primarily by sorcery. A mixture of soil and ants from a graveyard make a harmful concoction which can be placed in the path of a victim. Ngubane (1977: 144) has described the clinical picture of *amafufunyana* in the following way:

> She becomes hysterical and weeps aloud uncontrollably, throws herself on the ground, tears off her clothes, runs in a frenzy, and usually attempts to commit suicide. She reacts violently and aggressively to those who try to calm her. She is said to be possessed by a horde of spirits of different racial groups. Usually there may be thousands of Indians or Whites, some hundreds of Sotho or Zulu spirits.

There are other descriptions of *amafufunyana*, some of which conflict to some degree with Ngubane's description (for a full discussion see Swartz 1998: 162–164), but the dissociative features are clear and commonly reported. It is also the case that many psychiatric patients describe their condition primarily in terms of *amafufunyana* (Lund and Swartz 1998). Outbreaks of *amafufunyana* similar to outbreaks of hysteria (Leff 1988) have also been described, for example, at a girls' boarding school in a rural area (see Swartz 1986, 1987 for a review).

Ukuthwasa, in contrast to *amafufunyana*, is described as a positive possession state whereby a person is 'called' by ancestors to become a healer. This calling, which may involve considerable emotional distress and socially disruptive behaviour, typically includes prominent dissociative features of trance and communication with ancestors (Swartz 1998: 164–166), in common with other shamanistic experiences. In the 1970s, a number of South African authors were concerned to show that *ukuthwasa* is indeed a positive possession state and not a form of psychosis (Swartz 1998).

In the case of both *amafufunyana* and *ukuthwasa* there has been considerable debate in South Africa about whether the terms are used discretely to refer to particular disorders or clusters of symptoms, and currently there appears to be some consensus that the terms are used rather broadly and in connection with a number of experiences of emotional and other distress. Internationally, there are questions about whether the so-called 'culture-bound syndromes' refer solely or even exclusively to sets of recognisable symptoms and behaviours, or, more centrally, to ways of understanding consciousness and misfortune which resonate with core concerns of the society in which the culture-bound syndromes occur (Helman 1987; Hughes 1996; Lipsedge and Littlewood 1997; Swartz 1985). Recent important work on spirit possession in South Asia (Castillo 1994a, b) has demonstrated both the importance of early conceptualisations of trauma (and the work of Janet in particular) and an understanding of contextual factors for how we understand spirit possession.

Overall, though, there remains a separation in the literature between work on spirit possession in what are sometimes called 'less complex' societies, and the burgeoning interest in dissociation and possession in what is seen as a more complex, globalising world. Why is there this separation? There are many important compelling reasons for this. The most important is that interest in dissociation in 'complex' societies is relatively recent, and those who record the phenomenon are still in the process of recording its features. Related to this, possibly, may be the fact that dissociation and associated phenomena of memory and identity disturbance, are highly contested, as other contributions to this and a previous volume (Sinason 1999) show. The debates within dominant western cultures about the realities or otherwise of these phenomena, and of their extent, are still so new that looking outwards to other cultures has not yet become an issue. Consequent on this, there is a dearth of empirical cross-cultural and cross-national information on current manifestations of dissociation. There may also be an implicit political reluctance to explore the links between dissociation as a feature of postmodernity and dissociation as a defining phenomenon of the literature on possession – and, indeed, on mental health issues – in developing countries. The political problem, essentially, is that clinicians and others working in the field of dissociation in developed countries have enough to worry about in terms of the intellectual credibility of their work without being linked to the image of the primitive, the savage, and the unscientific world of indigenous healing in non-western countries. There may also be the dilemma of linking what is new in developed countries with what has been seen for some time as, if not humdrum, then at least common, in other countries for some time.

It is possible of course to speculate endlessly about this issue. Is there, however, anything more positive that we can put forward to suggest that the time has come to make links between spirit possession in developing countries and dissociation in the developed world? A key, and problematic, feature of the way that 'indigenous illnesses' or varieties of spirit possession tend to be portrayed in the transcultural psychiatry is that they are often presented as ahistorical and existing as fixed features of 'simple societies' (cf. Littlewood 1996; Littlewood and Lipsedge 1997). In this typification they share some features, of course, with the somewhat ahistorical presentation of all disorders in the dominant diagnostic systems, in spite of the fact that it can be clearly shown that disorders wax and wane with time (Leff 1988; Mezzich et al. 1996; Young 1995). There is something particular to the presentation of spirit possession, however, that is not shared by other disorders. Other disorders, such as for example schizophrenia and the affective disorders, are often regarded as timeless, as having existed throughout history, but also very much a feature of contemporary psychopathology. By contrast, spirit possession is not uncommonly seen as a relic of an ahistorical past – but, like, perhaps, catatonia and neurasthenia, a phenomenon which will disappear with greater 'civilisation' and social complexity. This formulation, which holds within it the implicit dualisms of a world-view which divides neatly between the 'developed' and the 'developing' worlds, the 'West' and the 'East' and so on (Boonzaier and Sharp 1988), may obscure key features of spirit possession which may make parallels with dissociation in the West easier to see.

If we think about spirit possession not simply as a product of an immutable, ahistorical past, but as a product of specific historical circumstances, then perhaps we can begin to see antecedents of such phenomena in these circumstances. There is of course a fundamental difficulty with the historical recording of such phenomena – in the history of psychiatry and anthropology they were 'discovered' intact by western explorers, and recorded as extant entities. But there have been some suggestions that *amafufunyana* may be related to colonisation and migration – even to the extent of its possibly having its origins in the twentieth century (Ngubane 1977). It has also been suggested that *ukuthwasa*, being more common in women than men, may relate to the gender politics of a society affected by migrant labour, in which men leave rural areas for work in the cities for most of the year (O'Connell 1980). The evidence presented for either of these arguments is not strong, but the assumption that these phenomena are ahistorical relics is generally not defended by evidence at all. Furthermore, there is some good anthropological work which links indigenous systems of healing and presentations of spirit possession to political concerns (Comaroff 1985; Reynolds 1996). There is also the suggestion from India that non-affective remitting psychosis (NARP), which arguably contains dissociative features, may relate quite closely to specific features of Indian gender politics (Collins et al. 1996).

What is striking about the construction of the 'primitive' world in which spirit possession is supposedly far more common (and archaic) than in the West is that this is also a subjugated world – a world of people who in many cases have been subdued by the West and then have become the objects of western scrutiny (Spivak 1990). Though it is of course incorrect to claim that western colonial subjugation had a monopoly on oppression and violence against large numbers of people, there is also no doubt of the role of violence and abuse in the establishment and maintenance of colonial subjugation. It may be precisely here that there is a link between dissociation as a 'new' phenomenon in the West, and spirit possession as a routine feature of transcultural psychiatric writing. The link, simply, is the link of violence and abuse. In the West, there seems little doubt that dissociation is linked strongly with trauma. In transcultural psychiatry, which often amounts to the description (some would argue, the *production*) of the pathologies of the subjugated, by contrast, there is often a complete elision of reference to trauma in the lives of the subjugated – an elision which may relate closely to the role of psychiatry as part of the apparatus of the colonial power (S. Swartz 1996). In South Africa, it is reasonably clear, for example, that much of the production of psychiatric knowledge on the mental health of migrant mine-workers obscured the possibility that their inhumane treatment as a captive labour force could contribute significantly to the development of psychopathological symptoms. Instead, the literature commonly presents the problems of South African mine-workers as problems of moving from an archaic culture into the rapidly-changing modern world (Swartz 1986). What we need to do in order to understand spirit possession more clearly is to explore its links with violence and abuse, and it may well be that in doing so we are able to find some key commonalities between spirit possession and dissociation as commonly discussed currently in the West. This is however only the first task.

A second important task is to think about the *representations* of dissociation and spirit possession in ways which may show further links. Much of the debate raging about dissociation in the West has less to do with the psychopathological phenomena in themselves than with the claims and counter-claims made for how they speak about the dilemmas of postmodern society – questions, as I mentioned at the outset of this chapter, of identity, violence and memory, as well as questions of legitimacy of representation. Who may rightfully speak for the abused, and what do we do if theoretically we believe that the abuse in itself may have effects which compromise the ability of the abused to speak accurately about themselves? Similar questions of course are being raised about who may accurately speak for the dominated and the colonised (Spivak 1990; S. Swartz 2000). The much-discussed 'crisis of representation' in the field of dissociation is just as much a feature of understanding psychopathology in the postcolonial world.

This is an exciting time, then, for thinking about dissociation and spirit possession together, and for linking phenomena which have seemed archaic relics of the past with what seem to be new features of the clinical landscape at the beginning of the twenty-first century. The questions are about abuse and violence and their consequences but are also about the representations of violence and abuse and their consequences. Under the theme of 'representation' we need to think as well about the ways in which violence and abuse may be obscured and rendered invisible. The process of making the invisible visible, though, as the work of Janet and Freud shows, is in itself not just a process of uncovering but fundamentally of defining and opening up a new discursive space. In thinking about dissociation and spirit possession together, we may begin to open up a new way of making connections, with all the difficulties and challenges, but also with all the possibilities that these connections can bring us.

NOTE

1 Throughout this chapter I use the distinctions 'western'/'nonwestern', 'developed'/'developing' and so on in the awareness that these distinctions are constructions we make of the world. The extent to which they are problematic for thinking about spirit possession will become clearer in the chapter.

REFERENCES

Boonzaier, E. and Sharp, J. (eds) (1988) *South African Keywords: The Use and Abuse of Political Concepts*. Cape Town: David Philip.

Castillo, R.J. (1994a) 'Spirit possession in South Asia, dissociation or hysteria? Part 1: Theoretical background'. *Culture, Medicine and Psychiatry*, 18, 1–21.

Castillo, R.J. (1994b) 'Spirit possession in South Asia, dissociation or hysteria? Part 2: Case histories'. *Culture, Medicine and Psychiatry*, 18, 141–162.

Collins, Y., Wig, N.N., Day, R., Varma, V.K., Malhorta, S., Misra, A.K., Schanzer, B. and Susser, E. (1996) *Psychiatric Quarterly*, 67(3), 177–193.

Comaroff, J. (1985) *Body of Power, Spirit of Resistance. The Culture and History of a South African People*. Chicago: Chicago University Press.

Hacking, I. (1994) 'Memoro-politics, trauma and the soul'. *History of the Human Sciences*, 7(2), 29–52.

Helman, C. (1987) 'Heart disease and the cultural construction of time: the Type A behaviour pattern as a western culture-bound syndrome'. *Social Science and Medicine*, 25, 969–979.

Hughes, C.C. (1996) 'The culture-bound syndromes and psychiatric diagnosis'. In J.E. Mezzich, A. Kleinman, H. Fabrega Jr and D.L. Parron (eds) *Culture and Diagnosis: A DSM-IV Perspective* (pp. 289–307). Washington, DC: American Psychiatric Press.

Kleinman, A. (1988) *Rethinking Psychiatry: From Cultural Category to Personal Experience*. New York: Free Press.

Kleinman, A. and Good, B.J. (eds) (1985) *Culture and Depression: Studies in the Anthropology and Cross-cultural Psychiatry of Affect and Disorder*. Berkeley: University of California Press.

Leff, J. (1981) *Psychiatry around the Globe: A Transcultural View*. New York: Marcel Dekker.

Leff, J. (1988) *Psychiatry around the Globe: A Transcultural View* (2nd edn). London: Gaskell.

Lipsedge, M. and Littlewood, R. (1997) 'Psychopathology and its public sources: from a provisional typology to a dramaturgy of domestic sieges'. *Anthropology and Medicine*, 4, 25–43.

Littlewood, R. (1996) 'Comments on culture-bound syndromes: I'. In J.E. Mezzich, A. Kleinman, H. Fabrega Jr and D.L. Parron (eds) *Culture and Diagnosis: A DSM-IV Perspective* (pp. 309–312). Washington, DC: American Psychiatric Press.

Littlewood, R. and Lipsedge, M. (1997) *Aliens and Alienists: Ethnic Minorities and Psychiatry* (3rd edn). London: Routledge.

Lucas, R.H. and Barrett, R. (1995) 'Interpreting culture and psychopathology: primitivist themes in cross-cultural debate'. *Culture, Medicine and Psychiatry*, 19, 287–326.

Lund, C. and Swartz, L. (1998) 'Xhosa-speaking schizophrenic patients' experience of their condition: psychosis and *amafufunyana*'. *South African Journal of Psychology*, 28, 62–70.

Mezzich, J.E., Kleinman, A., Fabrega, H. Jr and Parron, D.L. (eds) (1996) *Culture and Diagnosis: A DSM-IV Perspective*. Washington, DC: American Psychiatric Press.

Ngubane, H. (1977) *Body and Mind in Zulu Medicine: An Ethnography of Health and Disease in Nyuswa-Zulu Thought and Practice*. London: Academic Press.

Nuttall, S. and Coetzee, C. (eds) (1998) *Negotiating the Past: The Making of Memory in South Africa*. Cape Town: Oxford University Press.

O'Connell, M.C. (1980) 'The aetiology of thwasa'. *Psychotherapeia*, 6(4), 18–23.

Reynolds, P. (1996) *Traditional Healers and Childhood in Zimbabwe*. Athens, Ohio: University of Ohio Press.

Sinason, V. (ed.) (1999) *Memory in Dispute*. London: Karnac Books.

Spivak, G. (1990) *The Post-colonial Critic: Interviews, Strategies, Dialogues*. New York: Routledge.

Swartz, L. (1985) 'Anorexia nervosa as a culture-bound syndrome'. *Social Science and Medicine*, 20, 725–730.

Swartz, L. (1986) 'Transcultural psychiatry in South Africa. Part I'. *Transcultural Psychiatric Research Review*, 23, 273–303.

Swartz, L. (1987) 'Transcultural psychiatry in South Africa. Part II'. *Transcultural Psychiatric Research Review*, 24, 5–30.

Swartz, L. (1998) *Culture and Mental Health: A Southern African View*. Cape Town: Oxford University Press.

Swartz, S. (1996) 'Colonialism and the production of psychiatric knowledge in the Cape, 1891–1920'. Unpublished PhD thesis, University of Cape Town.

Swartz, S. (2000) 'Can the clinical subject speak? Some thoughts on a subaltern psychology'. University of Cape Town Department of Psychology Seminar Paper.

Young, A. (1995) *The Harmony of Illusions: Inventing Posttraumatic Stress Disorder*. Princeton, NJ: Princeton University Press.

Chapter 16

Multiple Personality Disorder and schizophrenia

An interview with Professor Flora Rheta Schreiber

Brett Kahr

THE LIFE OF FLORA RHETA SCHREIBER

On 3rd November 1988, Professor Flora Rheta Schreiber, a distinguished pioneer in the field of child abuse studies and psycho-biography, died in her hospital bed in New York City. Best known as the author of the landmark book *Sybil*, first published in 1973, Schreiber made an enormous contribution to the mental health field by calling widespread attention to the existence of multiple personality disorder, and to its traumatic origins.

During the last two years of her life, Professor Schreiber suffered from cancer of the colon, a very painful condition which required a great deal of invasive treatment which caused her much pain and suffering. Professor Schreiber entered hospital in Manhattan for a further bout of medical care, and during her convalescence in the autumn of 1988, she had a stroke, and then a heart attack, which proved fatal. I do not know Professor Schreiber's age at the time of her death; she very much believed that a real lady should never reveal such an intimate detail. I estimate her to have been some seventy years of age; but whatever her age, she died too soon, leaving many important projects unfinished, and many friends and colleagues bereft.

Flora Schreiber spent virtually all of her life in New York City, the only child of William Schreiber and Esther Schreiber, two rather liberal-minded librarians. As the daughter of two professional bibliophiles, it should not surprise us that Flora decided to devote her life to writing. From a very early age, she opted for a career in the literary world, and she steered clear of the kitchen. Flora often told me that when her mother had tried to teach her some basic cookery skills, Flora replied, 'If I were a boy, I would love to learn how to cook, but as a girl, I can't afford to'. Thus, the young Flora avoided the traditional domestic path so that she could immerse herself fully in her chosen trade. Indeed, Flora rarely ever entered the kitchen in adulthood, preferring the meals prepared by her loving and devoted cook, Flossie Simmons, who worked for Flora for many, many years. She also became a devotee of her local Chinese food delivery service.

Schreiber attended Columbia University where she studied English literature and related subjects. At one point, during the 1930s, she took a boat to

England to attend the Oxford Verse Festival, where she had the opportunity to meet W.H. Auden and T.S. Eliot. This proved a vital experience, and Flora appreciated the encouragement that she had received from both of these literary giants. Flora often reminisced about this early trip to England, and she often regaled her guests with the poignant story of her missing luggage. Apparently, when she arrived in England for the first time, she discovered to her horror that someone had sent all of her cases on to Cairo. It seems that a fellow traveller, also called Schreiber, planned a visit to Egypt by way of England, and he instructed his valet to ship all 'Schreiber' luggage to Cairo. When Flora appeared at her English hotel, she had to endure the embarrassment of having had all her evening dresses posted to the land of the Pharaohs; and, as a result, because the hotel staff would not let her wear her day dress in the main dining room, the young Flora had to take her meal alone in her room.

After Oxford, Flora acquired a certificate from the Central School of Speech and Drama in London; and upon completion, she returned to America, ever more determined to pursue a career in journalism. From a very early point in her career, she became interested in psychological matters. Although Flora never underwent a psychoanalytical treatment or a clinical training of any kind, her work always revealed an unusually profound sensitivity to psychological matters, so much so that most people did mistake her for a psychoanalyst, and this flattered Flora tremendously. In 1940, she published her first substantial article, 'Emily is in the House: Emily Dickinson as Revealed Through Her Imagery', a psychological study of the poetess Emily Dickinson, which appeared in the Spring issue of the periodical *Poet Lore*. Flora described this work as a 'psychograph', and it certainly serves as a lovely anticipation of her more substantial psychobiographical treatments of 'Sybil Isabel Dorsett', the multiple personality disordered patient whose life she chronicled with such tenacity (Schreiber 1973), and Joseph Kallinger, the American serial killer, who became the subject of her final book, *The Shoemaker: The Anatomy of a Psychotic* (Schreiber 1983).

Throughout the 1950s and 1960s, Schreiber established herself as a journalist who specialised in psychiatry and mental health. She also received a faculty appointment at the John Jay College of Criminal Justice at the City University of New York where she taught for many years with great distinction, rising to the rank of Full Professor of English and Speech and, later, as Director of Public Relations and special assistant to the President of the institution. As a columnist, Flora wrote countless pieces on all aspects of mental health; and she interviewed most of the key figures in post-war American psychoanalysis. She also greatly admired the work of Dr Murray Bowen, a leading figure in the field of family therapy and in the psychotherapeutic treatment of schizophrenia, often profiling his stimulating contributions.

Many people admired the quality of her work, and thus her reputation flourished. Flora received invitations to write important magazine features for women's journals, and she particularly enjoyed the articles that she wrote about the wives of the American Presidents. I believe Flora interviewed Eleanor Roosevelt, Bess Truman, Mamie Eisenhower, Jacqueline Kennedy, and Lady Bird Johnson. Flora conducted detailed and sharp interviews with these remarkable women before writing articles about them, so much so that Mrs Johnson, the wife of Lyndon Baines Johnson, once exclaimed: 'Being interviewed by Flora Schreiber is like undergoing psychoanalysis'. Even her interviews with the presidential spouses had a marked psychological slant, and Schreiber always did what she could to illuminate the psychological aspects of her subjects. Though articles on mental health issues are now quite common-place, in the 1940s and 1950s, they were not; and both Flora Rheta Schreiber and her close friend Lucy Freeman (1951), author of the uniquely popular book *Fight Against Fears*, deserve our thanks as true pioneers of responsible mental health reportage.

At some point in the late 1950s or early 1960s, Flora received a telephone call that would change her life, as well as the face of modern psychiatry. Dr Cornelia Wilbur, a psychoanalyst and psychiatric practitioner, phoned Schreiber to tell her about one of her patients, a young woman with no fewer than sixteen multiple personalities who had spent many years in treatment with Dr Wilbur. It seems that Dr Wilbur thought that the life story of this woman would be interesting for potential readers; and she enquired whether Schreiber would wish to write a book-length version of the case history. Wilbur very much appreciated Schreiber's work, especially after having seen a profile that Schreiber had already completed about Wilbur, in which Schreiber 'had written everything absolutely correct' (Wilbur and Torem 1993: xxix). Flora asked Dr Wilbur whether she had managed to integrate the sixteen per-sonalities; and Wilbur admitted that she had not yet done so. Flora then told her, 'Well, then, there's no book'.

Some years later, in 1962, Dr Wilbur rang Schreiber again, and she con-fessed that she had now succeeded; and that through intensive psychotherapeutic treatment, the sixteen separate personalities of the young patient had become fully integrated. Flora became preoccupied with this intriguing story, and she agreed to commence work on a book about the life of this extraordinary patient, whom Flora named 'Sybil'. Flora began to under-take an extensive and exhaustive series of interviews with Sybil, and she developed a very close personal relationship with her. Schreiber's own mother, Esther Schreiber, also came to know Sybil, and the three women spent a very great deal of time together.

To her everlasting credit, Flora Schreiber wrote the book version of Sybil's life not only on the basis of her interviews with Sybil and Cornelia Wilbur but, like a true investigative reporter, Schreiber actually arranged to meet with many of the individuals in Sybil's life, both past and present, to acquire inde-pendent, corroborative evidence of aspects of Sybil's childhood – something that a practising clinician cannot do. In this way, Flora succeeded in tracking down the whereabouts of Sybil's childhood paediatrician who confirmed that he had also suspected that Sybil's mother had perpetrated some form of extreme physical child abuse. In an era when memories and reminiscences of early abuse can so easily be dismissed as vestiges of the so-called 'False Memory Syndrome', Schreiber's methodology deserves particular attention as one of the first serious attempts to document the existence of child abuse, without needing to rely solely on the potentially subjective recall of the patient in question.

Flora became obsessed with Sybil's story, and she worked on the crafting of the manuscript with vigour. Schreiber told me that when she prepared the first draft of her grippingly written book, she would work for sixteen hours a day. She wrote by hand, and worked until her fingers became so tired that she could no longer grip her writing implement. After Schreiber had completed the book, she sent the manuscript to most of the major publishers but, in spite of her terrific track record as a writer, every single publishing house rejected the manuscript, approximately sixty publishers in all. Finally, a relatively obscure outfit in Chicago, Illinois, the Henry Regnery Company, expressed an interest in this seemingly bizarre tale of a woman with sixteen personalities. But during the negotiations, Henry Regnery's son-in-law took control of the publishing firm, and he lost interest in the manuscript until his wife coaxed him into taking on the project. As Cornelia Wilbur recalled, 'I was told that she, without doing the dishes or spending any time putting the children to bed, read the entire manuscript, and at 3 a.m. dropped it on top of her husband when he was asleep and said, "Publish this".' (Wilbur and Torem 1993: xxix). To everyone's great surprise, *Sybil* became an almost overnight sensation, quickly becoming a best-selling book, which remains in print today, almost thirty years after its initial publication.

Of course, many other investigators had written very illuminating tracts on Multiple Personality Disorder, ranging from such ancient writers as Paracelsus to such nineteenth-century figures as Robert Louis Stevenson (cf. Carlson 1981; Greaves 1993). More recently, the pioneer of object-relations thinking in Scotland, Dr Ronald Fairbairn, had written his MD thesis for the University of Edinburgh on the question of dissociation (Fairbairn 1929), and he elaborated upon these ideas in his subsequent work on dissociated identities in his little-known paper on hysterical states (Fairbairn 1954). One could extend the history of writing on multiple personality disorder almost indefinitely (cf. Shamdasani 1994). But none of these works captured the public imagination as compellingly as Flora Schreiber's book on 'Sybil'.

The success of *Sybil* created an enormous amount of pleasurable work for Flora Schreiber, and she developed a subsidiary career, lecturing all over America about the extraordinary story. A television film version appeared under the auspices of Lorimar Productions, with Joanne Woodward starring as the psychiatrist, Dr Cornelia Wilbur, and Sally Field playing the role of 'Sybil'. Flora had mixed feelings about the way in which Hollywood brought *Sybil* to the screen. She took ironic delight in reminding me that although she wrote the book which formed the basis of the screenplay, once she had signed the deal, she retained only the right 'to comment', but not the right to change a single word of dialogue of the teleplay.

If memory serves me correctly, after the publication of *Sybil*, Flora's lawyer, Arthur Abelman, contacted her, and he told her that he had just read about a newspaper article about a murderer called Joseph Kallinger, then awaiting trial in the Bergen County Jail, in New Jersey, for the vicious, fatal stabbing of a nurse called Maria Fasching. Abelman felt that if anybody could plumb to the roots of why a man would commit a murder, then Flora would be the perfect researcher, owing to her great psychological sensitivities. Flora first met Kallinger in 1976, and the two of them developed a strong bond. For the first time in his life, Kallinger felt that he had met somebody who maintained both a serious interest in him, and who could understand him in a special way. Before long, Schreiber had begun an intensive series of interviews with Kallinger, amounting to literally thousands of hours of tape-recorded talks over a 6-year period.

Relying both on interviews with members of the Kallinger family, and on extensive archival and documentary research into his childhood, Schreiber succeeded in reconstructing his life in extensive detail, perhaps more thoroughly than any other psychological investigator has ever done with a murderer. As with the case of Sybil, Flora Schreiber relied not only on personal reminiscences from Kallinger himself, but actually undertook the necessary field work to locate relatives, neighbours, and many other individuals who had played an important role during Kallinger's formative years. She even located a neighbour who had witnessed Kallinger's adoptive mother Anna Kallinger hitting him over the head with a hammer during his boyhood.

Eventually, Schreiber reconstructed Kallinger's horrific childhood, filled with grotesque forms of physical abuse and sexual molestation, both in the family home and outside. Quite importantly, from a methodological point of view, although Schreiber knew about child abuse from her work on the *Sybil* project, she did not hear about the abuse from Kallinger himself in the first instance. As she reported,

> My knowledge of the abuse of Joe as a child first came from outside sources and not from him. I had known him more than three years before, in response to my questions based on what these outside sources had told me, he reluctantly and slowly revealed the abuses he had suffered. Slowly I learned that I was dealing with the etiology of a psychosis that drove Joe to perform sadistic acts and to murder.
>
> (Schreiber 1983: 418–419)

In fact, Kallinger not only remained cautious in revealing details of his abusive childhood to Schreiber, but also, during the course of the interviews, he revealed that he had committed two other hithertofore unsolved murders, that of a small boy known pseudonymously in the book as 'José Collazo', and the other, his own son, Joseph Kallinger Jr.

Schreiber enlisted the co-operation of two eminent psychoanalysts, Dr Silvano Arieti and Dr Lewis Robbins, to help her understand the psychodynamics of paranoid schizophrenia. Both of these men assessed Kallinger, and they confirmed the diagnosis of schizophrenia. The American Academy of Psychoanalysis invited Schreiber to present a paper about Joseph Kallinger to its conference in Toronto, Canada, in 1982, and this pleased Flora immensely. She also published a short article about the case with Dr Silvano Arieti (Arieti and Schreiber 1981).

The publication of *The Shoemaker: The Anatomy of a Psychotic* (1983) caused an absolute flurry of vitriol in the media. Journalists began to spread rumours that Flora Schreiber had arranged a secret pact with Joseph Kallinger *before* the murders, arguing that as the best-selling author of *Sybil*, she could command a high fee for his memoirs, which they could split, and that Kallinger had committed murder for the main purpose of helping Schreiber to write another best-selling book. These allegations hurt Flora considerably, and she had to spend most of her lifetime's savings on expensive and ugly legal wranglings to protect her name and her reputation. Others criticised her mercilessly for having dared to take an interest in a multiple murderer; people regarded her stance of empathy and compassion towards Kallinger as absolutely reprehensible. Flora, in contrast, felt that she had actually made a real contribution to the understanding of the origins of murder, and she felt crushed that members of the public regarded her as shielding a murderer.

Flora and I first met in Oxford in 1984, during the promotion of the British paperback edition of her book, published by Penguin Books. She stayed for several days as my guest in Corpus Christi College, and she enjoyed a warm and welcome reception from numerous British colleagues, including Professor Rachel Rosser, now deceased, then Professor of Psychiatry at the Middlesex Hospital Medical School in London, who had arranged for Schreiber to deliver a lecture on the Kallinger case. Apart from a dreadful lunch at the Pride of Paddington pub, while waiting for a train, she enjoyed her trip to England immensely.

In her final years, she began to conduct preliminary research for a psychobiography of Benny Goodman, the famous swing musician, and also a psychoanalytical book on the Nazi, Rudolf Hess. Flora had also begun negotiations for a film version of *The Shoemaker*, as well as a stage musical version of *Sybil*. When I told her that I would find it hard to imagine that *Sybil* could be transformed into a musical comedy, Flora seemed surprised, and she began to expound upon all the ways in which questions of mistaken identity could be explored. She even showed me a copy of a list of potential song titles that she had generated for different scenes.

Sadly, Flora died on 3rd November 1988 before she could have done proper justice to any of these remaining projects. Many loving colleagues attended a memorial tribute in her honour. Professor Melinda Jo Guttman, a littérateur and theatre scholar who worked with Flora at the John Jay College of Criminal

Justice, delivered a moving speech. Professor Guttman (1998) also inherited some of Schreiber's jewellery. Marshall Coid, the well-known violinist, and leader with the orchestra at the New York City Opera, performed music in Flora's memory.

Schreiber never married. She did become engaged to Eugene O'Neill Jr, the son of the playwright Eugene O'Neill, during her youth, but the relationship collapsed. Although she never had her own family, she enjoyed her wide and varied circle of friends, and she attended to her network with great love. Flora will be much missed by her many friends and colleagues around the world who appreciated her warmth and generosity of spirit, and her fierce intelligence and bravery in psychological matters.

After her death, the case of 'Sybil', in particular, began to attract greater attention, as part of the growing Zeitgeist of the 'False Memory Syndrome', and amid growing numbers of allegations that psychotherapists had implanted false memories of abuse in the minds of their patients (cf. Borch-Jacobsen 1997). Eventually, the historian, Peter Swales, discovered the true identity of 'Sybil', and he revealed her name to *Newsweek* magazine (Miller and Kantrowitz 1999). As Flora Schreiber (1973: xiii) wrote in the 'Preface' to *Sybil*, 'This book goes to press over ten years after I first met the woman to whom I have given the pseudonym Sybil Isabel Dorsett. Sybil wants to maintain anonymity, and when you read her true story, you will understand why. But Sybil Isabel Dorsett *is* a real person.' It seems unfortunate that, in spite of the care and attention which Schreiber took to preserve the confidentiality of 'Sybil', this wish could not be respected.

I derive much pleasure from the fact that between 1990 and 1995, I organised an annual Flora Rheta Schreiber Memorial Lecture under the auspices of The British Institute for Psychohistory. Past lecturers included such distinguished clinicians as Donald Campbell, the late Dr Murray Cox, Dr Mervin Glasser, Dr Eileen Vizard, and Dr Estela Welldon, as well as the psychobiographer and politician Leo Abse. I still use her writing in my teaching, and I know that through new generations of students who find stimulation from *Sybil* and *The Shoemaker: The Anatomy of a Psychotic*, her work will continue to have a great impact.

THE INTERVIEW WITH PROFESSOR FLORA RHETA SCHREIBER

I first became personally acquainted with Flora Rheta Schreiber in 1984, towards the end of her life, when she lectured to the Oxford Psycho-Analytical Forum, a group that I had organised at the University of Oxford, to promote psychoanalytical ideas and scholarship. We developed a close friendship during the last years of her life, aided by the fact that I spent the 1985–86 academic year in the Department of Psychology at Yale University, and thus I had frequent opportunities to speak to Schreiber and to meet with her. As a research psychologist with a strong interest in the forensic field, Flora very much hoped that I would help her to plan a large interview study with serial killers, to ascertain whether other murderers shared the awful abusive history of Joseph Kallinger, the protagonist of *The Shoemaker: The Anatomy of a Psychotic*. She also hoped to enlist my assistance in writing a sequel to *The Shoemaker*, to try to understand the resistance to approaching murderers from a psychoanalytical point of view.

I had a greater interest, however, in another project. Flora possessed a veritable trunkful of letters which she had received in the wake of the publication of *Sybil*, all of them from men and women throughout the world who claimed that they too suffered from multiple personality disorder, and many of them bemoaned the fact that they could not find adequate psychological assistance. Some of the letters pleaded with Flora, urging her to write a book about them. Flora hoped to edit a book of these letters and, in July 1987, we began work on this project. Sadly, Flora became grievously ill soon thereafter, and it seemed inappropriate to continue the task. To the best of my knowledge, the letters have now joined the archives of the John Jay College of Criminal Justice in New York City, where Flora's papers will be preserved.

Knowing of Flora's increasing age, I thought it would be helpful to record an interview with her, so that she could still speak to us, even after her death. She agreed to an interview, which we recorded on the terrace of her Gramercy Park South apartment in Manhattan on Thursday, 25th June 1987. The interview has remained unpublished until this time, even though numerous inquisitive researchers have asked for copies. I found myself waiting, however, for the right vehicle in which to publish the text of the interview; and I suspect that Flora herself would have welcomed the opportunity to have her observations printed in an overtly psychoanalytical book.

I have made a number of very minor alterations to the text, to increase the readability of my oral interview with Schreiber. As we had recorded the interview on a hot summer's afternoon, which necessitated us being outside on Schreiber's balcony terrace, the sound of the New York City traffic had obscured a very small number of portions of the tape, rendering them inaudible, and thus requiring the occasional deletion. Otherwise, the text represents an accurate reflection of our conversation.

B.K. Good afternoon Professor Schreiber, it is a great pleasure to speak to you. I'm particularly interested in speaking to you about the very pathbreaking research that you have undertaken on the topic of child abuse. Now, you're not a clinician by training, you're a Professor of English Literature and Speech, is that right?

F.S. That is correct, and I've worked very extensively in theatre; and it seems to me that all these various disciplines converge into the sum and substance that is dealt with by the clinical psychologist or psychiatrist or psychoanalyst.

B.K. And what I find remarkable about your work is that in spite of the fact that you're not a clinician and that you have not had that formal background in clinical psychiatry or psychoanalysis, you have, nevertheless, made an extraordinary contribution to our understanding of child abuse and its clinical consequences in your two best-selling books – *Sybil*, which came out in 1973, and *The Shoemaker: The Anatomy of a Psychotic*, which was published a decade later in 1983, is that right?

F.S. That is correct.

B.K. Now, before we look at the causes and consequences of child abuse – and I'd like to ask you as well about your recommendations for what society can do to prevent the problem of child abuse – I wonder if you could recapitulate for us in a brief summary the major findings of your two important books, *Sybil* and *The Shoemaker*?

F.S. The major findings as they relate to the genesis of mental illness from child abuse? Yes, of course. Now, in the case of Sybil, she was a very badly abused child by a schizophrenic mother. Now the situation in Sybil is that of a mother who was loving on occasion and brutal on other occasions, presumably when she had a little psychotic break. The father loved Sybil very much but he was a completely peripheral personality, and he never intervened to stop the abuse. He trusted the child to be raised by this highly schizophrenic mother – he didn't know she was schizophrenic, but he did know she was mentally ill, and all the people in the community said, 'Hattie was "odd".'

B.K. Hattie is the mother?

F.S. Yes. But that is the basic story of her childhood. The mother abused Sybil in hideous ways. She had a little technique of inserting all kinds of foreign objects in the child's vagina, and she would hang the child up like an object, and she would have an enema bag on the ceiling and pour this enema water into the child's rectum, then put the child at the piano, bang on the piano while the child sat near it and would not permit the child to go to the bathroom. She locked the child in a wheat loft and literally put her there to die. Fortunately, the father had come home early that day and found the child, and saved her and wondered what had happened, how she had got into the hayloft. And Hattie said, 'Oh, Floyd did it, you know that boy down the street, he's always doing evil things.' Of course Hattie had done it. Hattie stuck a bead up Sybil's nose and then Hattie took the child to the family doctor, Dr Quinoness, and Dr Quinoness said, 'Well how did that happen?' 'Oh, you know how children are,' said Hattie, 'They're so clumsy.' And so on and so forth, ad infinitum. But what resulted from this was an intense hatred of the mother on the part of Sybil.

B.K. Obviously.

F.S. But Sybil was a well brought up little girl and she knew it was not nice to hate your mother. So she repressed this hatred and by the time she was three and a half, she had to have a modus operandi for survival and also a mask against this hatred, and so she became ill, she was in the Mayo Clinic in Rochester, Minnesota. And the day when the young intern said to her, 'I've got good news for you. You're going home tomorrow,' and this poor little girl could not have been told anything worse had he said, 'We're putting you in the gas chamber tomorrow'; it would have been much closer. And she jumped up and clung to him and said, 'Would you like a little girl?' He put her down and left the room, and she saw this retreating white coat. On the unconscious level, she decided she would not go home anyway. And that was the birth of the two central alternating selves – Peggy and Victoria, Vicky. Peggy later proliferated into two Peggys – Peggy Lou Baldwin and Peggy Ann Baldwin, but on that occasion, when Sybil was three and a half it was Peggy as one alter and Vicky as another alter. And they went home for Sybil. That was the beginning of multiplicity. People have often asked me whether this is Sybil's recollection of some sort of previous existence and all that kind of thing, and I resolutely answer, 'No, this can be explained in naturalistic terms', because Sybil erected a defence system, it was a defensive manoeuvre to protect herself against the hatred.

B.K. So in other words, when the external reality of the abusive mother and the abandoning, neglectful father became too powerful for Sybil, she split and developed these other personalities who could live her life for her.

F.S. She dissociated. I don't like using the word 'split' because it suggests schizophrenia. Sybil was not schizophrenic, she was suffering from what was established by Charcot as 'grand hysteria' with multiple personalities. But the function of these personalities was to defend Sybil against intolerable traumas.

B.K. Now Flora, you said that Sybil dissociated into different personalities?

F.S. To defend herself against hideous traumas, and to defend against the affect in her that those traumas engendered. But I want to make just one point which is very illustrative of this – Sybil accepted Hattie as her mother. None of the alters did. They would say things like, 'Her – she's Sybil's mother, she's not *my* mother', but they accepted what she had done to them. Sybil rejected what the mother had done and accepted the mother.

B.K. Now, did the alternate personalities express rage at the mother, the rage that Sybil herself felt?

F.S. Yes, they certainly did.

B.K. So in this way Sybil could be furious at her mother, and yet still remain the dutiful daughter?

F.S. Be the loving, dutiful daughter. But the alters were furious. But they weren't angry at their mother, because they denied that she was their mother. They were just angry at Sybil's mother, which is a very interesting sleight of mind.

B.K. Now let me ask you some questions about the actual child abuse. At what age did it begin, as far as we know?

F.S. Oh, early infancy. The earliest on record is at eight months old and these insertions of foreign objects occurred when the child was between one and two.

B.K. When you say 'on record', how was this child abuse documented?

F.S. Well, through Sybil's recollection, but also you can't pinpoint the time of this, this seems to be Sybil's recollection. But a gynaecologist whom Sybil visited in her adulthood told her that because of the internal injuries she would not be able to bear a child, so that is certainly testimony to the fact that those injuries took place.

B.K. Yes, how frightening. And the child abuse continued throughout Sybil's childhood and adolescence?

F.S. No, it stopped in childhood. It really continued through early adolescence but not much beyond that. And when Sybil went away to college, she was away from it all, and she was called back when her mother was having serious terminal cancer, and Sybil was very close to her mother then. She nursed her, and her mother was very loving, and apologised for some of the things she had done to her.

B.K. Let me ask you if I may Flora, when you wrote *Sybil* in the 1970s it really was one of the first books not only on the question of multiple personality disorder but also on the subject of child abuse. What impact do you think *Sybil* has had on the study of child abuse today? Do you think it opened some doors?

F.S. I hope it did, and there's a good deal of evidence that it did. To do a quantitative analysis would be impossible. We only know from letters and general remarks that it opened doors for individuals. They saw what they hadn't seen before, and my correspondence is replete with comments of that nature.

B.K. Now, after *Sybil* appeared, you started work on another book, another psychobiography of an abused child, and this time you chose not a case of multiple personality disorder, but rather, that of a multiple murderer, a serial murderer, Joseph Kallinger.

F.S. Well, I didn't make that choice, because when I signed the contract for what later became *The Shoemaker*, and when I first met Joseph Kallinger on 19th July 1976 in the Bergen County Jail, I had no idea that he was a multiple murderer, neither did the world. He was on trial at that point for a single murder that had taken place in Leonia, New Jersey.

B.K. So nobody knew about the other two murders as yet?

F.S. No, and I as little as anyone.

B.K. Now what prompted Joseph Kallinger to become a murderer?

F.S. Basically, the same thing that provoked Sybil into becoming a multiple personality, broadly speaking. He too was a seriously abused child. But in an emotional sense, the abuse was even worse.

B.K. So Joe suffered from both profound physical abuse and emotional abuse. Can you tell us about these two kinds of abuse?

F.S. Well, I want to compare the emotional abuse experienced by Joe with the emotional abuse experienced by Sybil. Sybil was with her own parents. She had a brutal mother who on occasion was a loving mother – she really had two mothers. Her father loved her very much although he was really very ineffective in preventing the abuse or taking a stand about it. Joe, on the other hand, had absolutely, literally, no love in his entire childhood from the time he was in the womb. While he was in the womb, his natural mother was making plans to have him adopted, taken from her. He was a love child, that is, she was in love with the man who was his father, but she had a husband of her own, and she was afraid that if Joe's identity were discovered, if there were a divorce action with her husband, then she might lose her daughter, who was the daughter of her husband as well as herself and who was fifteen months older than Joe. So Joe was to be sacrificed for this other child. So, she had nurtured Joe for three weeks, and she took him to the home of a friend, the only one who knew of his existence, and there she cooed to him, and sang to him, and gave him everything, nursed him, breast-fed him, did everything that a loving mother would do; and after that, she put him in a private boarding home, and then, when he was three months old, into an orphanage, St Vincent's, and when he was just a little over two, a couple over forty adopted him. They were unloving, wanting a child to adopt because they had a thriving shoe repair store, and they wanted to have a future shoemaker who would inherit their business and take care of them in their old age. There was no sense of adopting a child in the loving sense. There was no love, there was no feeling of any kind, and they were temperamentally worlds and worlds apart.

B.K. They adopted an apprentice rather than a child.

F.S. They adopted an apprentice, and put him into child labour when he was very, very little.

B.K. These were the Kallingers?

F.S. These were the senior Kallingers, Stephen and Anna. Throughout the years there was a good deal of physical abuse as well, but one further emotional abuse was that they would constantly say to him at the slightest childhood infraction, 'We will send you back' – back to the orphanage. So they were intensifying the insecurity of a child who was insecure to begin with.

B.K. In other words, Sybil always knew that she had a home to come back to, even though it was an abusive home.

F.S. Not to come back to, to be in. She never left it.

B.K. To be in, right. Sybil had a home to be in, but Joe was always under threat of being kicked out of his adopted parents' home.

F.S. Despite the abuses, Sybil was an adored only child.

B.K. So what did the Kallingers do to Joe in the household, physically and emotionally?

F.S. Well, emotionally it was very sterile, because they didn't love him. They told everyone they had adopted him, and that he was their good deed, and they threatened to send him back, intensifying his insecurity. And they didn't allow him out to play. The only time he left the house was to go to school and come home from school and then he was held by the hand by his unloving adoptive mother. There was no freedom, he had no friends, he was not allowed to bring any child into the house or go to any other child's house, indeed he was not allowed out of the house. Halloween was something he watched through the window, saw other kids trick-or-treating, and he never could go out and play anything. Neighbours told me that they'd wanted to take him out to play, but the Kallingers completely refused. The crowning instance of that nature took place when he was eight. He came home from school with his adoptive mother of course, and Joe walked into the room, and he went over to his adoptive father and said, 'Let me have a quarter, the class is going to the zoo this afternoon.' The father was about to give it to him and the mother said in German, 'Are you crazy, he is not to go.' And this was Joe's first act of defiance, and he said, 'But Daddy said I could go, and I'm going.' And she said, 'Zoo, you want zoo, I will give you zoo.' She took a hammer used in shoe repair work and banged him on the head. The blood flowed and he ran out of the room. Now this was not told me by Joseph Kallinger, certainly not by his mother or his step-father – they were dead before I entered the picture – but it was told me by a neighbour who was a customer; she was in the store when it happened.

B.K. So you had other evidence to corroborate the existence of the child abuse?

F.S. Well, lots of neighbours talked of this imprisonment, that this child could never go out to play.

B.K. And this occurred at the age of eight? Eight years old and his parents are beating him on the head with a hammer? How frightening!

F.S. His mother was beating him anyway. But there were other physical abuses. He was made to kneel on coarse sand paper until they said, 'Get up', usually for about an hour. The father hit him with an improvised cat-o'-nine-tails. The father hit him with leather from the shoe repair shop, and this went on and on, and they both put his hand over the kitchen stove and put up the flame. And the physical abuses, horrible as they are, are all the more horrible because of the emotional climate in which they took place. This child would have given anything for a sister or a brother or a companion, or even an aunt or uncle or grandparent. His entire childhood was spent with these two middle-aged people, humourless, bitter, cruel, and who regarded him not as a person but as an object.

B.K. What results did this abuse have?

F.S. One of the major episodes I have not reported yet, that's the so-called 'Bird Incident'. When he was six and three quarters he had a hernia operation. Before he went to the hospital the Kallingers said that he would suffer mightily because there would be a lot of pain and a lot of fear. He had heard women in the store talking about operations, so he went with a good deal of fear. But there was another fear and that was that they were really sending him back, because he found himself in another institution and it wasn't, in some respects, too different from the orphanage. But he looked at the surgeon as an instrument of power, exerting the same kind of power on a little boy's flesh as Stephen Kallinger the adoptive father exerted on leather in the shoe repair store. So knives became the instruments of power, whether in the shoe repair store or in the hospital. But when Joe came home from the hospital, the Kallingers sat him down on his kiddy chair under the chandelier in the living room and they said, 'We've got something to tell you. Dr Daly, the surgeon, operated on your hernia, but he did something else. There is a demon that lives in the bird (their euphemism for the penis), in the bird of little boys and men. And when the demon is removed, as Dr Daly removed your demon, you will always be a good boy and a good man, you will never get a girl into trouble, and you will never get yourself into trouble' – in other words, 'you are totally castrated'. Another incident had a good deal of shaping power. The Kallingers sent him on an errand from the store, that was the only way he could ever leave. And when he went on these errands he had a favourite spot in an abandoned tank in the old part of Philadelphia – Kensington – and he would sit in there and listen to the birds and watch the movement of the birds as he sat. And he was in a joyous frame of mind, this was part of his secret world, just as he had a secret world in the country cottage of the Kallingers, where he made his first identification with the butterflies, they were part of his secret world. And he fantasised that he had been a spirit that had lived before, and now had come to life again. He had been given birth to by another mother for the express purpose that the Kallingers would be sent to adopt him. And that fantasy died as the Kallingers became more brutal, and he accepted their brutality. But in the beginning it was an earnest, earnest plea, although they did not know about it, but an internal plea, for their love and their really wanting him. But back to the tank in Kensington. He was sitting there enjoying himself and then he became aware of three older boys – 'Ah, there's that shoemaker's kid', and they came over and held him down, one of them held a knife at his throat, another gave him a blowjob – and this was Joe's initiation into sex, he was eight, by strangers, forcibly, and with a knife at his throat. A knife which was already a symbol of power. I think the bird incident, and the incident in the tank are the two major influences on the developmental pattern as it applied to his particular crimes.

B.K. Can you elaborate on this further, and show how the physical abuse and the emotional abuse intertwined to create a murderer.

F.S. Well, the emotional abuse had led to rage, there was very intense rage. And that was cumulative. He brought rage to the Kallinger household, it was rage at abandonment by his natural mother. But the rage grew with the Kallingers' abuses. But more particularly he had been told that Dr Daly had removed the demon and Joe became very much aware of the power of the knife, the knife which conferred both sexual power and power in society, and he became absolutely obsessed with having both. When he killed the nurse in New Jersey, he had sent another man who was one of the hostages in this household, he hog-tied him and exposed his penis and got him ready for castration. Then he took Maria Fasching, the nurse, down to the basement and told her to chew off the man's penis. What I'm particularly concerned about is that the mechanism established in childhood became the mechanism of the three murders. They were replays of childhood incidents. I showed that in the Fasching murder, the murder of the nurse, he took her down to the basement and he said, 'You are to go in there', with this other guest who had been hog-tied, and whose penis had been exposed, 'You are to go in there and chew off his penis, or I'll kill you.' You see he was making her a delegate for his fantasy, for his obsession.

B.K. So, in other words, his parents had symbolically destroyed his genitals, any potency in his genitals, and this proved traumatic. And in the murders, he re-enacted this by way of mastery, by making it not his own genitals that were being destroyed, but someone else's.

F.S. Yes. And the whole point was that he was going to massacre the whole of mankind through the destruction of sexual organs. That was his principal delusion, his principal goal. So that within this framework he had ordered the nurse to chew off the man's penis 'or I'll kill you'. And she said, 'Kill me, I'd rather die.' She said, 'I don't want to live', and he struck her blindly with a knife. He never killed with anything else really. And so this was a very, very delusional moment, and the murder was part of the total plan for the destruction of mankind through the destruction of sexual organs. But he had asked her to be the delegate. He wasn't going to do it himself, and his idea was if she refused then he would get some other woman in the house to come down and be the delegate. But one of the hostages escaped and Michael came down – his son, that is – and grabbed him, and they left. He said, 'Action will take place now.'

B.K. So in other words they fled the scene before they could do any further damage to prevent being caught.

F.S. It was Michael who made them flee, because Joe wanted to stay and carry out more murders; his original plan was to kill everybody in that house.

B.K. So in the Maria Fasching murder, the nurse in New Jersey, he used a knife to perform symbolic castration, and he hoped that by threatening the nurse, she would perform an actual castration, by chewing off the male hostage's penis.

F.S. And until that moment there'd been a lot of emphasis on chew, chew, chew, in previous crimes, he was concerned with chewing.

B.K. Now tell me how these mechanisms worked in the other two murders.

F.S. Well, it's very clear in the José Collazo murder, this 10-year-old neighbourhood boy whom he'd never seen before, who they took to an abandoned factory. And in the abandoned factory, Michael, as delegate for Joe's obsession, did the actual killing of José, the actual killing was probably through suffocation; they put a sock in his throat and so on. But the further fact was that when the boy was dead, Michael, at Joe's behest, and in line with Joe's fantasy, sliced off a piece of the dead boy's penis. Joe put it in a plastic bag as a memento of success and as an early stage of world massacre through the destruction of sexual organs. He took the bag home and kept it in his store and it began to smell. After two weeks he threw it down the sewer. But it was a very precious memento of his world plan.

B.K. Now, is it true that both his parents were sterile?

F.S. We don't know that the mother was sterile, but we do know that his father was.

B.K. But they could not have a child together, so in effect, as a couple, they were sterile.

F.S. Yes, and Joe was a replacement for the child they couldn't have.

B.K. So what's the connection here between the sterile parents and the delusion to make everyone sterile by cutting off their sexual organs? That can't be accidental.

F.S. I think that's an important aspect of it. He was cutting off the sexual organs as a kind of retaliation because he had been told that his sexual organs, sexuality, his potency, had been destroyed in an earlier operation with the removal of the demon.

B.K. So is it fair to say that we have a chain of causality, beginning with the sterile parents? The sterile parents, angry and upset at their own condition, vented their rage on a little boy by telling him that he is sterile – in other words, if we can't reproduce, neither can you, and we've taken the demon out of your bird. And Joe, having been traumatised at such an early age took his revenge in this rather crazed fashion by attempting to take away everybody else's sexual potency. It's quite a frightening chain of causality, isn't it?

F.S. In the case of José, the boy was dead before there was a removal of a part.

B.K. But still you have the knife and the castration again.

F.S. Yes, it's the knife and the castration again.

B.K. And what about the third murder, that of Joe's own son?

F.S. Well in sequence it was the second murder. José Collazo was the first, Joey was the second and Maria Fasching was the third. But in the case of Joseph Kallinger Junior – Joey – as he was called, a son for whom Joe made enormous sacrifices, who he loved very intensely, on whom he spent a tremendous amount of time because Joey was always getting into trouble and Joe was always trying to get him out of trouble and so forth. But at any rate, he decided that Joey had to die, and had to die as a family sacrifice, because in the end he was going to kill every member of the family, Michael being next to last and Joe himself the last. He would then experience a glorious suicide, come to his apotheosis and become God. But before that, and that was to have been the end, Joe believed that some member of his own family had to be sacrificed to show that his family was no better than anybody else's family. And so he and Michael tied up Joey, all in the spirit of fun and games, and they tied him to a table in a used building under construction. And they had it all arranged. Michael, no, Joe was to come up with a knife and cut off Joey's penis while he was lying there, taking pictures and so on. Well, when it came to doing the cutting, Joe couldn't do it. This was his son, he loved Joey, and he couldn't cut off his penis. It was a moment of very intense conflict and he didn't do it. They left there without any kind of damage. The several attempts to kill Joey all failed because Joe lost heart, except of course the final attempt which did not involve castration directly. They tied him to a ladder and dropped him into a deep pool of muddy water and he was drowned. But the drowning was the substitute for castration, the castration that Joe couldn't perform on Joey. So nevertheless, the basic childhood pattern exists in each of the three murders. Even though totally abandoned and repressed in the third, nevertheless the drowning is a substitute.

B.K.   So would it be fair to say that every murderer brings his or her own psychological signature to the crime?

F.S.   I say that without real authority as I haven't studied every murderer, but I say it with rather strong intuition based on my very intensive exposure to Joseph Kallinger.

B.K.   Might it be fair to suspect that the Boston Strangler for example might have had a similar trauma with the neck or with strangulation and that this determined his mechanism?

F.S.   Very definitely.

B.K.   Because it can't be accidental that a serial murderer should use the same methodology over and over again.

F.S.   No, but fortunately, Joe could never have performed any of the world massacre, because he could never have killed three billion people. That in itself was a mathematical delusion.

B.K.   Tell us briefly now that Joe committed the murders, how was he caught, and what has happened to him since his arrest. How did the police find him?

F.S.   Well, they picked up evidence from the murder of the nurse. He had left a bloody shirt in Sylvan Park. The shirt had the name of Kallinger on it. It had been laundered and they put the customer's name. And he was fully aware of it, and Michael was aware of it, and Michael said, 'Don't throw that away, Dad, you'll get us caught.' But Joe insisted.

B.K. So Joe threw his bloodied shirt away. Why do you think he wanted to get caught?

F.S. Well I think there were deep unconscious reasons for that. He had been caught all his life, his entire life had been a trap, so I think he wanted to be in the trap.

B.K. It was what he was used to.

F.S. That of course is speculation on my part. He may have wanted to stop world massacre, it was a hell of a plan to go ahead with. That would have been more rational. But on an actual level what happened was the bloodied shirt and also various weapons they had discarded on the way to the park, with fingerprints and so forth, it was very telling evidence and when they had the bloody shirt analysed at the laboratory, they discovered Maria Fasching's blood. It was very clear.

B.K. Through basic forensic work they detected the murderer?

F.S. Yes, but he was not arrested for the murder of Maria Fasching. By this time word had got into these other communities where he had committed crimes. Harrisburg, Pennsylvania, and Camden, New Jersey, the Homeland section of Baltimore, Maryland, and Dumont, New Jersey, and when he was finally arrested, the police and other representatives of all these communities came to the Kallinger home for the arrest, but he was not arrested on the Fasching case, he was arrested on his invasion of the home in Susquehanna Township near Harrisburg, Pennsylvania. The arrest was on that. The home of Helen Bogin. That was where a bridge party had taken place. And he had bound the women who were there playing bridge. It was on that offence that he was arrested.

B.K. And eventually they charged him for murder as well?

F.S. That came later, when he was charged with breaking and entering into the main house in Leonia.

B.K. So eventually he was taken into custody.

F.S. On January 17, 1975.

B.K. Now he went through a battery of psychiatric examinations, I understand.

F.S. Not then. The point about this whole case is that it was resolutely believed that he was not psychotic, and it was only when he got to the Farview State Hospital that doctors there along with the world famous Dr Silvano Arieti whom I brought out there with Dr Lewis Robbins, clearly established that he was schizophrenic and that the murders were connected with the delusions and hallucinations of schizophrenia; but every single trial led to failure on his part. The insanity defence was denied in each case, when in fact it was not a plea, but an actuality. But no psychiatrist until those I have just mentioned recognized that fact, well that's not quite true. Dr Irwin Perr and Dr Jonas Rappeport did so in the Fasching trial, and again in the Joan Carty trial – she was a woman whom Kallinger had attempted to murder – they argued for the defence that he was psychotic. Dr Jonas Rappeport, a psychiatrist for the defence, said as soon as they had heard about the orthopaedic experiments, he knew that he was schizophrenic. The orthopaedic experiments had begun when he was fifteen and went right through the early years of his second marriage, and they were, God had ordered him to save mankind through orthopaedic experiments, that as a shoemaker he could save mankind through healing the pain in the feet through the proper orthopaedic devices. But when he burned the thigh of his daughter, Mary Jo, he concluded that the experiments had failed. He couldn't save himself as well as the rest of mankind.

B.K. So Joe was put into the Farview State Hospital which is a psychiatric hospital.

F.S. Well that was not until May 1978.

B.K. So he was put into the Farview State Hospital. Can you just tell us a little bit about what his life is like today and what kind of treatment, if any, he is receiving.

F.S. Well he has received comparatively little treatment. For a while he had one-to-one psychotherapy with Dr Ralph Davis, a clinical psychologist. And also with Dr Marcella Shields, a clinical psychologist. And they both did a good job with him. Since then, and this is four or five years ago, there has been no actual one-to-one therapy, and he is really regarded as bad rather than sick, in spite of the fact that there was this one incident in Farview a few years ago when a man got into Joe's bed at night, another inmate, and started fellatio with him, and Joe bit his penis in retaliation, right back to this prevailing motif. Well of course the Farview psychiatrist did not understand this at all. Joe was bad, Joe had hurt a man, etc. They're very judgmental and very non-analytical.

B.K. So in other words, he's receiving precious little treatment.

F.S. Oh, none.

B.K. It's very sad that even though here is a person who has injured, victimized other people because he himself was a victim, it's sad that the courts and the doctors, who should know better, are continuing this process of victimisation.

F.S. Well the court's treatment of Joe Kallinger has been absolutely outrageous.

B.K. All right, what lessons have we learned from *The Shoemaker*, if you had to sum up the main conclusions?

F.S. Well, to put it on a simplistic level, that child abuse of a serious nature can lead to crime – murder in this case – and that prevention of crime begins in the nursery.

B.K. It's a very interesting and frightening point that you raise, because most people would say that if we want to stop crime, then we should increase the size of the police force. But that doesn't deter people because the motivations to commit crime have started very early on in life.

F.S. You don't stop crime later after the criminal has committed the act; you stop crime in order to prevent the act from occurring.

B.K. Okay. Now you've presented in this last hour on the tape some very frightening material about two case studies examined in a great deal of depth. Unfortunately, psychiatry does not really spend much time decoding individual case studies. Doctors on hospital wards will see maybe twenty, thirty patients in a day, and they do not really have time to get down deep. But you have done two remarkably pioneering studies, detailed studies, in order to get to the bottom of people's problems – namely, that of Sybil, a victim of child abuse who later developed a fragmented condition known as multiple personality disorder, and also the case of Joseph Kallinger, who suffered from a psychosis, and who also became a mass murderer. Now each was a victim of child abuse, both physical and emotional. One thing that would be useful to know, both for clinicians and parents, is why two abused victims developed such different symptom pictures.

F.S. Well absolutely. In answer to the conditions of the abuse, they were totally different. We said earlier that Joe lived in this absolutely loveless environment. He was very vengeful, full of rage, and his responses grew out of those early incidents: the bird scene, when he was told that the demon had been removed from his bird and that he would always be impotent, and the scene in the tank where older boys, strangers, gave him his first sexual experience in terror, he was in terror, with a knife at his throat, and the knife for him became the symbol of power, both sexually and in a worldly sense. Both of these experiences were very important to him.

B.K. But why did Sybil become a multiple personality and not a murderer?

F.S. Because there was nothing in the childhood that indicated murder. There were no knives, there was nothing of that nature. And her multiplicity was a defensive manoeuvre to protect herself against the traumas of her childhood. Essentially she did not want to hate her mother because she'd been raised with the dictum that good little girls love their mothers. And Sybil, the waking self, always protested that she loved her mother. On the unconscious level, she hated her, and the alters expressed hatred for Sybil's mother, but they always denied that she was their mother.

B.K. So she was able to indulge in her murderous fantasies by having the other voices, the other personalities act this out. But why didn't Joe develop a multiple personality disorder too? What was the breaking point in the Kallinger case that actually turned him from the murderous fantasies, based on the hatred of the abusive parents, and what then made him actually go out and kill? Was it that his abuse was more intense, in some way, more traumatic?

F.S. Well, it was the delusion that he was ordered by God to kill. Sybil had no such delusion.

B.K. It is very tricky to tease apart . . .

F.S.   And Sybil did not even know that she was a multiple personality. Joe didn't know that he had committed these murders either. It is a matter of repression in both cases.

B.K.   I think the important point to stress, and let me know if you agree, is that without the abuse, both physical and emotional, Sybil would never have become a multiple personality and Joe would never have become a murderer.

F.S.   That's essential, and it is essentially true. The fact is that Sybil became a multiple personality to defend herself against the traumas that led to hatred of her mother.

B.K.   I'd like to know your opinion about public education on the topic of child abuse prevention. Now, you're in the fortunate position of being quite a vocal and widely read spokesperson because both of your studies of traumatic child abuse have been bestsellers. *Sybil* has sold how many millions of copies?

F.S.   Oh, I don't know recent figures. The last I heard, about seven million in the United States. And of course it has been published in eighteen foreign countries.

B.K.   Eighteen foreign countries! So it's very, very widely read. And it has been made into a film, yes?

F.S.   Well, filmed for television in the United States and a theatrical motion picture in foreign countries.

B.K.   Right, and *The Shoemaker*, too, is a bestseller.

F.S.   Well *The Shoemaker* was a bestseller in paperback in the United States and it has done very well in Germany in a publication by Schweizer Verlaghaus. And it has done very well, it was published by *Stern* magazine in many countries and it has been published in about five foreign countries additionally.

B.K.   So these books have reached an extraordinary audience all around the world. I think there must hardly be a person who has not heard about the book *Sybil*, really, I mean it is so well known. What do you think the effect is, of such widespread books arguing against child abuse and informing people about the widespread effects of child abuse? Is there any way that we can assess how much these books have changed public attitudes and whether it's worth it to keep knocking our heads to write these big books.

F.S.   Well I don't think you can possibly assess the extent of change. You can postulate that there has been change but you can't measure the extent of it.

B.K.   Have you any thoughts on advice to parents, to psychiatrists, to students, to trainees about prevention of child abuse.

F.S.   I think prevention, as I said earlier in this interview, begins in the nursery. And the thing is to have parents who are not abusive, which means parents who aren't psychologically sick. And that almost begins before the nursery, in their nurseries.

B.K. But what do we do when we have those traumatised parents who inflict pain on their children? Can they learn without going into treatment, because not everyone's going to go into long-term psychoanalysis.

F.S. I don't know what they can learn and I think some of the burden rests upon neighbours. In the case both of Sybil and of Joe, the neighbours were strangely silent, although they knew what was going on. The neighbour who told me about the zoo incident in the Kallinger story, told it to me probably thirty years after it had happened or more, but she never told it to anyone at the time, she didn't try to intervene with the Kallingers, she didn't tell the police, she didn't tell other neighbours. And the same thing is true in the case of Sybil. There were teachers in her school who knew she came to school bruised, and mangled. And the local family doctor saw these bruises. He'd say, 'Well how did Sybil get this?', and Hattie, her mother, would say, 'Oh doctor, you know how clumsy children are, she keeps falling, putting her hands out.' Hattie took Sybil to the doctor with a bead in her nose. He took it out. He asked, 'How did she get that?' Hattie would reply, 'She stuck it up', but of course *Hattie* had stuck it up.

B.K. So people knew what was going on in both the Sybil home and in the Joseph Kallinger home, but no one said anything.

F.S. No one did anything. So I think the reluctance not to interfere somehow has to be broken. It's not very pretty for me to snitch on my neighbour, but maybe snitching on my neighbour is the only practical solution.

B.K. There's the danger as well that this can reach witch-hunting proportions – 'Mr Policeman, I suspect my neighbour of massive abuse.'

F.S. It's very dangerous. As we know, in some of these instances, like the McMartin School in California, much of that may have been fictionalised, invented. You just don't know. It's a very, very difficult nut to crack, because you don't know what the answers are.

B.K. Well that's certainly been at the centre of many legal controversies during the last few years, with the child abuse reporting laws – can the courts come into your home and take your child away if you're suspected of being an abusive parent? Very tricky. What are the ramifications of being taken away from an abusive parent and put in a correctional facility; that can be traumatic too.

F.S. Taken away from abusive parents, put into a situation with abusive foster parents, or in an institution that is in itself abusive, is a terrible, terrible dilemma.

B.K. In terms of hands-on change that has resulted from your books, have you had any parents come up to you, particularly after the reading of *Sybil*, and say, 'You know, I was beating my children and I had no idea that this was so bad'. What have parents said to you?

F.S. Once on a call-in radio programme in Canada, a parent came on the air and confessed that she was like Sybil's mother. And she said, 'I will never do it again. Can I come and see you?' And I said yes. She came to the studio and talked.

B.K. Really. What was she like?

F.S. Outwardly very pleasant. The traditional witch is not the abusive parent. Hattie, Sybil's mother, was quite charming and intelligent, and she wrote poetry. She was a very gifted woman and a very brilliant musician.

B.K. Yet quite abusive as well. Tell me, this Canadian woman, did she give you any explanation as to why she felt compelled to beat her child? She was beating, yet she decided to stop as a result of your book *Sybil*.

F.S. No, not the book, the radio programme.

B.K. So these radio interviews really do influence the man and woman sitting at home. That must have been a very gratifying moment for you.

F.S. I'm not at all sure but I think that the programmes built around the books touch people more directly than the books themselves. I'm not saying this is always so but in many instances it proves so.

B.K. Well, that's fabulous. You must have felt very pleased that your testimony about the ill-effects of child abuse really influenced.

F.S. Well, it led to a confession, and a resolution to change.

B.K. That's very exciting. That certainly gives me encouragement to pursue things in the media and so forth. That's very important. You must have had other incidents like that. How many radio shows have you been on, promoting *Sybil* and *The Shoemaker*?

F.S. Radio and TV? Many hundreds.

B.K. So you've reached wide audiences.

F.S. In the USA, Canada, Great Britain, Germany.

B.K. So if they haven't read the book or seen the film, very likely they will have seen you promoting these on radio and TV.

F.S. There's been some exposure. Now there are many people who are not interested in the whole subject one way or another. They haven't been abusive, they haven't been abused, they're not multiple personalities, and they're not murderers. And they have rather narrow outlooks.

B.K. Have you had any people dispute your basic findings, saying, 'Oh well, maybe Sybil had a tough rap, but child abuse isn't so bad. It's good for toughening the character?'

F.S. Oh yes, we've heard that ad nauseam.

B.K. Have people said that to you?

F.S. To me? I remember one programme in Philadelphia, when someone got on the phone and said, 'Oh well, so what, I lived in Philadelphia and I know that Joseph Kallinger had a good home and he was dressed better than other kids. And they were very good to him.' Well they were very good to him in all sorts of superficial ways. Sybil's mother was very good to her in all sorts of superficial ways.

B.K. Three square meals, but lots of abuse too.

F.S. Even recently Joe talked about the good food he had in the Kallinger household. And he had better clothes than the other kids. The teachers asked Anna Kallinger to donate his clothes when he was through with them, when he'd outgrown them and so forth. But that is not the whole of life.

B.K. Physical needs are very different from psychological needs.

F.S. And I think both books illustrate that, because both children were abused physically, but they were also well fed, well clothed and so forth.

B.K. Well, it has been a great pleasure talking to you. You are a true pioneer in public education about mental health issues, especially the whole topic of child abuse, really breaking that field wide open, in my opinion. And I am sure that many of us are grateful for the terrific work that you have done and continue to do. I know you have been quite busy recently with the follow up to *The Shoemaker*. But tell us what you would like to do in the future to continue in this line. You are a specialist in psychiatric topics. You've completed two in-depth case studies. Where would you like to take this work now?

F.S. Deeper.

B.K. Deeper. In what form?

F.S. I don't have the answer. Possibly as a novel.

B.K. As a novel? Clearly, we haven't heard the last of Flora Rheta Schreiber.

F.S. Some people would have hoped that you had.

B.K. Thank you Professor Schreiber, it has been most gratifying.

F.S. Thank you. I enjoyed every moment of it.

ACKNOWLEDGEMENTS

I want to extend my deep gratitude to the late Professor Flora Rheta Schreiber, for agreeing to speak to me on tape, only one year before her death on 3rd November 1988. I also wish to convey my thanks to Ms Vivien Roberts for her very efficient and adept transcription of the cassette tape.

REFERENCES

Arieti, Silvano and Schreiber, Flora Rheta (1981) 'Multiple Murders of a Schizophrenic Patient: A Psychodynamic Interpretation'. *Journal of the American Academy of Psychoanalysis*, 9, 501–524.

Borch-Jacobsen, Mikkel (1997) 'Sybil – The Making and Marketing of a Disease: An Interview with Herbert Spiegel'. In Todd Dufresne (ed.) *Freud Under Analysis: History, Theory, Practice. Essays in Honor of Paul Roazen*, pp. 179–196. Northvale, New Jersey: Jason Aronson.

Carlson, Eric T. (1981) 'The History of Multiple Personality in the United States: I. The Beginnings'. *American Journal of Psychiatry*, 138, 666–668.

Fairbairn, W. Ronald D. (1929) 'Dissociation and Repression'. In Ellinor Fairbairn Birtles and David E. Scharff (eds) (1994) *From Instinct to Self: Selected Papers of W.R.D. Fairbairn. Volume II: Applications and Early Contributions*, pp. 13–79. Northvale, New Jersey: Jason Aronson.

Fairbairn, W. Ronald D. (1954) 'Observations on the Nature of Hysterical States'. *British Journal of Medical Psychology*, 27, 105–125.

Freeman, Lucy (1951) *Fight Against Fears*. New York: Crown Publishers.

Greaves, George B. (1993) 'A History of Multiple Personality Disorder'. In Richard P. Kluft and Catherine G. Fine (eds) *Clinical Perspectives on Multiple Personality Disorder*, pp. 355–380. Washington, DC: American Psychiatric Press.

Guttman, Melinda Jo (1998) Personal communication to the author. 6th September.

Miller, Mark and Kantrowitz, Barbara (1999) 'Unmasking Sybil: A Re-examination of the Most Famous Psychiatric Patient in History'. *Newsweek*, 25th January, 66–68.

Schreiber, Flora Rheta (1973) *Sybil*. Chicago, Illinois: Henry Regnery Company.

Schreiber, Flora Rheta (1983) *The Shoemaker: The Anatomy of a Psychotic*. New York: Simon and Schuster.

Shamdasani, Sonu (1994) 'Encountering Hélène: Théodore Flournoy and the Genesis of Subliminal Psychology'. In Théodore Flournoy. *From India to the Planet Mars: A Case of Multiple Personality with Imaginary Languages*. Sonu Shamdasani (ed.), pp. xi–li. Princeton, New Jersey: Princeton University Press.

Wilbur, Cornelia B. and Torem, Moshe S. (1993) 'A Memorial for Cornelia B. Wilbur, M.D., in Her Own Words: Excerpts from Interviews and an Autobiographical Reflection'. In Richard P. Kluft and Catherine G. Fine (eds) *Clinical Perspectives on Multiple Personality Disorder*, pp. xxv–xxxi. Washington, DC: American Psychiatric Press.

Information for DID sufferers and professionals working with this client group

RECOMMENDED BOOKS

Bentovim, A. (1995) *Trauma Organised Systems*. Karnac, London.
A clear exposition by a leading psychiatrist and family therapist of the way trauma can become an organising principle within a family (and an individual).

Bloom, S. (1997) *Creating Sanctuary, Towards an Evolution of Sane Societies*. Routledge, New York and London.
Sandra Bloom, a former President of the International Society for Traumatic Stress Studies provides a practical and theoretical rationale for residential treatment as therapeutic asylum. Her 'sanctuary' model does not exist in the UK.

Goodwin, J. and Attias, R. (eds) (1999) *Splintered Reflections: Images of the Body in Trauma*. Basic Behavioural Sciences, Basic Books, New York.
In examining how the body responds to past trauma the editors draw on the work of Bruce Perry, Richard Kluft, Nijenhuis and van der Hart, Barry Cohen, Anne Mills and Valerie Sinason.

Hacking, I. (1995) *Rewriting the Soul: Multiple Personality and the Sciences of Memory*. Princeton University Press, New Jersey.
Ian Hacking is a professor of philosophy and this important American book examines political and philosophical issues relating to dissociation, memory and abuse.

Mollon, P. (1996) *Multiple Selves, Multiple Voices, Working with Trauma, Violation and Dissociation*. Wiley, Chichester.
Phil Mollon, a psychoanalyst and consultant psychologist provides an impressive and thorough overview of dissociation, trauma and multiplicity. He provides a psychoanalytic perspective that takes the reader through the historical responses to this topic right up to the present day. As well as a sound theoretical background he provides a clinical overview and includes comments on the use of other or complementary therapies.

Perlman, S. (1999) *The Therapist's Emotional Survivor: Dealing with the Pain of Exploring Trauma*. Jason Aronson, New Jersey.
This is an honest helpful psychoanalytic book dealing with the secondary traumatisation clinicians face when they take on ritually abused dissociative patients.

Putnam, F.W. (1989) *Diagnosis and Treatment of Multiple Personality Disorder*. Guilford, New York.
One of the key texts of the last two decades.

Ross, C. (1994) *The Osiris Complex: Case Studies in Multiple Personality Disorder*. University of Toronto Press, Toronto.

Siberg, J.L. (1996) *The Dissociative Child*. The Sidran Press, Lutherville, Maryland.

Shirar, L. (1996) *Dissociative Children: Bridging the Inner and Outer Worlds*. W.W. Norton & Company, New York.
Two of the very few books dealing with extremely dissociative children.

Walker, M. and Antony-Black, J. (2000) *Hidden Selves: An Exploration of Multiple Personality*. Open University Press, Buckingham.
Moira Walker, a long-established clinician and writer collaborated with Jenifer Antony-Black, herself a survivor of childhood abuse and founder of the Quetzal Project in Leicester, in this innovative British book. A survivor called 'Liza' tells her own narrative about her abuse and multiple personality. Different clinicians from very different orientations provide their commentary on her narrative. These include Peter Dale (a sceptical perspective), Phil Mollon, Graz Kowszun and John and Marcia Davis from the University of Leicester.

De Zulueta, F. (1993) *From Pain to Violence, The Traumatic Roots of Destructiveness*. Whurr Publishers, London.
Utilising biological, neuropsychological, attachment theory and psychodynamic research, psychiatrist and group analyst Felicity de Zulueta takes the reader through attachment theory, violence as attachment gone wrong, and the psychology and prevalence of trauma.

KEY JOURNALS

The Journal of Psychohistory, edited by Lloyd de Mause, is an essential and brilliant journal bringing key insights on the impact of abuse in the past and its legacy and presence in the present. Themes around multiplicity are regular. (Website: www.psychohistory.com)

Journal of Trauma and Dissociation, the Official Journal of the International Society for the Study of Dissociation (ISSD), Haworth Medical Press. Volume 1, no. 1 came out in 2000 with an impressive array of research and clinical details.

CLINICAL AND SUPPORT LINKS

ACAL The Association of Child Abuse Lawyers is a non profit-making company set up for the benefit of lawyers and other professionals working with people who have been sexually, physically and emotionally abused in childhood as well as people with learning disabilities. They are also experienced in work with ritual abuse survivors who are dissociative. Tel: 01923 286 888.

The Clinic for Dissociative Studies Offers assessments, training, individual and group psychoanalytic psychotherapy. 10 Harley Street, London W1G 9PF, Fax: 0207 467 8312, Tel: 0207 467 8436.

CISTERS (Childhood Incest Survivors) PO Box 119, Eastleigh, Hants SO50 9ZF, Tel: 02380 369516 (answer machine only). Founded by Gillian Finch, this group offers mutual support for adult females abused in childhood, and offers workshops, newsletters and meetings.

First Person Plural A small UK organisation led by people with firsthand experience of dissociative disorders. It supports and informs people who experience dissociative disorders, their friends, family and professional allies; it encourages increased social recognition of dissociative disorders by health and social care professionals and enhances the general public's understanding and acceptance of people who experience dissociative disorders including Multiple Personality Disorder/Dissociative Identity Disorder. It produces a quarterly newsletter, offers a members' contact list, provides speakers and training.
    Write to Kathryn Livingston, First Person Plural, PO Box 1309, Wolverhampton WV6 9XY, email: fpp@collective1.fsnet.co.uk and Website http://members.aol.com/Fpplural/fpp.html

Mosaic Minds This is a new DID website found at http://www.MosaicMinds.org

The Pottergate Clinic for Dissociation 11 Pottergate, Norwich, Norfolk NR2 1DS. Tel/fax: 01603 660029, Web page http://www.dissociation.co.uk/organ.htm
    The centre offers full diagnostic assessments, individual therapy, consultancy, training and research. Remy Aquarone, the Centre Director, is UKCP and BCP registered and has worked with dissociative clients for the last 12 years.

RAINS (Ritual Abuse Information and Network Support) For professionals and carers who support survivors; Tel: 01483 898600.

SAFE Supports survivors of ritual abuse through a helpline, Tel: 01722 410889, and through a quarterly newsletter, *Safe Contact*.

SMART ISSUE An on-line journal with details of books, research, conferences and other news linked to ritual abuse, dissociation, mind control. It is America-based. Editor: Neil Brick; email: SMARTNEWS@aol.com

SURVIVE.ORG.UK Website for survivors of rape and child abuse set up by the ISSD; International Society for the Study of Dissociation.

TACT – Trauma Aftercare Trust A charitable trust offering help to people suffering from the after-effects of trauma. It offers a treatment programme throughout the UK, a helpline and training. There is also a quarterly newsletter. Helpline: Tel: 01242 890 306, Fax: 01242 890 498.

The Traumatic Stress Service, Maudsley Hospital This service specialises in the treatment of PTSD. Tel: 0207 919 2969.

Other recommendations include the Samaritans, 'Childline' and local church groups.

Index

Note: page numbers in *italics* refer to figures, page numbers in **bold** refer to tables.